Praise for
# *The Spy Who Loved Us*

"I enjoyed this book enormously and learned a lot. *The Spy Who Loved Us* is a fine read and a gripping story; but, most of all, it is an object lesson in why human intelligence and a great spy will always trump the most sophisticated espionage and surveillance technology. It's not the simple accumulation of information that counts. It's the recognition of what's important and then knowing what to do with it."

—TED KOPPEL

"The story of Pham Xuan An is the revelation of a remarkable life and a remarkable man. Fictional accounts of practitioners of the Great Game—the craft of spying—come nowhere near the real thing that was practiced by An. In *The Spy Who Loved Us,* An is revealed as a man of split loyalties who managed to maintain his humanity. Cast prejudices aside and you will discover a true hero, scholar, patriot, humanist, and masterful spy."

—MORLEY SAFER, correspondent, CBS *60 Minutes* and author of *Flashbacks: On Returning to Vietnam*

"Relevant, instructive, funny. The shock of the double never goes away. Neither does the gullibility of the arrogant intruder."

—JOHN LE CARRÉ

"This is a brilliant book about a man and his times. It strengthens the feeling I got from meeting him late in his life that Pham Xuan An was one of the most impressive people I have ever encountered. He was a man of wisdom, courage, and clear-headed patriotism. He was also—even if it seems ironic to say this under the circumstances—a man of extraordinary integrity. He loved us at our best even while confronting us at our worst."

—DANIEL ELLSBERG, author of
*Secrets: A Memoir of Vietnam and the Pentagon Papers*

"Thomas Bass tells a fantastic tale of intrigue, espionage, and friendship. His book reads as if it came from the farthest shores of fiction, and I wouldn't believe a word of it if I hadn't met so many of its characters and didn't know the story to be true."

—H. D. S. GREENWAY, editor, *The Boston Globe*, and Vietnam war reporter for *Time Magazine* and the *Washington Post*

"Every veteran, every scholar, every student, everyone who survived the Vietnam war is advised to read this book and reflect on its wisdom. In his thoughtful, provocative biography of one of the most successful espionage agents in history, Thomas Bass challenges some of our most fundamental assumptions about what really happened in Vietnam and what it means to us today."

—JOHN LAURENCE, Vietnam war reporter for CBS News and author of *The Cat from Hué: A Vietnam War Story*

"This is a chilling account of betrayal of an American army—and an American press corps—involved in a guerrilla war in a society about which little was known or understood. The spy here was in South Vietnam, and his ultimate motives, as Thomas Bass makes clear, were far more complex than those of traditional espionage. This book, coming now, has another message, too, for me—have we put ourselves in the same position, once again, in Iraq?"

—SEYMOUR HERSH, author of *Chain of Command: The Road from 9/11 to Abu Ghraib*

"Thomas Bass has rendered a sensitive, revealing portrait of the strangely ambivalent personality I knew during the Vietnam war. In doing so he provides us with unique insights into the nature, conflicting sentiments, and heartbreak of many Vietnamese who worked with Americans, made friends with them, but in the end loved their land more and sought, as their ancestors had for a thousand years, to free it from all trespassers."

—SEYMOUR TOPPING, former Southeast Asia bureau chief and managing editor of *The New York Times*

# THE
# SPY
# WHO
# LOVED
# US

Pham Xuan An, Ho Chi Minh City, February 2005.
Photograph by James Nachtwey.

# THE
# SPY
# WHO
# LOVED
# US

### THE VIETNAM WAR
### AND PHAM XUAN AN'S
### DANGEROUS GAME

## THOMAS A. BASS

PublicAffairs • New York

Maps by Jeffrey Ward.

Portions of this book first appeared in *The New Yorker*.
The author wishes to thank James Nachtwey and the Richard Avedon Foundation
for permission to reproduce the photographs on pages iv and x–xi.

PublicAffairs books are available at special discounts for bulk purchases in the
U.S. by corporations, institutions, and other organizations. For more informa-
tion, please contact the Special Markets Department at the Perseus Books
Group, 2300 Chestnut Street, Suite 200,
Philadelphia, PA 19103, call (800) 810-4145, ext. 5000, or e-mail
special.markets@perseusbooks.com.

Text set in 11.75 New Caledonia

Library of Congress Cataloging-in-Publication Data

Bass, Thomas A.
The spy who loved us : the Vietnam War and Pham Xuan An's
dangerous game / Thomas A. Bass. — 1st ed.
p.   cm.
Includes bibliographical references and index.
ISBN 978-1-58648-409-5
1.  Pham Xuan An, 1927–2006. 2.  Vietnam War, 1961–1975—
Secret service—Vietnam (Democratic Republic) 3.  Espionage, North Viet-
namese—Vietnam (Republic) 4.  Spies—Vietnam (Democratic
Republic)—Biography.  5.  Journalists—Vietnam (Democratic
Republic)—Biography.  I. Title.
DS559.8.M44B38 2008
959.704'38—dc22
[B]
                              2008021344
First Edition
10 9 8 7 6 5 4 3 2 1

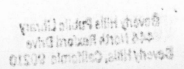

*For Tristan and Julian*

He felt as though he were turning his back on peace forever. With his eyes open, knowing the consequences, he entered the territory of lies without a passport for return.

GRAHAM GREENE,
*The Heart of the Matter*

Pham Xuan An,
*Time*
correspondent,
whispering
in the ear of
Robert Shaplen,
*New Yorker*
correspondent.
TO THE LEFT,
Cao Giao,
*Newsweek*
correspondent.
TO THE RIGHT,
Nguyen Hung
Vuong,
*Newsweek*
correspondent, and
Nguyen Dinh Tu,
*Chinh Luan*
newspaper.
Continental Hotel,
Saigon,
April 17, 1971.

Photograph by
Richard Avedon.

# Contents

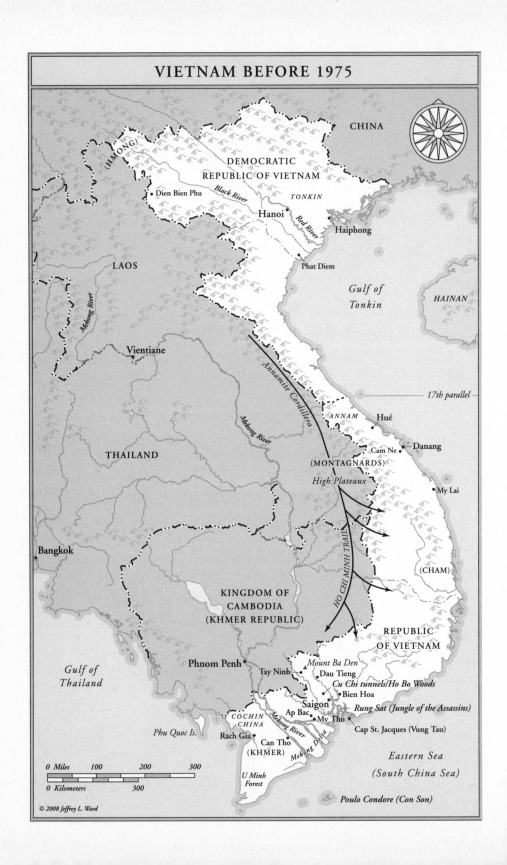

# VIETNAM BEFORE 1975

CHINA

(HMONG)

DEMOCRATIC
REPUBLIC OF VIETNAM

Dien Bien Phu

Black River

TONKIN

Hanoi

Red River

Haiphong

Phat Diem

Gulf of
Tonkin

HAINAN

LAOS

Mekong River

Vientiane

Annamite Cordillera

Mekong River

17th parallel

ANNAM

Hué

Cam Ne

Danang

(MONTAGNARDS)

THAILAND

High Plateaux

My Lai

HO CHI MINH TRAIL

Bangkok

(CHAM)

KINGDOM OF
CAMBODIA
(KHMER REPUBLIC)

REPUBLIC
OF VIETNAM

Phnom Penh

Mount Ba Den

Tay Ninh

Dau Tieng

Cu Chi tunnels/Ho Bo Woods

Bien Hoa

Gulf of
Thailand

Saigon

Ap Bac

Rung Sat (Jungle of the Assassins)

COCHIN
CHINA

Mekong River

My Tho

Cap St. Jacques (Vung Tau)

Phu Quoc Is.

Rach Gia

Can Tho
(KHMER)

Mekong Delta

Eastern Sea
(South China Sea)

U Minh
Forest

| 0 Miles | 100 | 200 | 300 |
|---|---|---|---|

| 0 Kilometers | | 300 |
|---|---|---|

Poulo Condore (Con Son)

© 2008 Jeffrey L. Ward

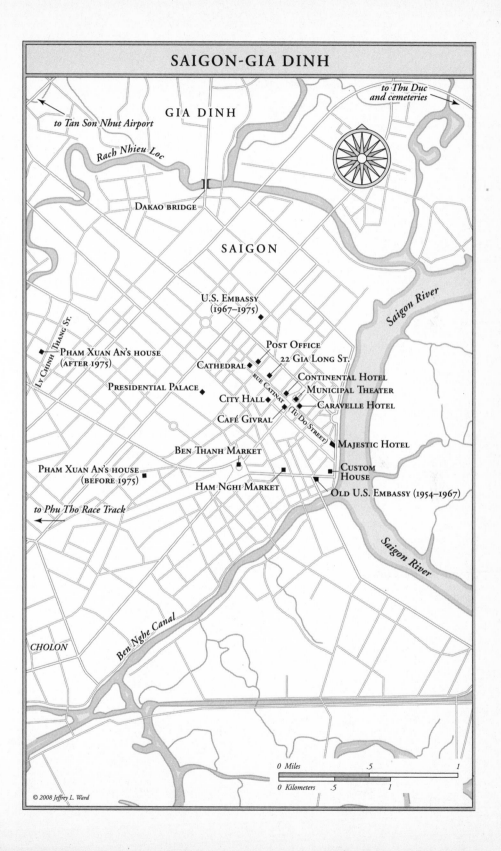

# SAIGON-GIA DINH

GIA DINH

*to Tan Son Nhut Airport*

*to Thu Duc and cemeteries*

*Rach Nhieu Loc*

DAKAO BRIDGE

SAIGON

*Saigon River*

U.S. EMBASSY
(1967–1975)

POST OFFICE

PHAM XUAN AN'S HOUSE
(AFTER 1975)

CATHEDRAL

22 GIA LONG ST.

*RUE CATINAT*

CONTINENTAL HOTEL

PRESIDENTIAL PALACE

MUNICIPAL THEATER

CITY HALL

CARAVELLE HOTEL

*(TU DO STREET)*

CAFÉ GIVRAL

MAJESTIC HOTEL

BEN THANH MARKET

CUSTOM
HOUSE

PHAM XUAN AN'S HOUSE
(BEFORE 1975)

HAM NGHI MARKET

OLD U.S. EMBASSY (1954–1967)

*to Phu Tho Race Track*

*Saigon River*

CHOLON

*Ben Nghe Canal*

0 Miles        .5        1

0 Kilometers    .5       1

© 2008 Jeffrey L. Ward

# *Foreword*

"A merica is good only at fighting crusades," wrote General
David Petraeus in his doctoral dissertation on "The American Military and the Lessons of Vietnam." Submitted to Prince-
ton University in 1987, Petraeus's work attacked what had
become the military's conventional wisdom on the lessons of
Vietnam. He characterized this as an "all or nothing approach,"
which boiled down to the doctrine that the United States should
fight only conventional wars with overwhelming support from
a crusading public. Petraeus rejected this "business as usual approach." He argued instead that the United States was likely to
find itself in the midst of other irregular wars fighting two,
three, many Vietnams. Petraeus went on to compile the army
field manual on counterinsurgency published in 2006. The following year, given the chance to conduct fieldwork on his aca-
demic specialty, he was appointed commander of U.S. forces
in Iraq.

Wars are not only crusades; they are also affairs of the heart.
Wars are fought for love, which we have known ever since
Helen of Troy launched a thousand ships full of smitten men

willing to die on her behalf. American humorist P. J. O'Rourke captured this truth in an essay he wrote on Vietnam in 1992: "In the early evening in Hué, the girls from the secondary schools come home from classes, fleets of them bicycling through the streets, all dressed in white *ao dais*, trim shirtdresses worn over loose-fitting trousers. Not for nothing do the remaining Catholic churches ring the Angelus this time of day. I wonder if it changes the nature of a society for beauty to be so common."

After exclaiming over the "huge aggregate percentages of sirens and belles" in this Edenic country, O'Rourke writes, "Now I understand how we got involved in Vietnam. We fell in love. . . . [We] swooned for the place. Everybody, from the first advisers Ike sent in 1955 to Henry Kissinger at the Paris peace talks, had a mad crush on Vietnam. It broke their hearts. They kept calling and sending flowers. They just couldn't believe this was goodbye."

Before beginning my story about Vietnam and America (with sideways glances toward France and other parts of the world), let me say that this book is about war and love, the lessons of Vietnam, counterinsurgencies, and other conflicts called irregular. It is about spies and journalists and the confusion between them. Some would claim that journalists helped to lose the war in Vietnam. In this case, I am claiming that a journalist helped to win the war—for the Vietnamese. This discomfiting book is about knowledge and deception and the ineluctable incertitude of knowing where one shades into the other. It offers no verities to be redacted into the new lessons of the Vietnam war. It is the simple life of a complex man. The truth is in the details. We begin.

# A Cautionary Note
# on Agent Z.21

H ere is Pham Xuan An now," *Time*'s last reporter in Vietnam cabled the magazine's New York headquarters on April 30, 1975. "All American correspondents evacuated because of emergency. The office of *Time* is now manned by Pham Xuan An." An filed three more reports from Saigon as the North Vietnamese army closed in on the city. Then the line went dead. During the following year, with An serving as *Time*'s sole correspondent in postwar Vietnam, the magazine ran articles on "The Last Grim Goodbye," "Winners: The Men Who Made the Victory," and "A Calm Week Under Communism." An was one of thirty-nine foreign correspondents working for *Time* when the Saigon bureau was closed and his name disappeared from the masthead on May 10, 1976.

Recognized as a brilliant political analyst, beginning with his work in the 1960s for Reuters and then for the *New York Herald Tribune* and the *Christian Science Monitor,* and, finally, as a *Time* correspondent for eleven years, Pham Xuan An seemed to do his best work swapping stories with colleagues in Givral, a café on the old rue Catinat. Here he presided every afternoon

1

as the best news source in Saigon. He was called "dean of the Vietnamese press corps" and "voice of Radio Catinat"—the rumor mill. With self-deprecating humor, he preferred other titles for himself, such as *"docteur de sexologie," "professeur coup d'état,"* "Commander of Military Dog Training" (a reference to the German shepherd that always accompanied him), "Ph.D. in revolutions," or, simply, General Givral.

We now know that this was only half the work An did as a reporter, and not the better half. An sent the Communist government in Hanoi a steady stream of secret military documents and messages written in invisible ink, but it was his typed dispatches, now locked in Vietnam's intelligence archives in Hanoi, which will undoubtedly rank as his *chef d'oeuvre.* An wrote four hundred and ninety-eight reports (the official figure revealed by the Vietnamese government in 2007), averaging about one per month, during his fifty-five-year career as an intelligence agent.

Using a Hermes typewriter bought specially for him by the North Vietnamese intelligence service, An wrote his reports, some as long as a hundred pages, at night. Photographed and transported as undeveloped rolls of film, An's dispatches were run by courier out to the Cu Chi tunnel network that served as the Communists' underground headquarters. Every few weeks, beginning in 1952, An would leave his Saigon office, travel twenty miles northwest to the Ho Bo woods, and descend into the tunnels to plan Communist strategy. From Cu Chi, An's dispatches were hustled under armed guard to Mount Ba Den, on the Cambodian border, driven to Phnom Penh, flown to Guangzhou (Canton) in southern China, and then rushed to the Politburo in Hanoi. An's writing was so lively and detailed that General Giap and Ho Chi Minh are said to have rubbed their hands with glee on getting these reports from Tran Van Trung—An's code name. "We are now in the United States' war room!" they exclaimed, according to members of the Vietnamese Politburo.

As Saigon fell to the Communists, An was hoping to be evacuated to the United States. This was not because he feared Communist reprisals, as everyone assumed, but because Vietnamese intelligence planned to continue his work in America. They knew there would be a war-after-the-war, a bitter period of political maneuvering in which the United States might launch covert military operations and a trade embargo against Vietnam. Who better to report on America's intentions than Pham Xuan An? In the last days of the war, An's wife and their four children were airlifted out of Vietnam and resettled in Washington, D.C. An was anxiously awaiting instructions to follow them when word came from the North Vietnamese Politburo that he would not be allowed to leave the country.

An was named a Hero of the People's Armed Forces, awarded more than a dozen military medals, and elevated to the rank of brigadier general. He was also sent to what he called a "reeducation" camp and forbidden to meet Western visitors. His wife and children were brought back to Vietnam a year after they left. The problem with Pham Xuan An, from the perspective of the Vietnamese Communist Party, was that he loved America and Americans, democratic values, and objectivity in journalism. He considered America an accidental enemy who would return to being a friend once his people had gained their independence. An was the Quiet Vietnamese, the man in the middle, the representative figure who was at once a lifelong revolutionary and ardent admirer of the United States. He says he never lied to anyone, that he gave the same political analyses to *Time* that he gave to Ho Chi Minh. He was a divided man of utter integrity, someone who lived a lie and always told the truth.

"An's story strikes me as something right out of Graham Greene," said David Halberstam, who was friends with An when he was a *New York Times* reporter in Vietnam. "It broaches all the fundamental questions. What is loyalty? What is patriotism? What is the truth? Who are you when you're telling these truths? There was an ambivalence to An that's almost impossible for us to imagine. In looking back, I see he was a man split right down the middle."

In his 1965 book on Vietnam, *The Making of a Quagmire*, Halberstam, with unintentional irony, described An as the linchpin of "a small but first-rate intelligence network" of journalists and writers. An, he wrote, "had the best military contacts in the country." Once Halberstam learned An's story, did he bear him any grudges? "No," he told me, when I called him to discuss An's wartime duplicity. "It is a story full of intrigue, smoke, and mirrors, but I still think fondly of An. When you mention his name, a smile comes to my face. I never felt betrayed by An. He had to deal with being Vietnamese at a tragic time in their history, when there was nothing but betrayal in the air."

In 2005 I published an article about Pham Xuan An in *The New Yorker*. Shortly after the piece appeared, I signed a contract to develop the article into a book. What I thought would be a simple assignment turned hard as I became enveloped by yet more intrigue, smoke and mirrors. I began to suspect that I had fallen into the same trap as An's former colleagues. They had swapped ignorance for willful ignorance and remained charmed to the end by An's smiling presence. Was he a "divided man," as Halberstam maintained, or was he a "man of the revolution," as the Vietnamese say, with the rest being his cover? Was he an accidental Communist or a Communist *tout court*, who worked at his job until the day he died?

As I dug deeper into this project, I realized that An, while presenting himself as a strategic analyst, someone who merely observed the war from the sidelines, was actually a master tactician involved in many of the war's major battles. He was an award-winning soldier bedecked with medals, a central player in a long string of military engagements marking Communist victories and American defeats. An had not received four medals—as I reported in *The New Yorker*—but *sixteen*. These were not ceremonial citations. All but two of them were battle medals, awarded for valorous service in Vietnam's wars against the French and Americans.

Ever since our first meeting in 1992, An had put me off the trail to discovering what he actually did during the First and Second Indochina Wars and what he continued to do as a "consultant" for Vietnam's intelligence services until his death on September 20, 2006. He hid these facts from outsiders, with the brilliant sleight of hand and charming humor for which he was famous. When my inquiries became too pointed, he turned from assisting my book project to trying to block it. His superiors in military intelligence had given him permission to talk to me for a magazine article. He had been fond of *The New Yorker* from the days when he worked as assistant to Robert Shaplen, the magazine's Far Eastern correspondent. An must have told his bosses, "It's only a magazine article. I'll spin the story, maybe at greater length than usual, but without giving away anything we don't want to give away." They had allowed him to undertake this assignment, supposedly limited in scope, but they explicitly denied him permission to work with me on a book. As soon as the article was published, An put an end to our meetings and hastily arranged for another "official" biography to be written, one designed to keep his cover securely in place.

An was a brilliant conversationalist. His method throughout his life had been to disguise his activities through talk. How could someone so voluble and open about his life be a spy? How could someone so funny and pointed in his remarks about human stupidity be a Communist? This method worked so well that it became ingrained in his personality. There was no way to shut him up. An talked and talked, and in the end, for a mere magazine article, we had recorded sixty hours of taped interviews. Many more hours of conversation were transcribed in the written notes of our meetings. As I replayed these tapes and reread my notes, the variations in An's narrative began to intrigue me. Only once, for example, among a dozen descriptions of the "crash course" that had trained him as a Viet Minh soldier, did An reveal that he later commanded a platoon, which on at least one occasion had fired on French soldiers. This was not the work of a strategic analyst but the act of a partisan.

I am sorry to report that this book also benefited from An's death. The control he exercised over the story of his life ended in the fall of 2006. Intelligence sources, both in North and South Vietnam, began revealing previously undisclosed information. This included details about An's involvement in some of the war's major battles and campaigns. We learned, for example, that he had won a First Class military medal for providing advance warning of U.S. plans to invade Cambodia in April 1970. The warning allowed Communist forces, especially the military command, to escape to the west. Another First Class medal had been awarded for revealing South Vietnam's plans to invade southern Laos in February 1971. Here An's tactical involvement led to a crushing military defeat for Republican forces.

The information revealed since An's death confirms that he was privy to a breathtaking array of military intelligence. Some of the new information was released accidentally, some intentionally. In either case, I began receiving a steady stream of messages, notes, photos, and other documents about a man who, seventeen years after I first met him, continues to surprise. An's cover will finally come undone only when someone gets the chance to read his collected *oeuvre*—the intelligence reports he sent to Ho Chi Minh and General Giap, which made them clap their hands with glee and exclaim over the verve and narrative grip of the Tolstoy in their midst, known to them by his code name as Z.21.

During our meetings over the years, An knew that he was speaking to me at greater length than was required for a magazine article, even a feature story written with the leisurely scope that was once afforded to Robert Shaplen. But An had his cover, and I had my cover, at least until *The New Yorker* article was published. After this, neither of us could pretend that we were talking to each other for anything other than a book, which An had not been authorized to do. When I went to visit him for the last time, in January 2006, we were preparing for what I thought would be a long night of conversation, the usual mix of stories and jokes, when he told me this would be our last meeting. There was no going back on his decision. We would never see each other again.

I knew by this point that An was working with another "official" biographer. "What's the difference between my book and this other book?" I asked. "Your book is being written from inside Vietnam," he said, implying that I had access to sensitive information that should not be revealed. I took this as a compliment to my Vietnamese research assistants, whose legwork and tenacity were sometimes as remarkable as An's back in the days when he was the hardest-working journalist in Vietnam.

I was hurt by An's decision not to see me again, and I took the news personally, until I learned that he was acting on orders from above. His story was meant to be spun as Halberstam had told it. In this version of An's life, created for Western consumption, he was a nationalist, inadvertently caught up in his country's history, a strategic analyst who had looked down on the war from the Olympian heights of *Time*. A different picture is presented here, of a master tactician and committed fighter for the Communist cause. I have written the *unauthorized* biography of a spy. Although An withdrew his support from this project—along with some of his American friends who took up the cudgels on what they thought was his behalf—I persist in thinking that if this book says anything true about Vietnam and its prolonged wars or the nature of war in general, An would secretly be smiling on it.

On several occasions I nearly abandoned the project, and even as this book goes to press, the fundamental questions remain just that—questions. If I were talking to An about this dilemma, as I often did, he might crack a joke or launch into an anecdote from Vietnamese history or suggest I read a book, such as Nguyen Khai's 1983 novel about An's life, *Thoi Gian Cua Nguoi* (The Time of Man). Conversations proceed like this in Vietnam. They are circuitous and languorous, before shifting, almost imperceptibly, into moral tales that simultaneously amuse and instruct.

I have told this story in Vietnamese style, fluid in point of view and sense of time. Pham Xuan An is dead. He was hooked to a ventilator for several weeks before his lungs collapsed for good in the fall of 2006, ending all those years of conversation. David Halberstam is dead. He survived a lifetime of covering wars in Africa and Asia before dying in the passenger seat of a car that was struck at an intersection in Menlo Park, California, in 2007. For as long as I can still hear them, I will keep their voices in the present tense. The reader should be warned, though. There is no one true story of Pham Xuan An's life, because his life contained multiple truths. Even his name is a warning. *An* in Vietnamese means "hidden" or "secret."

During the twenty years it fought the Vietnamese, the United States never understood the people or the culture of Vietnam. South Vietnam was to be remade in America's image. *Terra incognita* preceded *terra nova*. America's disregard for its enemy cost it dearly. It lost the war, with fifty-eight thousand soldiers killed and hundreds of thousands wounded, and it lost its naïveté about its invincible military might.

America's enemy did not make the same mistakes. The Vietnamese studied their adversary. They cultivated an agent who could think like an American, who could get inside the American mind to learn the country's values and beliefs. The Vietnamese needed a spy in the enemy camp, although not a common, second-story man. They needed a strategic spy, a poetic spy, a spy who loved Americans and was loved by them in return. After gaining their confidence, he would pick the lock most prized in military strategy—the lock to their dreams and ambitions, their myths about themselves, and their role in the world.

For this assignment, the Vietnamese put their faith in one man, who would become their most important spy and one of their greatest military weapons. As a lesson in warfare and as a way to understand the Vietnamese, there is no better lens than the life of Pham Xuan An. Instead of being called "the spy who loved us," he could equally well be called—as one of my editors suggested—"the most dangerous man in Vietnam." While reading this book, I recommend keeping both lenses at hand or, better yet, popping one in each eye.

# Baptism
# by Fire

Ho Chi Minh City—or Saigon, as it is still commonly called—is a single-mindedly commercial place. Filled with pushcarts and vendors selling everything from soup to CDs, the streets are roaring rivers of two-stroke motorcycles. The exhaust fumes are so thick that Saigon's famously beautiful women have started covering their faces with scarves. "We are all Muslims now," says Viet, my Honda man, who drives me around the city on the back of his motorcycle.

Approaching An's house—a villa in District Three, a densely settled neighborhood near the train station—we pass an intersection full of motorcycle repair shops and come to a street that specializes in selling tropical fish, including the Siamese fighting fish that An admires. I tug on the bell that hangs from his green metal gate. As the dogs start barking, I peer through the grill to see An shuffling down the driveway on this sunny day in January 2004. A wispy figure, he wears a white, short-sleeved shirt with a ballpoint pen in the pocket, gray trousers that flap around his legs, and rubber sandals. He arrives winded but smiling and greets me with a handshake

that involves only the tips of his fingers. Recently hospitalized
with a collapsed lung, the result of a lifetime of smoking Lucky
Strikes, seventy-seven-year-old General Givral, with his full-
toothed grin, looks as puckish as ever.

I had first visited An in the early 1990s when I was in Vietnam researching a book on Amerasians—the children of American soldiers and their Vietnamese lovers. When the book was
published, I sent him a copy, and I sent him other books when
mutual friends of ours visited Vietnam. An knew that I was interested in hearing his story. He was a gracious host to the visitors who were allowed to see him after Vietnam adopted *doi
moi*, its version of perestroika, in the late 1980s. He would
spend hours explaining Vietnamese history and culture, but
he was silent as a sphinx on one subject—his life as a spy. Late
in 2003, I received a message that he might finally be willing to
talk, not formally but in friendly conversations. These began at
Tết, the lunar new year, and resumed for another couple of
weeks at the onset of the rainy season in May 2004. I saw An
again in March 2005 and then the following year before Tết.

An leads me through his garden, a tropical enclave lush
with star fruit and bushberry trees. It is perfumed with frangipani and splashed with color from the flowering apricot blossoms and orchids. A hawk and three fighting cocks stare at us
from cages under the trees. We stop in the middle of the garden to admire a porcelain statue of one of An's beloved German
shepherds. An credits Edward Lansdale, military intelligence
agent and supposed model for Graham Greene's "quiet" American, with teaching him how to use dogs in his work. "I trained
my dog so that he could alert me when the police were searching
people's houses, even a kilometer away," An says. "He was a
good spy." An, with his puckish humor, also points out that the
superintelligent, Lansdalian dog in his garden has three testicles.

An's wife, Thu Nhan, is sweeping the front porch with a
short-handled broom. She is a pleasant, round-faced woman
who wears her hair tucked into a bun. Ten years younger than

An, she is busily cleaning before the rush of visitors who will be coming for the Tết holiday, including their daughter, who lives in California. Hanging on the porch and from poles set in the driveway are cages containing An's laughing thrushes, golden-fronted leaf birds, magpies, canaries, and other songbirds. A blue Indian mynah with a yellow bill announces in Vietnamese, "Grandfather, telephone call for you!" The bird is mimicking the voice of An's grandson, who lives with him along with An's three grown sons.

We kick off our shoes and enter the large room that once served as An's office and library, as well as his reception and dining room. Lining the far wall are the glass-faced shelves that house his books. A Chinese landscape painting hangs above a green upholstered sofa and chairs. Below the open windows sits a fish tank that holds the third component in An's menagerie. "Dogs are loyal," he says. "Birds are always hopping around in their cages, keeping busy. Fish teach you to keep your mouth shut. Unfortunately, while I was in the hospital, most of my fish died."

The room has been changed since I last visited. In the alcove near the front door, in place of An's desk and filing cabinets and the piles of magazines and papers which used to reach toward the ceiling, sits his son's piano. Later I discover what happened to An's office when he and I walk past the family altar and out through the kitchen into the driveway at the back of the house. "Here is where my wife threw all my papers," he says, pointing to two gray filing cabinets and a desk piled with yellowing documents. All that protects them from the elements is a narrow plastic roof.

As we stare at the papers heaped in the driveway, An laughs. "My wife tells me it's time to make room for the younger generation, but I can't die yet. There's nowhere for me to go. I can't go to heaven because I have told too many lies; hell is reserved for crooks, but there are so many of them in Vietnam, it's full."

An has pendulous ears, a high, square-domed forehead, close-cropped dark hair, and lively brown eyes. His left eye is slightly larger than his right, as if he were simultaneously taking both the long and short view of the world's affairs. Photographs of him from the 1950s show him wearing narrow suits, white shirts, and black trousers. An looks like one of the nice, clean-cut young men who joined fraternities and mastered social drinking. He was taller than the average Vietnamese, a scrappy boxer and swimmer who once thought, after failing his school exams for the second year in a row, that he might become a Vietnamese gangster.

"I don't want to talk about myself," An says frequently. "There is too much to remember." Then without skipping a beat he begins recalling in minute detail scenes from fifty years ago. He leans forward in his chair. He gesticulates with his fingers, which are long-boned and nearly translucent with age. He shapes the air in front of him as if it were a doughy ball, taking a punch at it from time to time. He divides his remarks into Confucian triads and pentads while waving his fingers through an arc that represents one of the *déesses,* the protective goddesses to whom he credits his success in life. An can also talk for hours about world events, drawing parallels between Vietnam and the Iraq war ("techniques first developed in Asia have been moved to the desert") or evaluating the world's intelligence services ("The Americans are masters at gathering intelligence, but they don't know what to do with it").

Pham Xuan An was born in the Vietnamese Year of the Cat, at the Hour of the Buffalo, on September 12, 1927, twenty miles northeast of Saigon, in the Bien Hoa psychiatric hospital, which at the time was the only European medical facility in Cochin China open to Vietnamese. As the firstborn son of a *cadre supérieur,* an educated member of the colonial administration, he received a French birth certificate, an unusual privilege.

"They had one doctor to take care of the crazy people who were pregnant," An says. "It's because I was born in an insane asylum that some people say my blood was infected by the 'virus' of Communism. *An was born in a psychiatric hospital? That's why he follows the Communists. He's crazy!*"

An is a great fabulist. He uses animal stories and proverbs to poke fun at people's pretensions. His humor acknowledges life's absurdities and embraces its contradictions, but sometimes I wonder if it isn't also a shield, a kind of protective carapace to keep interlocutors at bay. Why *did* An become a Communist? Does he joke about it because the question is too serious to be treated any other way?

Originally from Ha Dong, the heart of North Vietnam in the densely populated Red River delta lying between Hanoi and the coast, An's great-grandfather, Pham Xuan Ong, a silver- and goldsmith, was recruited by the Nguyen dynasty to make medals for the royal court at Hué in central Vietnam. An's grandfather, Pham Xuan Duong, rose through the Vietnamese civil service to become a teacher and eventually director of a primary school for girls. In the photograph that stands as the centerpiece of An's family altar, Duong wears a gold medal on his chest. Given to him by the emperor, the large tulip-shaped medal, called the *kim khanh*, signifies that An's grandfather holds a rank equivalent to a secretary in the government. An shows me a picture of himself as a baby with the medal hanging around his neck. I ask if he still owns his grandfather's *kim khanh*. "It was sent to Ho Chi Minh for the gold campaign," he says, referring to the massive bribe that Ho paid the Chinese army in 1946 to convince them to withdraw from northern Vietnam after World War II.

After graduating from the University of Hanoi, An's father, Pham Xuan Vien, worked as a cadastral surveyor establishing property lines and tax rolls in Vietnam's southern frontier. Vien laid out roads in Saigon and canals through the U Minh forest, along the Gulf of Siam. While surveying in Cambodia, he met An's mother, another emigrant from the north, an industrious woman with a second grade education who could read and write. The work of a colonial surveyor in southern Vietnam involved press-ganging peasants into carrying surveyor's chains through the Mekong marshlands and building towers in the jungle to establish sight lines. "When you do land surveying and build canals and roads, you see the poor Vietnamese workers eking out their living," An says. "You see the French system of forced labor, beatings, and other abuses. The only way to oppose these abuses is to fight for independence. The Americans did the same thing in 1776. When my father saw how badly the French treated the peasants, it was natural for him to fight for Vietnamese independence. My father became a patriot. My family was always patriotic in their desire to remove the French from Vietnam."

As a *cadre supérieur,* An's father held one of the highest ranks available to a Vietnamese in the colonial administration. There was no engineering school in Indochina (for this advanced training one had to study in France): so Pham Xuan Vien had been schooled as an *agent technique,* which was the functional equivalent of a civil engineer. Born in Hué in central Vietnam and educated in the north, Vien spent his entire career in the south, building France's colonial infrastructure. At the time, the south was the Vietnamese frontier, much of it still covered in jungle. Other parts were accessible only by boat. Working his way through seasonal flood plains, mangrove forests, and rice paddies buffeted twice yearly by monsoons, Vien served in the vanguard of what the Vietnamese call the *nam tien*—the march to the south.

The Viets, one among Vietnam's fifty-four ethnic groups (although by now the dominant group), have been expanding southward from their home in the Red River valley near Hanoi for the past five thousand years. But it was only after the Mekong wilds in the south had been overlaid with roads and plantations that the Viets could finish their march. Pham Xuan An, like his father, had served the *nam tien*. In fact, he could be said to have brought it to its end. A unified Vietnam stretching from the Chinese border to the Gulf of Thailand could exist only after all of Vietnam's invaders—Chinese, French, Japanese, American, and Cambodian—had been expelled and Vietnam had fought the last of its Indochinese wars. Only then would the *nam tien* be complete.

Like many Vietnamese, An traces his ancestry to southern China. "That's where we lived before we were pushed out," he says. "We migrated from Hanoi to central Vietnam, the area of the Cham and Cambodians, before we moved farther south into Cochin China. My ancestors followed the same history as the rest of the country, moving from the heartland in the Red River delta south into the lowland areas."

Soon after arriving at the royal court in Hué, An's family began its ascent from manual laborers to colonial cadres. While Pham Xuan Ong, the family patriarch, was a craftsman, shaping gold and silver into plants and animals so elaborately detailed that they seemed to take on a life of their own, his children used their position at court to secure jobs as teachers and administrators. The school directed by An's grandfather, Duong, was one of the first in the country to teach *chu quoc ngu*, or modern Vietnamese writing—an adapted version of the Latin alphabet developed in the seventeenth century by French missionary Alexandre de Rhodes. Vietnam's original system of writing, *nom*, based on classical Chinese characters, was banned by the French in 1920. Duong's school was part of a strategy to reset Vietnamese history to year zero. With a new language and literature, Vietnam would become the sole Asian country with a Roman alphabet. To help reshape the consciousness of its Asian subjects, France introduced the guillotine into Vietnam and began using it with revolutionary fervor. The French ultimately failed to impose their political will on Vietnam, but their linguistic revolution was a success. A country that was largely illiterate, due to the difficulty of mastering Chinese calligraphy, is now almost universally literate.

An's uncle also directed an elementary school. Another uncle became a civil servant working for the post office, while his aunt married an *agent technique,* who, like An's father, had graduated from the University of Hanoi. An's successful, upwardly mobile family might have been expected to feel beholden to the powers that had trained and employed them, but instead of supporting the French, they resisted them. They ran the schools, built the roads, and delivered the mail, but at the same time they were patriots who opposed French colonial rule in Vietnam. They were quiet revolutionaries, not the ones who went to prison or fought in the Viet Minh resistance, but their fervor was deep and unwavering, and it would come to fruition—with devastating effect—in the revolutionary career of Pham Xuan An.

The Viets are a fierce tribe whose history consists predominantly of battles against enemies from the north (Genghis Khan and the Chinese and Japanese), the east (Portugal, France, and America), and the west (Laos, Khmers, Indians, and Thais). The list of Vietnam's warriors, including women warriors, is long, and so too is the duration of their struggles. The Vietnamese fought for a thousand years to oust one Chinese occupation.

Patriotism in colonial Vietnam was inadvertently fostered by the French. They taught the Vietnamese about nationalism, including the idea of the nation-state and its aspirations to express the spirit of a unified people. Vietnam's school curriculum was devoted to studying the French Revolution and its happy conclusion in a republic devoted to *liberté, egalité,* and *fraternité.* The French never intended for the Vietnamese to embrace these ideas as their own. They were talking about *France,* not Vietnam. But once the nationalist ideal began bleeding into the colonies, not even the guillotine could cauterize it.

"To make a living, you had to work for the French regime, but none of the Vietnamese wanted their country dominated by foreigners," An says. "Our history is full of battles against invaders. We borrowed our language for fighting this struggle from the French, but it was motivated by our love for our own people—the same force that motivates any country to fight for its independence."

The French divided Vietnam, like Gaul, into three parts. Tonkin in the north included Hanoi and the port city of Haiphong. The central region of Annam was simultaneously the birthplace of revolutionaries, such as the Tay Son brothers and Ho Chi Minh, and home to the quaint royal court in Hué. Cochin China in the south was comprised of Saigon, the Michelin and other rubber plantations at Dau Tieng, and the great rice-growing domains of the Mekong delta. A unified Vietnam stretching from the Chinese border to the Gulf of Siam had never existed. Nor did the French *want* it to exist. They outlawed the word *Vietnam*—because it referred to the idea of a unified country—and arrested anyone who used it.

"The map of Vietnam was made by the French," An says. "Before they arrived we had no nation. The high plateaus belonged to the Montagnards. Other parts belonged to the Cham or Khmer."

I am speaking with An one day when he walks to the buffet next to the dining room table, opens the top drawer, and shuffles through a collection of old photographs and letters. "Here it is," he says, holding out his police identity card from the colonial era. Because his father's family came from central Vietnam, known to the French as Annam, the Sûreté (French criminal investigation department) has identified An as an Annamite.

"All the Vietnamese opposed the French occupation," An tells me. "Insurgencies were always popping up in one area or another." He launches into a story about the depth of anti-French sentiment in colonial Vietnam. Like many of his stories, this one, stretching back over successive generations, involves an interlocking mosaic of family and social relations so tightly knit that I can barely tease out the strands. To help me, An gives me a handhold for keeping track of the narrative as it slips backward into Vietnamese history.

Today's point of reference is Nguyen Thi Binh, whose name is mentioned frequently in An's stories. Binh and An, both born in 1927, were childhood friends. Their fathers were classmates at Hanoi University and worked together as engineers in Cochin China. Binh and An might have married if their paths had not diverged during Vietnam's interminable wars. Imprisoned for two years by the French, Binh became foreign minister of the National Liberation Front (the coalition of southern revolutionaries whose armed forces were known as the Vietcong), and she led the NLF delegation at the Paris peace talks. In 1992, after serving as Vietnam's minister of education, Binh was elected vice president of Vietnam. During the tumult immediately following the end of the Vietnam war, she helped An get his family reunited in Saigon, but today's story stretches even farther back in time.

Binh's grandfather, scholar and anticolonial agitator Phan Chu Trinh, believed that France should honor its democratic principles by replacing Vietnam's mandarin rulers—of which he was one—with modern laws and institutions. After peasant tax revolts erupted in 1908, Trinh was sentenced to death, but instead was shipped to Poulo Condore, the Devil's Island prison camp also known as Con Dao. Thirteenth-century explorer Marco Polo was the first Westerner to discover this archipelago of sixteen mountainous islands in the South China Sea—or Eastern Sea, as the Vietnamese insist on calling it. With their windswept nesting grounds for turtles and dugongs, the islands have a lonely, spectral aura enhanced by their long years of use for imprisonment and torture. It was here that the infamous "tiger cages," first built by the French and later adopted by the Americans, became the symbol of the cruel U.S. presence in Vietnam.

After three years on Poulo Condore, Trinh graduated to exile in France, where he worked as a photo retoucher and coauthored articles signed "Nguyen Ai Quoc," Nguyen the Patriot, which at the time was an alias for Nguyen Sinh Cung, later known as Ho Chi Minh. When Phan Chu Trinh died in 1926, thousands of people swarmed into the streets in Saigon and Hanoi, demanding an end to French colonial occupation. An's father helped organize these demonstrations, and An followed his father's example in the 1950s, when he too used the funeral of a Vietnamese patriot to launch a series of street demonstrations and strikes.

When we meet, An and I usually sit in his living room. Sometimes we walk to the bookshelves that line the back of the room. One day An takes me behind the shelves into a narrow corridor where his family altar is located. It holds the usual sticks of incense and bowls of fruit and jumbled collection of photos which honor the dead. Vietnam is a country that celebrates death days instead of birthdays. "The Vietnamese are not Buddhists," An says. "They are animists. The religion they practice is ancestor worship. This is why the Tết holiday is so important to the Vietnamese. It is the occasion when you invite the souls of the dead to come back to visit the living."

"We believe we have three souls," An says, "spiritual, sentimental, and material. The spiritual soul distinguishes humans from animals. The sentimental soul comes from the heart. The material soul comes from the abdomen. It explains why humans are bad, why we kill people and are corrupted.

"When you die, you report to the emperor of hell. If you have committed too many crimes, you are forced to stay there. In any case, you will stay in hell for three days after your burial. Then your family comes to visit your grave with a black chicken. If the chicken cries, it is let out of its cage and allowed to run free. Called 'the opening of the grave,' this releases the sentimental soul. You can use a black dog for this ritual, but it costs more. If the dog returns to your home, it will bring your sentimental soul with it. We celebrate this event by placing a photo of the dead person on the family altar."

Placed in the center of the altar is the photograph of An's grandfather, showing him dressed in a tight-fitting tunic and wearing around his neck the gold medal from the emperor. Nearby are the photographs of other ancestors, whose stories An begins to tell. His grandfather had three wives. His first wife bore him four children, including An's father, who was the second of three sons. His third wife bore him three children. His second wife, childless, left An's grandfather and then married into an aristocratic family in the north and gave birth to To Huu, who became one of North Vietnam's greatest poets and politicians.

"At that time, the French allowed you to have three wives," An says. "In the old days, you could have five wives and seven concubines. That's why I always wanted to live in the old times," he jokes.

An's father, Vien, also had two wives, actually one wife and a concubine. Before Vien met An's mother, he had a daughter with a peasant girl in Rach Gia, the southern town at the edge of the U Minh forest. For a brief time in 1941, the girl came to live with An's family, but she soon got homesick and left. An never saw her again.

Like his father, An's mother was part of Vietnam's southward march. She came from the coal mining region near Haiphong, and her family hailed originally from China, where her grandfather, like An, was an avid bird lover. As a little girl, she tended his skylarks—Chinese birds that are carefully bred to produce the finest singers and dancers.

"Where is a photo of your father?" I ask An, as we stand in front of the family altar.

"It is here," he says, reaching for a picture toward the back. The photo shows a stern man wearing black spectacles and a dark Western suit and tie.

"I can't stand up too long, particularly when it's hot," An says, returning the photo to its original position. I wonder if his father's censorious gaze is also making An gasp for breath.

Born in 1900, An's father was educated in the girls school run by An's grandfather—a rare exception to the strict colonial rules regarding single-sex education. After high school, Vien went north to Hanoi for his training as an *agent technique,* a civil engineer. The engineers divided their tasks into different specialties: mapping, surveying, dredging canals, building roads. An's father excelled in mapping. He spent most of his working life in the jungles and wild areas of Cochin China scouting out the plan of attack for his colleagues, who arrived later to build South Vietnam's public works. An himself mastered these skills when he started mapping battlefields during the Vietnam war. One of his most important jobs at *Time* was to submit weekly coordinates for all the troop emplacements and battles in the ongoing war.

In spite of their privileged position as civil servants, An's family members were not oblivious to the suffering around them. Forced labor and an immiserated peasantry formed the base of the colony's economy. Ngo Vinh Long, in his book *Before the Revolution: The Vietnamese Peasants Under the French,* describes how Vietnam's rubber plantations functioned as slave labor camps, with annual death rates higher than twenty percent. Stiff taxes on the peasantry, *corvée* labor, an elaborate system of police controls and prisons, periodic famine in the countryside followed by peasant revolts and swift reprisals—this was the political economy that ground the vast majority of Vietnamese into poverty. At the same time, the French built roads and schools throughout the countryside, and the mail was delivered with remarkable celerity. This economic system operated like a great machine for converting jungle into rubber and rice plantations, and it also provided the leisure for French *colons* to spend their afternoons sipping Pernod on the terrace of the Continental Palace hotel.

Vietnamese opposition to French colonial rule took a variety of forms. Some Vietnamese wanted to ameliorate the brutality of the French system while maintaining a Franco-Vietnamese alliance to keep the Chinese at bay. Others called for throwing off the French colonial yoke. An's immediate family wanted to bring the colonial era to an end. "If you are a teacher, every day when you face your students, you can see that their families are poor, and you know why they are poor," An says. "My grandfather saw the consequences of the French occupation, and he couldn't help but be opposed to it."

An's father also saw the consequences. "My father mapped the forest by laying out chains, which is hard to do in the jungle," An says. "He had to build towers for sight lines and rely on *chaineurs*, who included prison laborers and peasants too poor to pay their taxes." After mapping the area around Bien Hoa, Pham Xuan Vien was transferred to Rach Gia. This vast area of swamps and mangrove forests bordering the Gulf of Thailand marks the end of the road in Vietnam's southward march. As far from civilization as you can get, the area is sparsely settled by refugees from China and Cambodia and by pirates who cruise offshore in the gulf. Surrounding Rach Gia is the U Minh forest, an aqueous domain filled with various species of Melaleuca water palms and cajeput groves. Thousands of fish traps, triangular cages made from bamboo sticks, float in the water. The slender white trunks of the cajeputs thrive in the marshes, as do a large variety of insects, including honeybees whose combs are avidly collected. The French tried to drain these swamps and canalize them into rice plantations, but they never fully tamed the U Minh badlands. The forest was a staging area for the Viet Minh. It served the same purpose for the Vietcong, and it was here that Pham Xuan An was trained as a revolutionary soldier.

As a child, An traveled through the vast, watery reaches of the U Minh forest on his family's sampan, which was loaded with his father's surveying equipment and maps. At night the family docked in canal-side villages, where local authorities loaned them huts in which they cooked dinner and slept. One evening before An's second birthday, the family was crossing the estuary of a big river that opened onto the ocean when the twin spouts of a marine tornado began racing toward them. "It looked like the black necks of two geese intertwined with each other," An says. The boat survived the storm, but An's mother, then pregnant with An's sister, decided that a waterborne life was too dangerous for her firstborn son, and An was sent to live with his paternal grandparents in Hué.

They lived in a brick house, built by An's father, which was occupied by An's grandfather and his first and second wives and An's half uncle and aunt. After delivering her second child in Hué, An's mother rejoined her husband in the south. "I was abandoned there to live with my grandfather at the age of two," An says. He is not using the word *abandoned* by accident. This first separation from his parents would be followed a few years later by another separation, which An calls his exile.

It was two years before An saw his parents again. They came to Hué on the death of his grandmother, and after the funeral, they took An back to Cochin China. No longer living on a boat, the family occupied a house in Gia Dinh province outside Saigon, which at the time was a provincial city of a few hundred thousand souls surrounded by rice fields, rubber plantations, and forests. Few roads had been cut through the countryside (An's father was charged with mapping where they would go), so people traveled the area on jungle paths, mostly on foot and occasionally by tilbury, a small two-wheeled cart pulled by a horse.

And so began An's lifelong love affair with Saigon. He spent hours along the Saigon River, swinging in the banyan trees and jumping in the water. He made friends with the workers in the Ba Son shipyard who cast him fanciful metal coins to play with. He rode the trolley to Cholon, the Chinese district, and then rode back to the movie theater near the bridge at Da Kao, where he watched films of Johnny Weissmuller playing Tarzan. "It was a beautiful dream of freedom in the jungle," An says of those movies. "I thought under Communism I would live like Tarzan. I put this dream into the revolution."

"Look at Tarzan!" An exclaims. "What does he have? Only his loincloth. When you are a Communist you become Tarzan, king of the jungle." This is Communism as a pure state of nature, a Rousseauian idyll. It is the high school philosophy version of Communism, which An acquired from books sent to students in the colonies by the French Socialist Party. "Yes, I am a Communist," he says. "Communism is a very beautiful theory, the most human theory. The teaching of God, the Creator, is the same. Communism teaches you to love each other, not kill each other. The only way to do this is for everyone to become brothers, which may take a million years. It's utopian, but it's beautiful."

As a political analyst, An knew that Communism was a failed god, responsible for millions of deaths in the twentieth century, and he knew intimately the limits of the Communist regime under which he lived. But An the patriot made a choice when he was young to fight for an independent Vietnam. The most effective force in leading this struggle against the Japanese, French, Americans, Chinese, Cambodians, and other invaders of his divided country was Communist. "Here in Vietnam, which organization did you have to join in order to carry on the fight for your country?" he asks. "You had no choice but the Communist Party."

An was happy to be reunited with his parents in Saigon, but school was another matter. Enrolled in the French primary school, he had to take a big exam at the end of third grade. If he failed the exam, he had to repeat the class. If he failed again, he flunked out of school. The exam was so important that, on the day it was given, police surrounded An's classroom and locked the doors against parents who might try to bribe the teacher.

"I failed the exam," An says. He laughs remembering this scholarly setback, a full-throated, hearty laugh. "The school where I did my best work and spent my happiest days was *école buissonnière*," he says, using the French term for playing hooky.

The father of one of An's classmates was a coffin maker. At night, An slipped out of the house to sleep with his friends in the empty coffins. (When business was slow, the coffin maker thought it lucky to have his surplus stock temporarily occupied.) "It was cozy inside our coffins, and I slept quite well," An says. "My father would go out looking for me. When he discovered I had been sleeping in my friend's coffins, he would whip me."

"Other nights, I went out with my friends to look for ghosts. We hid near the cemetery, beside a stand of bamboo. They say that at night, when ghosts appear, they make a noise, and if you look at a grave, you can see the spirit rising from the body. This is actually the mist that rises when the rains begin to fall, but we thought the first exhalations of mist were the spirits of dead people rising from their graves. So we would lie in wait, and at night, when the wind blew, the bamboo would knock together and make a clicking noise, like bones shifting in their coffins. This was the sound that told us to get ready, the ghosts are coming."

As I listen to him tell this story, An reminds me of Tom Sawyer, conjuring with spirits and getting into mischief, while back home his father, playing the role of Aunt Becky, is preparing to tan his backside.

Five kilometers outside of colonial Saigon, the forested area where An lived would turn pitch black and silent at night, except for the plaintive cry of the peanut vendor as he made his rounds from house to house, selling cones of roasted peanuts for a few pennies apiece. An was sometimes allowed to buy a cone of peanuts as a special treat. One night, with heavy monsoon rains beating on the roof, he heard the peanut vendor's distant cry. An summons up the plaintive voice from his youth: *yang rang yang, yan cau boi mang, mang dao rang.*

Opening the door, An discovered that the peanut vendor was a boy his own age. His only protection against the monsoon rains was a conical cap and cape made from the leaves of water coconuts.

An had returned to his homework and was munching his roasted peanuts. When his father asked him what he thought of the peanut vendor, An replied, "He's a boy like any other boy."

"Do you think so? Then why are you sitting here, in this comfortable room? Why are you reading books under an electric light while he is outside in the dark, wearing nothing but a cape made of coconut fronds? He is earning money to feed his family. His mother and father are poor. Why don't you take advantage of your lucky situation? Why do you fool around all the time, day and night, night and day? I beat you to make you study, for your future benefit."

Neither beatings nor lectures improved the headstrong youngster. "He whipped me. So I didn't study," An says. "My father was afraid I would turn into a Saigon hooligan, a *du con Sai Gon*. That's why he exiled me to Truoi. Already in third grade you had to read and write French. Even mathematics was in French. History was taught in French, and it was mainly French history. I was doing well in math, but I failed the French oral dictation, and that was the part they took most seriously."

"My father sent me to Hué, and my grandfather sent me to Truoi," An says, describing what he calls his exile. "Truoi was a very poor area, with only one primary school for many villages. The head of the school was the adopted son of my grandfather. His wife was also a teacher in the school. I stayed with them for a year. I took the exam and failed again. My father was so mad! I had spent a whole year enjoying life, doing nothing."

Living among people so poor that they ate roasted cicadas for meat and lit their homes with rendered rat fat was supposed to scare An into working harder in school. Instead, he delighted in playing hooky and larking around the countryside. After flunking his exams again, he was caned by his father and brought back to Saigon for a stricter regime.

One morning, after I pull the bell at his gate and An walks through his garden to greet me, I find him looking tired and dispirited. "A friend died last night," he says. "This is happening all the time now."

"Old people lose their teeth," he says. "What they should lose instead, since they have no use for them, is their balls."

"I really wanted to grow up to be like Tarzan. To have a pretty girl and live freely in the jungle. Now they make me live in a house. I have to put on a tie to go to meetings and weddings and funerals. Tarzan never put on a tie."

"I thought you wanted to grow up to be a Vietnamese gangster."

"When you're a good gangster, people like you. You can help them. You fight for the weak against the bullies who dominate them."

"What happened to your project?"

"My grandfather said no. My father said no. That's why he exiled me to Truoi, when he noticed that I was trying to become a Saigonese gangster. Seeing the hard life of the peasants, I was supposed to mend my ways, but I enjoyed it. Do you know why? Because my father wasn't there. I wasn't being whipped by him with his rattan cane."

An was brought back to Saigon for a final try at passing his exams. He returned to swimming in the river and larking about town, but things had changed. War was looming in Asia. The world was shifting around him.

"I had a friend, a Vietnamese boy, who was a French citizen. His brother was drafted by the French in 1938 to serve in the French army. Before he was shipped to Europe to fight the Germans, he was detained in the military barracks near the zoo. Every weekend my friend and I would walk from Gia Dinh to the barracks, carrying a big bunch of bananas. His mother wanted him to have them. This might be the last native food he ate before going to die in Europe."

An tells few stories about his mother, but one concerns a family dispute that occurred when he was ten or eleven years old. "The most beautiful women in the world are French," said his father. "No," said his mother. "American girls are the prettiest."

An's father was surprised to have his opinion contradicted, since he was an expert on the subject. As a respected member of the French civil service, he was occasionally summoned to judge local beauty contests at provincial fairs, and according to him the French girls—not the Vietnamese or *métisses*—were always the most beautiful.

"I asked my mother, 'How do you know American girls are beautiful?' 'Look at the movies made in Hollywood,' she said. 'In their manner, their speech, their gestures, the American girls are prettier than the French girls. So when you grow up, you should go to America and marry a woman like this. You will be happy. Don't marry a French girl. They are arrogant.'"

To prove his point, An's father sent him to watch *Les Misérables,* a movie about an impoverished French family with a pretty young French girl as the heroine. An appreciated this lesson from his father, but the movies he really loved were American films with Charlie Chaplin and Laurel and Hardy and, of course, his great favorite, Tarzan.

In 1938 An's family moved from Saigon to Can Tho, the bustling colonial city that was the economic and cultural capital of the Mekong delta. An's father, replacing a Frenchman who had been mobilized, was officially elevated to the rank of engineer, and An, in spite of his failed exams, was admitted to fourth grade, where he finally mastered the devilish French *dictée.* Sitting at the confluence of two rivers in a skein of waterways and canals, Can Tho presides over a region known as Cuu Long, or Nine Dragons. This is a reference to the nine branches of the Mekong River which traverse this verdant floodplain. The city is filled with floating markets and edged with orchards growing durians, mangosteens, and oranges. Rife with coconut palms and groves of sugar cane, the area is dominated by the emerald green paddies that make this the rice bowl of Southeast Asia. Can Tho was originally settled by Khmer krom—downstream Cambodians—who ruled until the end of the seventeenth century, when the Nguyen lords began to expand their influence southward. By the 1860s, the French had taken control of the delta and set to work draining and canalizing the marshy land into rice plantations—a project begun eighteen centuries earlier by Indian traders.

An was a happy-go-lucky schoolboy, but World War II was approaching. Desperate for conscripts, the French tried to draft the colony's able-bodied men, even people as old as Pham Xuan Vien, An's father. In 1938 Vien was called to Saigon for a physical exam, which he failed. In 1940 the Japanese occupied Indochina. The French colonialists were left to run their own form of Vichy government, which put a French face on Japanese rule.

An spent his high school years at the Collège de Can Tho, which trained boys through the tenth grade. He remained an indifferent student, but he was beloved by teachers who admired his independence and inquisitiveness. They saw in him a new kind of Vietnamese—agile, quick on his feet, adventuresome. The world was turning topsy-turvy with war and revolutionary fervor. The French colonial era was collapsing. The Vietnamese understood that mastering the French *dictée* would not be enough to guarantee success in this new world. A couple of An's teachers, pinning their hopes on this devilish boy, tried to push him forward.

An sensed that the French world in Asia was dead, although it would be another fifteen years before the body was finally carried offstage. He began taking private English lessons from a Vietnamese Protestant minister who had been trained in Singapore, and he became an avid student of American culture, being particularly impressed by its revolutionary history, its films, and its legendary Chicago gangsters.

In 1941 An's father was transferred back to his old territory near the U Minh forest. An's family, which now included his younger sister and two younger brothers, moved to Rach Gia, while An stayed behind in Can Tho. His French teacher, Truong Vinh Khanh, assumed the role of An's absent father. Khanh was the loving and appreciative counterpart to the stern Pham Xuan Vien. Deeply cultured in Vietnamese and French literature, Khanh was also a sportsman and, like An, he had a keen sense of humor. A French citizen from a wealthy landowning family, Khanh had an unusual appreciation for the United States, which he sensed would be the next major influence shaping Vietnam.

Khanh had the worldly tolerance required to appreciate a student like An, who never worked hard enough to get more than middling grades but possessed an abundance of good humor and animal spirit. The two of them exercised every day with Khanh's punching bag and sparred in his boxing ring. "I loved him so much. He taught me all sorts of things," says An.

An's American friends claimed him as one of their own, but his early training was deeply French. Whenever he had difficulty finding a word in English, it was the French term that came to mind. His sense of Vietnamese nationalism and his early training in Marxist theory and Communism were borrowed from France. "We students knew about patriotism and nationalism, and how did we know these things?" An asks. "Because we were taught by the French."

"In our first year of secondary school we were allowed to learn Vietnamese for only an hour a week. The rest of the instruction was in French. They taught us about the French Revolution, the origins of France, French solidarity, French wars, the history of World War I and France's other wars against Germany, French religion, Catholicism, the royal court and nobility, French law. There was a strong emphasis on civic education," An says, referring to the idea of a united people, with rights incarnated in a constitutional state.

Khanh supplemented An's readings in French literature with the stories and fables of Jean de La Bruyère and Jean de La Fontaine. An loved these stories about humans and animals which reveal that the only difference between them is human pride and pretension, which put us at a disadvantage when compared to the noble simplicity of other animals. "When I feel a little unhappy I read the *Fables* of La Fontaine, because he's a *professeur universel*," An says. "Another favorite of mine is Jean de La Bruyère. He's a very optimistic writer. He teaches you how to smile, to be happy. Professor Khanh introduced me to these writers. That's why I owe him a lot."

"He thought I should go study in France. 'There is no jungle in France,' he said. 'You won't have any friends calling you out to play. There will be no swimming in the river, no boxing, fighting, training every day. You will have to become serious, like the French.'"

Khanh came up with another idea. "Since the only school at which I excelled was *l'école buissonnière*—playing hooky—he thought I should become a gangster. 'You will never be a good student,' he told me. 'To speak French, all you need to do is learn three words. To learn English, learn another three words. For the rest, you should learn how to fight. You should become the leader of the gangsters in Cochin China. This will make you highly respected by your friends and family.'"

"'The best gangsters are in Chicago,' he said. 'You should become a Vietnamese gangster, but learn how to do it from the Chicago gangsters.' He told me to go to the United States and learn about technology, the modern way of doing things. He said the Chicago gangsters, when they fight, always use *poing américain,* brass knuckles. He taught me how to make them. You pour hot lead into a mold and then cool it with water. You can break someone's skull very easily."

Khanh and his pupil spent hours swapping jokes and fabulous stories about An's future training as an American gangster. One of Khanh's stories involved the Chicago stockyards. With

a smile tugging at his lips, An tells me about Chicago's miraculous machine for killing pigs, which Khanh considered the
apex of American technology. "In Vietnam, we tie down the pig
and cut its throat with a knife. We collect the blood. We open up
the abdomen of the pig and clean out the entrails. In America,
you never touch pigs. They're dirty. They're inhuman. The
Americans are very clean people. They have beautiful Yorkshire pigs, Berkshire pigs, which are much bigger than Vietnamese pigs. Each one weighs over a hundred kilos."

Telling me this story, An begins to grunt like a Yorkshire pig
on its way to slaughter. He is a brilliant mimic. I am hearing a
perfect Yorkshire grunt here in Saigon. "At the stockyards,
where the pigs are killed, an American wearing fine shoes and
a necktie opens a gate leading to a big metal machine. He
pushes a button. The pig falls down. The machine finishes him
off. The dirty pig goes in one side of the machine and comes out
the other, all cooked and nicely arranged on a plate. Sausage,
ham, salami—it's all prepared in this wonderful machine."

"On the far side of the machine sits a big gentleman wearing a tuxedo and bowtie. In front of him is a table set with
white linen, crystal goblets, fine china and silver, and a good bottle of wine. The food comes out of the machine and lands on his
plate. He tastes a morsel. He sips his wine. He puffs his cigar.
He pauses and with a nod of his head—but only if it meets his
highest standards—the food is whisked away for delivery na-
tionwide to all the markets in America.

"If he's not happy, he shakes his head and someone pushes
another button. The food is transported off his plate, back into
the machine. Do you know what happens then? Out the other
side of the machine walks the Berkshire pig!

"I went to Chicago and tried to find this machine," An says,
referring to his travels across the United States in the 1950s.
"My professor was dead by then, or I would have written to tell
him that I couldn't find this miraculous machine anywhere
in America."

In the context of wartime Vietnam, Khanh's recommendation that An become a gangster was not far-fetched. Vietnam has a long tradition of criminal gangs. The French used criminal enterprises to finance their colonial administration, and they put gangsters in charge of running the country. In colonial Vietnam becoming a gangster could indeed "make you highly respected by your friends and family."

Preeminent among Vietnam's modern gangsters was Le Van "Bay" Vien. An illiterate, bullnecked assassin who was adept at Sino-Vietnamese boxing, Bay Vien was chief of the Binh Xuyen river pirates who controlled the opium traffic and all the casinos and houses of prostitution in Saigon. A graduate of the Poulo Condore prison camp, he would rise to become the unofficial mayor of Saigon, the city's richest man, its de facto police chief, and a general.

In one sense, the entire history of Vietnam—all fifty centuries of it—can be seen as a long succession of rival war bands and gangsters. Vietnam is a great crossroads, a veritable stew of cultures, all of which seem to have staked out this territory because it was as far from home as one could get. Vietnam was where you went after a failed revolution in China, India, Cambodia, or France. It was the land of pirates, exiles, war lords, and criminal gangs, all fighting each other in the dark obscurity of the country's jungles and tropical flood plains.

Vietnam is named for the Nam Viets, or "southern" Viets, who were forced to migrate from the Mekong headwaters in Tibet into the Red and Black river valleys. As the Viets continued to move south, they bumped into groups of people from India, Cambodia, and Malaya who had settled in the rich, rice-growing regions of the Mekong delta. The contentious history of the delta emerges from obscurity in the first century C.E., when the Indianized civilization of Funan was established. Funan had walled cities replete with libraries and silversmiths and a strong fleet, which allowed it to control Vietnam's coastal waters. To the north of Funan, another Indianized culture took root in Champa.

As described by William Cassidy, who has written a lively account entitled *Southern Viet-Nam's Criminal Traditions* (1991), "What we know today as Saigon began as a collection of villages some eighty kilometers inland from the coast, known originally as Prey Kor, or 'the Land of Forests,' a refuge and hiding place from and for the pirates that harassed seagoing traffic to the south and river traffic to the west. The area presented a vortex of piracy and banditry. The Malay pirate fleet operated inland from Poulo Condore. The Champa pirate fleets operated southward from below Hué. Funanese and Cham bandit gangs monopolized the overland routes."

By 1859 a new band of pirates—the French—had captured Saigon, and by 1862 Emperor Tu Duc had ceded a big chunk of Cochin China to his new European overlords. Cambodia fell in 1863, and by 1884 the entire region was under French control. The French suppressed coastal marauding, preferring to control sea traffic and tax it for themselves. This forced Vietnam's gangsters to move inland, where they became river pirates, hiding in the swampy regions southeast of Cholon—Saigon's Chinatown. In Cholon itself the river pirates ran bordellos, opium dens, and gambling halls. The staging area for their criminal activities was an area called Rung Sat, the Jungle of the Assassins. Here, in the hamlet of Binh Xuyen, coalesced a yeasty mix of swamp bandits, Cholon street thugs, escaped contract laborers from the Michelin rubber plantation, and members of various criminal associations linked to Chinese Triads and Vietnamese secret societies.

By the early 1930s, the Binh Xuyen pirates had welcomed into their ranks a young street hoodlum named Bay Vien. He was captured by the French and imprisoned on Poulo Condore, but he got a lucky break when the Japanese assumed control of Vietnam in 1941. They released the Binh Xuyen gangsters from Devil's Island and began employing them as a useful tool for ruling the country. After the Japanese coup d'état on March 9, 1945, when French citizens in Vietnam were rounded up and thrown in prison, Bay Vien emerged as a government police official.

The Japanese occupation of Vietnam shadowed An's teenage years. He saw the Japanese as a belated addition to the long line of invaders who had tried to rule his country. If anything, the Japanese were even more brutal than the French. Other Vietnamese allied themselves with this new political force, excited by the prospect of Asians ruling Asia—a racial platform that the Japanese exploited to good effect.

"The Japanese talked of 'Great Asia' and 'Asia for East Asians,'" An says. "They wanted to kick all the white people out of Asia. Eventually South Korea and Hong Kong were the only two places where the Caucasians still had their foot in the door. The Japanese considered this their great achievement."

Vietnam's political parties and even its religious sects began to hew the Japanese line. "The Japanese were very smart," An says. "They invented the Hoa Hao religion. They co-opted the Cao Dai religion. They set up the Dai Viet political party and recruited students into the Vietnamese Kuomintang (VNQDD), influenced by Sun Yat-sen. They were also very smart in using the French against the Communists. They knew the Vietnamese Communists opposed them, so to keep order and mobilize the economy to serve the Japanese forces, they left the French in place to do their bidding."

Part of this mobilization involved converting Vietnam's rice crop to fuel for Japan's military machine, which resulted in two million Vietnamese starving to death. The charade of French rule in Vietnam ended in 1945 with the Japanese coup d'état. As An watched the French citizens of Can Tho being beaten and forced to sit in the town square without water all day before being thrown into prison, the scene left him with a visceral distaste for the Japanese and their colonial legacy in Asia.

Caught up in the patriotic fervor sweeping over Vietnam at the end of World War II, when the country seemed poised to shake itself free from the defeated French and retreating

Japanese, An dropped out of school in the spring of 1945 and joined the Communists. "Our first enemy was the Japanese, who were occupying the country," he says. "The Communist leaders were particularly keen to recruit students who knew how to read and write. We were young and patriotic."

"At that time, we knew for sure that the Communist leaders would sacrifice their lives for the good of the country. The majority of them were educated, like Ho Chi Minh and Dr. Pham Ngoc Thach, who had a French wife. My own primary school teachers joined the Communists. It was the best organization. All the others claimed they were fighting the French, but when the French returned, they stopped fighting, like the Dai Viet, which had been created by the Japanese to fight with them. After the war, the Dai Viet joined the French or Americans and worked secretly for the CIA. Some of them tried to join the Communists but were boycotted, which doesn't seem right to me. It's not good if you become suspicious of everybody. In that case, you have poisoned yourself.

"The Communists made many mistakes," An admits. "The Communism of Stalin and Mao—I don't like that kind of Communism. They invented their own form of Communism. They propagated their own theories for their own benefit.

"Do you remember what happened to the son of Deng Xiaoping, the secretary of the Communist Party in China?" An asks. "The Red Guards threw him out of a window and broke all the bones in his body. Now he is paralyzed from the waist down. Marx didn't teach them to do that. I don't think so."

Whenever An and I talk about his Party allegiance, it is the benevolent gods of Communism whom he chooses to worship. "Communism teaches you to love each other, like Jesus Christ taught his followers. He's a kind of Karl Marx, I guess."

"We were fighting not for Communism but for independence and the unity of Vietnam," An says. "That's what the majority of Vietnamese wanted. This is different from fighting for Communism."

At the end of World War II in the fall of 1945, Vietnam was overtaken by the short-lived euphoria of what was known as the August Revolution. In Hanoi, Ho Chi Minh, quoting America's Declaration of Independence, declared the country free and united before a cheering crowd of a million people. Ho ruled the Democratic Republic of Vietnam for a handful of days, until the Chinese moved in from the north and the British landed troops in the south. The British rearmed the French, who stormed Saigon's government buildings and soon gained the upper hand in splitting off Cochin China from the rest of Vietnam. In November 1946 the French navy bombarded Haiphong, killing as many as six thousand Vietnamese civilians. The French resumed control of Hanoi and forced Ho Chi Minh to flee into the countryside. It would be another decade before he returned to power in the north and another thirty years before Ho's revolutionary forces regained control of the south.

"We were bitterly disappointed in the British," An says. "We were even more bitterly disappointed when the French returned to power. After the August Revolution, almost all the students in the high schools and universities joined the struggle. Even the children of landowners and the French *métis* joined, like my friend whose father was my physics teacher. He was a Vietnamese who had graduated from university in France. His wife was French. Their son, who was half Vietnamese, half French, joined the revolution."

An tells me another story about a *métis* who joined the fight against the French. His father was a major in the Expeditionary Corps. His mother was Vietnamese. Their son, who looked more French than Vietnamese, tried to fool the enemy by donning a French uniform and leading an attack on the southern city of My Tho. He was captured and faced a death sentence.

"'I have captured your son,' said the French major to his Vietnamese wife. 'Do you want me to release him or send him to the military court?'"

"'I would like you to save his life,' she said.

"'I will lose my job. I will be dismissed from the army.'

"'Yes, but I love him very much, and he loves his country. He is a patriot.'"

On the next beat, An starts rewriting the dialogue.

"'He loves *two* countries. The country of his mother, and the country of his father.'

"In the end, the major released his son," An says. "He lost his rank and returned to France. His son was regrouped to North Vietnam and stayed there until 1975, when he returned to the south. By then he had lost everything, all of his father's estates and property. Today he lives in Saigon, a poor man. This happened to many children of landowners. Their parents were killed by the Communists during the revolution, but they continued to serve their country."

In September 1945, An signed up for a "crash course" in soldiering taught by the Communists near Rach Gia. For a hundred recruits there were only fifty weapons, including some muskets left over from World War I. Trainees had to pick up spent cartridges to make new bullets. Although he was involved in fighting first the Japanese and then the French, An dismisses this experience as little more than running errands. But a government Web site, recounting his activities as a Hero of the People's Armed Forces, describes An as "a national defense combatant who participated in all battles in the western region of South Vietnam," and it is not until March of the following year—six months after enrolling in his crash course—that An undergoes what he calls his *baptème de feu*.

"This course was reserved for the peasant class and the children of workers," An says. "I was considered an intellectual. My father was a *fonctionnaire*, a *cadre supérieur,* which was considered a pro-French element."

The Communists were also suspicious because An owned land. Doubting that his son would get far in school, An's father had bought him a tract of land near the U Minh forest. An visited his land from time to time, where he witnessed firsthand the hardships of peasant life in the countryside. These visits provided An with a good excuse for traveling into remote areas and also provided him with a source of income—most of which came, ironically, from the Americans.

"My father said the only way to help me was to make me a landowner. So in 1941 or 1942 he bought me seventy hectares of land in Rach Gia, plus thirty hectares of concession. This was rice tract land, very rich in rice paddies. Unfortunately we didn't have a chance to exploit the land because the revolution came in 1945."

An's land near the U Minh forest would later become a landing zone for the American military, which touched down here when ferrying troops into the region by helicopter. When he was a journalist accompanying soldiers on commando raids into the forest, An landed here several times.

"In the end, do you know who paid me for my land?" he asks. "Uncle Sam. In 1970 the Vietnamese government instituted land reforms. They would get rid of the owner class. They would show people they could do better than the Communists. The Americans footed the bill. They gave me a lump sum payment for forty percent of the value, and then every year after that they gave me another portion. I was supposed to receive the final payment in 1975, but I didn't have a chance to get it because the Communists came.

"If Uncle Sam hadn't bought my land, the Communists would have come and seized it. It would have been socialized and become the property of the government. I would have become the owner of *all* of Vietnam, possessing *all* the land in the country. I would have become Tarzan living free in the jungle, owned by nobody and everybody. This would have made me a happy man."

An laughs uproariously at his own joke. History dealt him the best of both worlds. He got Uncle Sam's cash in his pocket, and then he got to swing happily through the Communist jungle of collective ownership. "You know, God is always changing his mind," An says. "He never decides anything properly."

An's instructors in Rach Gia were guerrilla fighters from North Vietnam who had been incarcerated by the French on Poulo Condore. "The French system for controlling Vietnam was quite simple," An says. "They built a big palace for the provincial governor and next to it they built a prison, and next to that they built a courthouse. They captured you, took you to court, passed sentence on you, and threw you in prison, where the governor and his subordinates could watch you. It was all very logical."

"In addition to the main prison in each province, there were many concentration camps and prisons scattered throughout Indochina. In order to be a leader you should have spent time in one of these prisons. These people had been captured because they loved their country." When An uses the word *captured*, it is one of the rare instances when he employs a revolutionary term for its Western equivalent, in this case, *arrested*. The old *Time* reporter is discreet about tipping his hand with politically loaded words.

"The Communists who made propaganda in the prisons were well trained. They knew how to recruit members from among the other nationalist parties, the VNQDD, the Hoa Hao, and the Cao Dai. These people were also patriotic, but they were vague. They didn't have any ideology. The Communists were ideologues. This was very important. They had a system for acting on their nationalist sentiments, a plan of action. When you 'graduated' from prison, this was the first step to being promoted."

I have asked him to tell me this story before, but only once does An let slip that he saw combat in at least one battle as a Viet Minh platoon leader. "One day I was assigned to fight the French. I led my platoon out into the field. We set up an ambush along the road. This was in the hot season, April 1946. The

French had signed an agreement not to move through this area, which was controlled by our forces. They were breaking the agreement."

"I had thirty people in my platoon. We were armed with guns, grenades, and pistols. We had French shotguns, what they call 'Flauberts,' which are bird-shot rifles used by children to shoot pigeons, and some double-barreled shotguns. The French came marching down the paths alongside the canal. There were two columns of troops moving toward us. In between them was a boat, with machine guns ready to rake the sides of the canal.

"We had taken up a position on a bridge over the canal. I ordered my platoon to fire on the French, but we were too far away to hit anyone or see if anyone was hit. The French called in air cover, and when the plane arrived, I ordered my platoon to withdraw. This was my *baptême de feu*," An says, using the French term to describe his baptism by fire. "I never shot a gun again during the war."

An's real *baptême de feu* came in 1947, when he realized that even the people he loved would have to be sacrificed for the revolution. By mid-1946, he had left the countryside and returned to Can Tho. He was walking down the street one day when he ran into his beloved French teacher, Truong Vinh Khanh, who had been appointed by the Japanese to be director of the Lycée de Can Tho and had just been named minister of education in the newly created state of Cochin China. Surprised and pleased to see his old student, Khanh asked An what he was doing.

"I have just returned from the countryside, from my land," An told him. "The French are back, and most of the revolutionaries are gone. So I'm looking for a job. Maybe I'll go to Saigon or join the military school at Vung Tau."

While An tells me about this encounter, I notice that he is already wearing his protective coloration as a spy. He is pretending to be a landowner concerned about defending his property from the Viet Minh. Then he floats the idea of enlisting in the newly formed officer training school of the Franco-Vietnamese colonial army.

"An, don't be stupid," Khanh told him. "A soldier gets killed very easily. Stay here in Can Tho, and the next time I return, I'll take you to Saigon and give you a scholarship to go to France and finish high school. When you grow up you'll be able to learn properly. Now you're too crazy."

An laughs heartily, remembering his old teacher and his former craziness. The scholarship to France never materialized. The opportunity disappeared when Truong Vinh Khanh was ambushed by the Communists and killed in a roadside attack. They were aiming for the prime minister, a Cao Dai optometrist named Le Van Hoach, but they got Khanh instead.

"In 1947, in broad daylight, outside My Tho, the Communists ambushed a whole convoy of government officials," An says. This bold move was the first major attack organized by Tran Van Tra, the young military commander who later led the assault on Saigon during the Têt Offensive in 1968. By 1975, Tra would emerge as deputy commander of the Ho Chi Minh campaign, the last battle in the Vietnam war.

It is hard to imagine the pain An must have felt when he learned that the Communists had assassinated his French teacher. The moment reveals with blinding clarity the tragedy of modern Vietnam. An was caught up in a war, an actor who had taken sides. He knew that many people, including friends and family members, would die in this conflict. He had no choice but to carry on. "It's not a matter of reason or justice," a French military officer says to the British journalist who is the protagonist in *The Quiet American*. "We all get involved in a moment of emotion and then we cannot get out."

# The Work
# of Hunting Dogs

When France regained control of Vietnam in 1945, An's father, Vien, was afraid to return to his post in Rach Gia. He took refuge in Can Tho for a year, until he thought it safe to resume his old position. He had encouraged his surveyors and the rest of his staff to join the Viet Minh, and they had fought the Japanese, the British, and now the French. The colonial administration doubted Pham Xuan Vien's allegiance, since he had declined an offer of French citizenship in 1942. By 1947 they were using tougher measures.

"My father got into a lot of trouble with the French security in Rach Gia," An says. "They called him in for interrogations, day after day, night after night. Everyone who worked for him had abandoned the French zone and joined the revolution. They put the blame on him. He was intimidated by the French. He was scared. He couldn't sleep. That's why he got tuberculosis." By 1947 Vien's health was so precarious that he was admitted to the tuberculosis ward at Cho Ray hospital in Saigon.

"This was the year I was supposed to go back into the jungle to join the revolution," An says. "I went home to see my father before I reported for duty. My mother told me that he had been hurt by the security people. 'He is sick. You better go see him, before you leave for the jungle,' she told me."

When An went to Saigon, his father asked him to stay and take care of him. An did so willingly. Vien had a lung removed and remained in Cho Ray hospital for two years. It was probably in the TB ward that An acquired the scarred lung tissue that remained after his own bout with tuberculosis. "I got a little bit of the *grisaille* from my father, the infiltration of microbes. This is why I got a deferment from the Vietnamese army, until they were sure I had been cured."

An used his time in Saigon to read books and study English. When the United States Information Service opened an office on the rue Catinat near the Grand Hotel, An signed up for the first language course. In 1949 he made another attempt at finishing high school. Thanks to the intercession of his former math teacher, who had been named director of the Collège de My Tho, An was allowed to reenroll in school. Located in an amiable market town seventy kilometers southwest of Saigon, My Tho was the delta's second *lycée* devoted to preparing students for the *baccalauréat*.

Instead of finishing school, An got caught up in organizing student strikes and demonstrations. In 1950 Cochin China's schools were closed as students rallied for two mass demonstrations, one against the French and another against the Americans. Known as the Tran Van On demonstrations, these protests—borrowing a page from An's father's generation—were organized around the funeral of Tran Van On, a fifteen-year-old high school student at Saigon's *lycée* Pétrus Ky who had been killed by the French police. (One story says he was shot during a protest in front of the governor's palace; another says he was bludgeoned to death.)

An returned to Saigon for the big demonstrations, which were held in January and March 1950. The United States had sent two destroyers to Vietnam carrying war matériel. They were anchored in the Saigon River at the foot of rue Catinat, the main street in Saigon, which runs from the Catholic church past the Continental Hotel and down a tree-lined promenade to the waterfront. The military display included the USS *Boxer*, an aircraft carrier moored off the coast that launched a formation of war planes. The American pilots buzzed the student demonstrators in Saigon. Although the First Indochina War would continue for another four years, the United States was already positioning itself to succeed France in Vietnam.

"It looked as if all of Saigon had joined the students in their demonstration, as the funeral procession wound its way from Pétrus Ky high school to Cho Ray hospital, to pick up the body of Tran Van On and carry it to the cemetery," An says. "The crowd was even larger for the second demonstration in March. All the elements of society joined, the workers, clerks, market vendors; everyone poured into the streets.

"We were protesting the agreement signed by France and the United States in 1950. The Americans would foot the bill for the French Expeditionary Corps on two conditions. The French had to establish a Vietnamese armed force. There had to be a real Vietnamese army, not just Vietnamese troops serving under French command. The French also had to set up a real Vietnamese government. Not the kind of phony front they were used to operating with, but a real government, with some autonomous power of its own.

"The American policy of self-determination, saying that each sovereign country should have its own democratic government, is actually a messianic policy that America tries to impose on the rest of the world. This is why the Americans tried to create a country called South Vietnam, which was assembled out of the former colonies of Cochin China and Annam." The United States, according to An, prefers to rule the world through client governments that are nominally independent but do Washington's bidding. The French saw this system as messy and cumbersome, if not dangerous, because Vietnamese puppets were prone to cutting their strings and dancing to their own tune.

When France dispatched its best general, Jean de Lattre de Tassigny, to carry out this new plan for fighting the Viet Minh, An and his fellow students met de Lattre in 1950 with another round of street protests. "I was one of the organizers. Because I knew how to dodge the police, I was not arrested or killed. I was lucky. Many of the other organizers were not so lucky."

It was during the Tran Van On demonstrations that An began working with Dr. Pham Ngoc Thach, a French-trained medical doctor and Communist Party member who was "in charge of intellectual proselytization and student politicization" in Cochin China. A specialist in treating tuberculosis, Thach went on to become Ho Chi Minh's personal physician and North Vietnam's minister of health. (The number one cause of death for Communist soldiers during the French and American wars was malaria. Thach would die of malaria in 1968 while he was in the jungle searching for a cure.)

An had been introduced to Thach by a fellow student, Do Ngoc Thanh, better known by his alias Ba Hoc Sinh. "He was the leader of the student group in Saigon, before he was captured by French security. They tortured him to death and threw his body in the Saigon River. I was very upset when my friend was killed." A member of the Communist Party since the age of seventeen, Ba tutored An in socialist ideology. He was also a member of the Marxist Club in Saigon, which met at the house of French educator Georges Boudarel. Later Boudarel went into the jungle to join the Communists, where he too worked for Dr. Thach.

"Ba gave me all sorts of books published by Editions Sociales in France. The first book I read was *L'Economie*. Then I read about the history of the Bolshevik Party and Leninism. I wasn't a member of their Communist reading group, so I read all these books on my own.

"When my friend was captured, I realized I was in danger. His sister came to let me know that he had been arrested. I burned all the revolutionary books and documents he had given me. It took me the whole night to burn them."

Diaries written by Jack and Bobby Kennedy describing their trip to Indochina in 1951 offer a candid assessment of the Vietnamese revolution. John F. Kennedy, who was then a third-term congressman from Massachusetts, his twenty-six-year-old brother, Robert F. Kennedy, and their sister Patricia visited Vietnam in 1951 on a fact-finding trip designed to beef up JFK's résumé as he prepared to run for the senate the following year. Flying into Saigon on October 19, they were greeted at the airport by an impressive array of troops and tanks, a display not intended for them but for de Lattre de Tassigny, who was also visiting Saigon. "People seem sullen and resentful," Bobby noted in his journal. The countryside was held by the guerrillas, not the French. "Could hear shooting as evening wore on. Great many assassinations."

The Kennedys noticed right away that the French Indochina War was not being fought by the French. Certainly the French were throwing their best officers and many billions of francs into the conflict, but of the one hundred and fifty thousand colonial troops in Indochina, only fifteen percent came from metropolitan France. Of the eighteen thousand soldiers in the French Foreign Legion, for example, ten thousand were Germans who had fought in World War II. To avoid starving to death in the internment camps set up at the end of the war, they had volunteered to fight in Asia. Supporting this force were another one hundred and fifty thousand native troops.

By the fall of 1951, the Viet Minh had launched three major attacks on French forces in the Red River delta in the north. After ten thousand men were killed—many of them from aerial attacks with American-supplied napalm—the Viet Minh abandoned a general offensive and adopted guerrilla warfare.

It would be another three years before they attacked the French again in open battle at Dien Bien Phu, a lonely fort in a mountainous valley one hundred and eighty miles west of Hanoi.

On the first page of his journal Bobby described Ho Chi Minh as "an old Communist agitator" who had no popular support in Vietnam. The following day, after his first briefing, he had changed his mind: "If poll taken today, at least 70% of people throughout whole of Indo China would vote for Ho Chi Minh merely because he fights the French. The populace where fighting is taking place are all in favor of Ho Chi Minh. Sometimes they will help the Viet Nam troops, but they attempt to give the French troops wrong information, if they give them any."

The only Vietnamese the Kennedys interviewed was an unnamed journalist who complained that Vietnam was overrun by French *colons*. Bobby concurred. "Too many streets with French names, too many French flags, too many French in high places," he wrote. The journalist told the Kennedys about Vietnam's long-standing hatred of the Chinese—the reason why Ho Chi Minh would never bring Chinese troops into the war. Unfortunately, this lesson had been forgotten by the time John F. Kennedy became president of the United States in 1960.

The Kennedys were invited to dine, in evening dress, with His Majesty Bao Dai, the former emperor whom the French had brought back to run the State of Vietnam. "Had dinner with President at his palace—armed guards with revolvers in full view around the corridors," wrote JFK. "After dinner a small elephant was brought in [to the dining room] and spent some time there."

Two nights later, the Kennedys dined with General de Lattre de Tassigny, who was particularly worried about the Red River delta, home to seven and a half million Tonkinese, "good fighters and workers," de Lattre said, "the best people in S.E. Asia." De Lattre outlined an early version of the domino theory. "If the Commies gain control [of the Red River delta] they will turn the flank of all S.E. Asia. They can infiltrate into Laos and from there into Burma and down into Malaya. By this means Communism will hit Cochin China before the troops arrive."

Flying north to Hanoi for a "very impressive army show," the Kennedys spent the afternoon touring little hilltop fortifications in the Red River delta. The Kennedys lunched in one of these forts with a French colonel who said he was "optimistic . . . about the successful end of war, although this might not occur during our lifetime!!" Bobby recorded this observation with double exclamation marks.

"We are not here to help French maintain colonial rule, but to stop Communists," wrote John F. Kennedy in his journal. His brother was more honest in his assessment. "We are here to help French maintain colonies. French suspicious of U.S. intentions."

With the schools on strike and politics occupying his time, An never returned to high school. His father had taken early retirement at a reduced pension, and with no one else to support the family, An went to work. He moonlighted at various jobs, including driving a *cyclo-pousse*—a bicycle-mounted rickshaw—before he was hired as a bookkeeper at the CalTex oil company.

In 1950 An scored high marks in the competitive exam used to recruit civil servants. He left his bookkeeping job to become one of fifty people trained by the Indochinese government to work as customs inspectors. "There were ten for North Vietnam, called Tonkin, ten for central Vietnam, called Annam, ten for Laos, ten for Cambodia, and ten for Cochin China," An says. In 1950 he reported for work at the Saigon customs house at the harbor. For a normal person, this would have been a lifetime sinecure, leading to a happy retirement feathered by the usual bribes and kickbacks. But An was too smart for this limited career and too restless. He continued studying English and dreamed of traveling to the United States. He liked many of the Americans he met, often befriending them, but he was also convinced that the colonial powers occupying his country had to be defeated by any means possible. Only then could Vietnamese and Americans truly be friends.

During the Tết new year celebration at the end of January 1952, An was summoned by his Communist superiors to report to the jungle. He was excited, thinking he was finally being called to the war zone for action. He expected to be issued a gun and get to work fighting the enemy. "Already by 1947 I had decided I was ready to go into the jungle," An says. "But because my father was sick, I had to stay in the city and take care of him." Before he left Saigon, An was instructed not to quit his job at the customs house, curiously, and he was told to pretend that he was merely traveling out of town for the Tết holiday.

After journeying to Tay Ninh near the Cambodian border, An spent the night in a remote village before being picked up by a guide. They walked all day through the forest. "The French were continually sweeping through the area on military operations. It was hard to slip in and out. You sometimes had to wait for days before it was safe to move through the jungle."

An had already been here while visiting his younger sister, Pham Thi Cuc, who had moved to the jungle three years earlier to become "the Voice of Nam Bo," a radio broadcaster for the Communist network. An sometimes brought her food and medicine and stayed overnight at the radio station, hidden under the jungle canopy. (In 1955 An's sister moved to North Vietnam to work for the state-run coal mines.)

"It was a very hard life in the jungle," An says. "They didn't have enough food. They ate manioc and foraged for edible leaves. If they were lucky, they got rice. They made bread out of cassava, which you can eat when it's hot, but when it's cool, it's very tough, very difficult to chew. The French had Moraine spotter planes, which flew over the jungle looking for smoke or other signs of habitation. If they saw anything, they bombed it.

So you had to bake your bread in termite nests and vent the smoke through piles of leaves on the forest floor."

According to An, their only pleasure came from drinking homemade beer, of which there were two kinds: *standing* beer and *sitting* beer. "Standing beer was made from the urine of men. Sitting beer from the urine of women. After you took this urine and put yeast in it, it tasted like any other beer," An assures me, "but men usually preferred to drink standing beer, and women preferred sitting beer."

An was bunked in with his sister at the Viet Minh radio headquarters when Dr. Pham Ngoc Thach, secretary of the Cochin China Communist Party, arrived. Thach was responsible for setting up what came to be known as COSVN, the Central Office for South Vietnam. The advance element of the Communist Party's Central Committee, COSVN directed the war in the south. As the two men talked, An was disappointed to learn that he would not be joining his sister in the forest. Instead, he was being recruited to work as a spy in Thach's newly established military intelligence service. "I was the first recruit," An says. He found his new assignment ignoble. "Spying is the work of hunting dogs and birds of prey," he told Thach.

"I had been beaten by the riot police during the student demonstrations in Saigon, and I had no desire to be a stool pigeon or an informer," An says.

"You have to fight for your country," Thach told him. "Whatever we want you to do, you have to do it. You have no choice. You are fighting for the people. Any position is honorable, unless you are working for the enemy."

"I was supposed to follow the implantation of the Americans in Vietnam," An says. "To face the future, we had to start learning about the American intervention." Thach ordered two instructors to come down from the north and tutor An in military intelligence. One was trained by the Russians, one by the Chinese, but An found both of them pretty much useless. "Basically, Dr. Thach said I was on my own. I should borrow books from the Americans and the French that discussed intelligence and apply them as best I could."

While An describes this scene to me, his birds start screeching, as if they are trying to transport us back into the jungle on that fateful day. They sound like a mocking menagerie, hooting like chimpanzees and meowing like cats. They even bark like An's dogs. When I listen to the tape of our conversation, I strain to hear An's voice through a nonstop chorus of peeping, chirping, singing, calling. The birds repeat the same notes over and over again, with one bird giving out what sounds like a mayday distress call, "Help me, help me, I'm drowning." A microphone hidden in An's wall would record nothing but this idiotic din of screeching, babbling, cooing, complaining birds.

The first problem An confronted on slipping back into Saigon as a newly recruited spy was how to avoid being drafted into the French colonial forces. The Communists feared that An would end up as a colonel—not high enough in rank to be a good source of information. The sleepy world of the Indochinese customs house yielded little news, so An began moonlighting as a press censor at the Saigon post office. Here he was told to black out the dispatches written for British and French newspapers by Graham Greene, a "troublemaker" the French assumed was working for British intelligence.

Sitting under the soaring iron columns and revolving ceiling fans that decorated this impressive building designed by Gustave Eiffel, An worked at the post office in the late afternoon. Journalists posting stories from Saigon faced delays from faulty transmissions and other technical problems, but their biggest hurdle lay in the censor's office. An, a self-taught English speaker with a loose grasp of the language, was instructed to censor dispatches from Graham Greene, one of the great literary ironists of the twentieth century.

"The French gave us orders to watch Graham Greene very closely," An says. "He had worked for British intelligence dur-

ing World War II. Then he came out to Indochina to cover
the war. While he was in Asia, smoking opium and pretending
to be a journalist, the Deuxième Bureau assured us he was a
secret agent in MI6, British intelligence. We were also ordered
to watch very closely anyone who worked for the CIA.

"One day Graham Greene came to the post office to file a
story. His report was placed on my desk. It was a long report.
'What do I do with this?' I asked my supervisor. 'You have to be
very careful,' he said. 'If there are any words you are not sure
about, just cross them out. Your English isn't very good, but
there's nothing he can do about it. He can't argue with you. So
just go ahead and cross out the words. Mark it up and then give
it to the man who types the telegram. They never give him a
chance to argue anyway.

"To file a good story, you have to use a pigeon," An says, referring to a courier who flies dispatches out of the country and
files them in Hong Kong or Singapore. "Greene himself wrote
a story about how he used to pigeon articles out of Vietnam for
David Chipp, the Reuters correspondent in Indochina. I later
worked under David Chipp when he became chief of Reuters
in Southeast Asia. When I talked to him about this, he told me
that *he* was the one who pigeoned articles out of Vietnam for
Graham Greene.

"When Greene was in Saigon he smoked a lot of opium," An
says. "He got it from Mathieu Franchini at the Continental
Hotel. It wasn't illegal to smoke opium back then. I never met
Graham Greene. I saw him at the post office or down at the
Continental, having an aperitif on the terrace, but if I had
started talking to him, I would have got in trouble with the
French military security, the OR, the Office des Renseigne-
ments. These people were planted everywhere."

Aside from censoring Greene's dispatches, An also witnessed
the event that provided the centerpiece for *The Quiet American,* which was published in England in 1955 and in the United
States a year later. "I was on my way home from the customs

house," An says, describing what he saw on January 9, 1952. "We had a long break at lunchtime for a siesta, before going back to work in the afternoon. Sometimes when there wasn't much to do, I would go swimming in the pool near the Majestic Hotel and then go home for lunch. That day I told my boss I wanted to leave early to watch the parade honoring a French regiment that had fought in Korea. It was being rotated home, with a stop in Saigon to march down rue Catinat to impress people. This was the most important street in Saigon, lined with lots of elegant shops. A reviewing stand had been set up in front of the cathedral, and the whole city was planning to show up to watch."

An was riding his bicycle up the rue Catinat toward the Continental Hotel. Ahead, he saw a large crowd gathered near the fountain that decorated the Place Garnier. Facing this square in the center of Saigon were café Givral, the municipal theater, the Continental Hotel, and other Saigon landmarks. Neither An nor the spectators knew that the parade had been canceled. Suddenly An saw people flying through the air and heard the massive explosion that turned the plaza into a bomb site full of dead bodies and wailing survivors. He arrived at the scene to find windows shattered and lots of injured bystanders calling for help.

Featured as the climax of *The Quiet American,* the bombing was the work of General Thé, a Cao Dai warlord who was supported by the Americans as a "third force" meant to lead Vietnam into a future that was neither Communist nor French. In Greene's novel, Alden Pyle, the CIA agent who is financing Thé, considers this act of urban terrorism the unfortunate price one had to pay for advancing the cause of Vietnamese freedom. "The French G2 got a tip that General Thé had planted a bomb," An says. "So at the last minute they canceled the parade. Maybe they got the information too late. Maybe they wanted the bomb to go off and embarrass the Americans by having them kill lots of innocent civilians. Anyway, many people were lining the streets, waiting for the parade, when the bomb went off. It shattered the windows in the café Givral and the pharmacy next door. I watched as the police rushed in to help the wounded."

Except for its private army of several thousand soldiers, the Cao Dai were a peculiar choice for American patronage. The religion was founded in 1926 by a Vietnamese civil servant who had been enlightened during a spiritualist séance. The Cao Dai had a pope and female cardinals who presided over a holy see, eighty kilometers northwest of Saigon. Greene described the Cao Dai church as "a Walt Disney fantasia of the East, [full of] dragons and snakes in Technicolor." Represented by the divine, all-seeing eye, the religion included among its saints Joan of Arc, Descartes, Shakespeare, Pasteur, and Lenin.

Soon after its publication, An was given a copy of *The Quiet American* by Mills C. Brandes, a CIA case officer in Saigon, who would later serve, it appears, as chief of station in Thailand. Brandes thought the book would help An learn English. "Many Vietnamese believed this story about the Americans coming to Vietnam and trying to set up the Cao Dai as a 'third force,'" An says. When *The Quiet American* was made into a movie, An published a review of it. When the book was filmed for a second time in 2001, An served as an adviser on the film and as the model for one of its central characters—the Communist assassin who kills CIA agent Alden Pyle.

To escape his "manic-depressive temperament," Graham Greene began traveling in Asia in 1950. He was covering the Communist insurgency in Malaysia as a correspondent for *Life* when he flew to Hanoi in January 1951 to visit an old friend who was stationed there as British consul. Greene immediately fell in love with Vietnam. He would return three more times to report on the war and gather material for *The Quiet American*. As Greene wrote in *Ways of Escape*, the second of his two autobiographies, "In Indochina I drained a magic potion, a loving cup which I have shared since with many retired *colons* and officers of the Foreign Legion, whose eyes light up at the mention of Saigon and Hanoi."

"The spell was first cast, I think, by the tall elegant girls in white silk trousers; by the pewter evening light on flat paddy fields, where the water buffaloes trudged fetlock-deep with a slow primeval gait; by the French perfumeries in the rue Catinat; the Chinese gambling houses in Cholon; above all by the feeling of exhilaration which a measure of danger brings to the visitor with a return ticket: the restaurants wired against grenades, the watchtowers striding along the roads of the southern delta with their odd reminders of insecurity: 'Si vous êtes arrêtés ou attaqués en cours de route, prévenez le chef du premier poste important.'" [If you are detained or attacked en route, alert the station chief at the next guard post.]

On this first visit to Vietnam, Greene met the man who would become the model for the quiet American. Greene was in the marshes of Ben Tre in the Mekong delta, visiting "the happiest of the warlords in Cochin China," the Eurasian colonial Leroy, who provided his visitors with an evening of dancing on his private boat. "I shared a room that night with an American attached to an economic aid mission—the members were presumed by the French, probably correctly, to belong to the CIA. My companion bore no resemblance at all to Pyle, the quiet American of my story—he was a man of greater intelligence and less innocence, but he lectured me all the long drive back to Saigon on the necessity of finding a 'third force in Vietnam.' I had never before come so close to the great American dream which was to bedevil affairs in the East as it was to do in Algeria."

Greene returned to Vietnam in October 1951, eight months after his first visit. Again he was on assignment from *Life*, this time to write about the French war in Indochina. Also in October Greene was featured on the cover of *Time*. His leonine head was superimposed on a dark tunnel resembling a vagina, at the end of which glowed a Christian cross. The caption at the bottom of the cover read:

Novelist Graham Greene
Adultery can lead to sainthood.

Greene left Vietnam in February, hoping to travel to the United States to see the filming of his novel *The End of the Affair*. But his request for a visa was denied on the grounds that he was a Communist. (He had been a member of the Party for six weeks as a college prank.) When Greene was accidentally granted a visa by a U.S. consular official in Saigon, the man was sent scurrying through town to find the author in his room at the Continental Hotel. After knocking the door and asking to see Greene's passport, the man whipped out a stamp pad and marked the visa canceled.

When he was later allowed to travel to the United States on a short-term visa, Greene attended mass with Claire Booth Luce, wife of Henry Luce, chairman of Time Inc., and he delivered his magazine assignment to Luce's editors at *Life*, who killed the story. As Greene wrote in *Ways of Escape*, "I suspect my ambivalent attitude to the war was already perceptible—my admiration for the French Army, my admiration for their enemies, and my doubt of any final value in the war."

Returning to Vietnam in December 1953, Greene spent a "doom-laden twenty-four hours" at Dien Bien Phu, the upland fortification in the mountains west of Hanoi. Five months after Greene's visit, the Viet Minh overran the fort. The battle marked a major turning point in world affairs, said Greene, who believed it was the first time in the history of Western colonialism that Asian troops had defeated a European army in fixed battle. Of the fifteen thousand French expeditionary soldiers defending Dien Bien Phu, three to four thousand were killed on the battlefield and another ten thousand were captured by the Viet Minh. Half of these men would die on a five-hundred-mile forced march down from the mountains to the coast. The day after the Communist victory, the international conference convened to end the Indochina war opened in Geneva.

"Dien Bien Phu was a defeat for more than the French Army," Greene wrote in *Ways of Escape*. "The battle marked virtually the end of any hope the Western Powers might have entertained that they could dominate the East. The French, with Cartesian clarity, accepted the verdict. So, too, to a lesser extent, did the British: the independence of Malaya, whether the Malays like to think of it or not, was won for them when the Communist forces of General Giap, an ex-geography professor at Hanoi University, defeated the forces of General Navarre, ex-cavalry officer, ex-Deuxième Bureau chief, at Dien Bien Phu. (That young Americans were still to die in Vietnam only shows that it takes time for the echoes even of a total defeat to circle the globe.)" When asked by the *Sunday Times* to write about the most decisive battle in world history, Greene chose Dien Bien Phu.

Greene visited Vietnam for the last time in 1955. Scheduled to meet Ho Chi Minh for an interview but feeling a bit under the weather, he resorted to his customary cure—smoking a few pipes of opium. "The pipes took away the sickness and gave me the energy to meet Ho Chi Minh at tea."

"Of those four winters which I passed in Indochina, opium has left the happiest memory, and as it played an important part in the life of Fowler, my character in *The Quiet American*, I add a few memories from my journal concerning it, for I am reluctant to leave Indochina forever with only a novel to remember it by." Greene's remark in *Ways of Escape* is followed by eleven pages describing his opium smoking, which began during his first visit to Vietnam in 1951. "A French official took me after dinner to a small apartment in a back street—I could smell the opium as I came up the stairs. It was like the first sight of a beautiful woman with whom one realizes that a relationship is possible: somebody whose memory will not be dimmed by a night's sleep."

Pham Xuan An was formally inducted into the Communist Party in 1953 at a ceremony in the U Minh forest presided over by Le Duc Tho. A graduate of Poulo Condore, Tho was in charge of the southern resistance against the French. He would later spend four years negotiating with Henry Kissinger at the Paris peace talks. Tho's younger brother, Mai Chi Tho, as head of security for the Communist forces in the south, was An's boss.

"They asked me to join the Communist Party because I worked in a sensitive section," An says. "If I hadn't joined, they wouldn't have trusted me. They explained all the measures they took for security reasons, and I had to study the resolutions of the Party congresses. The Indochinese Communist Party had been officially disbanded, but it continued to work underground. The Communists feared the loss of popular support if they operated openly, so they carried out their activities in secret."

An had provisionally joined the Party the preceding year during a ceremony in the jungle near Cu Chi. "There is a probationary period of three to six months for a worker to join the party," An explains. "For a member of the middle class, a student, or someone who works for the government, the probationary period is at least a year, before you move from alternate to become a full member of the Party."

An did his homework, reading Party resolutions and the works of Marx and Engels, but he drew his real political lessons from Karl von Clausewitz, the nineteenth-century Prussian general who fought Napoleon at Waterloo and then, as director of the Prussian war college, wrote his unfinished masterpiece, *On War*. What An found most compelling in Clausewitz is the idea of total war, which includes attacking the citizens and property of an enemy nation in every way possible. An often returned to this idea, explaining over and over again the importance of the idea of total war to Vietnamese strategy.

"To fight a strong opponent from a foreign country, you have to carry out a prolonged war," he says. "You have to mobilize all the human beings and resources of your country toward one end—defeating this opponent. Faced with this general mobilization, the enemy will eventually conclude that carrying on its war is no longer profitable. It will decide on its own to withdraw. This is how you win. You do not defeat the enemy. You *cannot* defeat them. You are too weak, but by carrying out a prolonged war, you will eventually wear them down so that they leave of their own accord. The Chinese call this *people's warfare*. The Viet Minh learned it from the Chinese. They think the idea was invented by Mao Tse Tung, but it is actually a lesson from Clausewitz."

I am surprised when An tells me that the Vietnamese never won the Vietnam war. "No, the United States did not lose the war," he says. "We were fighting what Clausewitz called total war, where the entire nation is mobilized to fight an aggressor. According to Clausewitz, this war ends only when the aggressor calculates that his gains will never outweigh his losses. At this point, he will pull out. This is the only way for a weak country to fight a strong power. The Chinese improvised on this idea, but Clausewitz is our real teacher."

"This is exactly what happened," An says. "The Americans went away. That's all. We fought until the French left the country. We fought until the Americans left, and then we overthrew the puppet regime. We didn't beat the enemy militarily. Even Dien Bien Phu was just one battle that the French lost in a much larger war. The Americans didn't lose the war in Vietnam; they withdrew. It wasn't even their war to lose. It was the war of their puppets. The Americans built the country. They were the kingmakers, but then it collapsed. It wasn't the fault of those who built the house that it collapsed. It was the fault of those who lived in it."

After An's induction into the Party, Le Duc Tho served tea and cakes. "He made a little speech, saying that I was still a young man and that the war would soon be over. He knew the major powers were gathering to discuss arranging an armistice in Korea, and he thought the war in Vietnam would soon be resolved as well. He knew the Americans were replacing the French, but he had no way of knowing that the Second Indochina War would last as long as it did."

Following Tho's speech, he asked the cadre to introduce An to marriageable women in the Party. "They would introduce me to several girls, and I would choose among them."

"Did he introduce you to any girls himself?"

An chuckles at the thought of Vietnam's future prime minister functioning as a dating service. "No, he ordered his men to do it."

"They did introduce me to girls, and I liked one of them," An says. Before I can ask for her name, he launches into the story of another relationship. "The first girl I loved was an eleven-year-old classmate in Can Tho named Pauline Taget. She was a beautiful *métisse* whose father worked for the police. She joined the revolution. She was captured. Her father intervened to release her. After that, she lived with a man in a relationship organized by the revolution until he was killed in 1947 or 1948. At his funeral, Pauline insisted on draping over his coffin the revolutionary flag, the red flag with the big star in the middle."

I ask An if he has any photos or documents recording the moment when he joined the Party.

"No, you didn't sign anything," he says. "There was just this small ceremony. That's why many people later on had no way of proving that they were members of the Party. They had to go through the process all over again. My liaison officer, Nguyen Thi Ba, had to join the Party three times, even though she had been working for the Communists since she was a young girl of eighteen."

When not serving him tea and cakes and introducing him to eligible girls, An's Communist handlers could be stern. They held one black mark against him. He was a landowner who collected rent from peasants, a petit bourgeois oppressor of the working class. As described by his Vietnamese biographers, An had two tails, both of which he had to chop off.

"You are a petit bourgeois guy, but one who in his blood wants to be a hero, who has a passion for the movies, so it's easy to botch the work," An's handlers told him. "The son of a petit bourgeois has a tail. That tail is a bourgeois lifestyle, an arrogant and condescending speech and behavior toward the people, especially poor people whom they call the lower class. Even if you are clever enough to hide it, sooner or later the tail will protrude; it's very disgusting. You must find a way to cut it off."

After this lecture, An reported to the docks every day to eat lunch with the stevedores. This effort at worker solidarity was guided by the motto of the "three togethers": eat together, work together, rest together. An thought he was making good progress, until one day he revealed the second tail to be chopped off.

An punched a Frenchman in the nose. The lout was abusing some workers when An grabbed him by the neck and flung him to the ground. Instead of being praised for revealing "the tail of a patriot," he was chastised by the Communists. "An intelligence agent cannot be impatient and egoistic. It's not permissible to act like the boss defending his workers. Having been charged with secret work in the bowels of the enemy, if you show an unwillingness to associate with colleagues, turn down bribes, refuse to go for drinks or flirt with girls, how can you get anything done? Only a Communist guy would be so serious and determined. How can you fight if you show your tail like that?"

In spite of his freelance work at the post office for the Deuxième Bureau, An was drafted in 1954 into the Armée Nationale Vietnamienne. To avoid getting shot during the waning days of the French colonial war in Indochina, he played on the family connections by which business gets done in Vietnam. He asked his cousin, Captain Pham Xuan Giai, for help. "He was the head of the family," An says of Giai, the eldest son of his father's elder brother. Eight years older than An, Giai was born in Hué. Trained as a military officer by the French, he fought alongside Ho Chi Minh in 1945 and then switched sides the following year, going back to work for the French. Captain Giai was ambitious and smart, earning quick promotions as he moved through the ranks of the French intelligence services until he emerged as head of G5, the psychological warfare department of the army general staff.

Giai made his cousin an adjutant, the highest-ranking noncommissioned officer, and put him to work at army headquarters on the rue Gallieni, near Cholon. This is where Colonel Edward Lansdale found An when he came to offer his services—and money—to Captain Giai. Lansdale, a former advertising man and expert in psychological warfare, had been sent to run the CIA's covert operations in Vietnam. Officially arriving in Indochina soon after the French defeat at Dien Bien Phu, Lansdale found G5 and the rest of the old colonial military apparatus in a shambles. The southern forces were totally demoralized, with no idea what to do with themselves, until Lansdale and his innocuously titled Saigon Military Mission began turning Cochin China into a country called South Vietnam.

Finding a promising student in the young Pham Xuan An, Lansdale and his colleagues began teaching him the tradecraft that he would employ for his next fifty years as a Communist spy. "I am a student of Sherman Kent," An says, referring to the Yale professor who helped found the CIA, including what today is called the Sherman Kent School for Intelligence Analysis. "Strategic intelligence," Kent wrote in his classic text *Strategic Intelligence for American World Policy* (1949), is a "reportorial job" based on studying the personalities of world leaders. "It must know of their character and ambitions, their opinions, their weaknesses, the influences which they can exert, and the influences before which they are frail. It must know of their friends and relatives, and the political, economic, and social milieu in which they move."

Pham Xuan An, the psyops intelligence agent, was beginning to acquire the reportorial method that he would later employ so brilliantly as Pham Xuan An the *Time* correspondent. "People usually have one career, while I had two, the job of following the

revolution and the job of being a journalist," An told writer
Nguyen Thi Ngoc Hai. "These two professions were very contradictory, but also very similar. The intelligence job involves collecting information, analyzing it, and jealously keeping it secret,
like a cat covering its droppings. The journalist, on the other
hand, collects information, analyzes it, and then publishes it to
the world."

In addition to the writings of Sherman Kent, An was given
Paul Linebarger's classic text, *Psychological Warfare* (1948).
"The Communist magic is a strong, bad magic," writes
Linebarger of the "hostile operators" at work in psywar. "Psychological strategy is planned along the edge of nightmare." As
a quadruple agent who was moonlighting for France's Deuxième Bureau while working for his cousin's indigenous Vietnamese intelligence organization and its CIA sponsor, and at the
same time reporting to his Communist handlers, An was beginning to live along the edge of his own personal nightmare.
"I was never relaxed for a minute," he says. "Sooner or later as
a spy, you'll be captured. I had to prepare myself to be tortured.
This was my likely fate."

It was scant solace that most of An's colleagues in G5 were
in a similar predicament. "The guy in the office who worked for
the CIA was fighting against my cousin, who worked for the
Deuxième Bureau. They were keeping track of each other's
activities, reporting back to their bosses on what was happening.
But they were good friends. They played around all the time.
This is the Vietnamese way, pure Vietnamese. We were thrown
together like a bunch of crabs from the world's five oceans."

"When we weren't spying on each other, we smoked opium
and played together as friends. That was just the way things
worked. I had to compartmentalize. It was hard. First you do
it by reflex, and then, after a long period of time, you become
accustomed to it. I always had to be vigilant. My cousin, my
boss, was pro-French. So I had to pretend to be on the French
side, while I was actually against the French. I was also against

the interventionists, the Americans, while at the same time I was working for them. But you can't kill all the time. When the war was over, these were the people I would have to live with."

Among this farrago of spies were two men who would become An's fast friends. Cao Giao was a bespectacled man with a wispy goatee who worked for the Communists. Nguyen Hung Vuong, who had the caved-in face of an opium addict, worked for the CIA. An and his colleagues spent so much time together, palling around town and sipping coffee on the rue Catinat, that they came to be known as the Three Musketeers. They tipped each other jobs and information and remained loyal friends throughout Vietnam's numerous wars. In the beginning, An played little brother to his more experienced colleagues, as they taught him what they knew about the business of spying.

Born in 1917 into a mandarin family south of Hanoi, where his father worked as an official in the French judiciary, Cao Giao was irrepressible and brilliant. He had a rapier wit that spared no one's feelings. In turn, every political party that came to power in Vietnam would throw him in jail and torture him. He never recanted, never shaved the truth. Up to the day he died in exile in Belgium in 1986, he belonged to an intellectual aristocracy, like a Renaissance courtier forced to flee from one principality to another but always dawdling a bit too long at the café, lingering over one final story, one last joke, so that time and again he was captured by invading forces which always presumed he was on the wrong side. "He was the kind of man who goes to jail all the time, under any regime, just go to jail," An says, laughing at the thought of poor Cao Giao offending everybody.

The first to throw him in jail were the French. Cao Giao had allied himself with the Japanese when they invaded Vietnam. With their slogans about Greater Asia and Asia for the Asians, he thought they might hold the key to liberating his country. "This was my first lost cause," he quipped. Cao Giao then went to work for the Communists. Among the crucial tips he gave them was advance notice of the Japanese coup d'état against the French. "He was the only source for this information," An says. "He contributed a lot to the revolution, particularly under the Japanese occupation and the French."

Nonetheless, when the Communists come to power in the north, it was their turn to arrest Cao Giao and torture him for having worked for the Japanese. Eventually he fled to the south. Here Cao Giao got in trouble with Ngo Dinh Diem, another collaborator with the Japanese who had emerged as America's ally against the Communists. On being released from Diem's torture chambers, Cao Giao went to work for *Newsweek*. He was the inseparable twin of his fellow Vietnamese journalist at *Time*, but while the discreet An never got in trouble with any-one, Cao Giao was a lightning rod for suffering. By 1978 he was being tortured again in Saigon's infamous Chi Hoa prison, this time for supposedly collaborating with the CIA. After four years in prison, including thirteen months in solitary confine-ment, Cao Giao was finally allowed to fly into exile.

While Cao Giao was a born storyteller whose round, nut-brown face was invariably animated with a smile, his colleague, the frail, stoop-shouldered Vuong, spoke in a cadaverous whisper that made him sound as if he were trying to disappear from the space in front of you. He had a head full of straight, graying hair and the transparent, papery skin of an *opiomane*. Born in 1923 in Kunming, southern China, into a Vietnamese family who worked for the French, Vuong was a brilliant student who passed his high school exams in Hanoi before going on to study med-icine. In August 1945, after a brief stint as a censor, he left Vietnam for Hong Kong. Then he traveled to Thailand, where he became friends with Pham Xuan Giai, An's cousin. While Giai was attached to the Deuxième Bureau, Vuong was work-ing for the CIA, first in Thailand, Laos, and Hanoi, and then fi-nally in Saigon, where Giai recruited him to work for G5.

"Vuong, who worked for the CIA, was fighting against my cousin, who worked for the Deuxième Bureau," An says. "They were keeping track of each other's activities, reporting back to their bosses on what was happening. But they were good friends who played around together. There is nothing wrong with that. Each one had his own responsibilities. I learned a lot of things from these people. No one ever suspected that I was working for the Communists. I was so innocent and so open. Anything I didn't know, I would just ask about. Since no one had taught me about intelligence, I had to ask those who knew about it to teach me."

From his cockpit at G5, An was getting a global introduction to psyops. "They had borrowed from the British and the French various ideas about counterinsurgency warfare," he says. "From the British, they relied mainly on the ideas of Sir Robert Thompson and his experience in Malaya. From the French, they relied on the ideas of Colonel Roger Trinquier, an expert in counterinsurgency warfare, first in Vietnam and then in Algeria. He had been a professor at a high school in France, and then in World War II he became a military man. Trinquier was the first person to work out a plan for fighting the war in Indochina. He is the key to understanding the French strategy of counterinsurgency. His ideas were later adopted by the Americans. You should read Trinquier if you want to understand what we were doing back then."

Born in 1908 in the French Alps and trained as a schoolteacher, Trinquier got his start in 1934 as a young military officer fighting Vietnamese pirates and opium smugglers in the wild territory known as the Land of One Hundred Thousand Mountains, which straddles the Chinese-Vietnamese border. He was imprisoned by the Japanese during World War II. After the war, Trinquier devoted the next fifteen years of his military career to fighting wars of independence, first in Vietnam and

then in Algeria. According to Trinquier, revolutionaries prevail not because they win their wars, but because the politicians
sell out the military at precisely the moment when it is winning
the war. If this complaint sounds familiar, it would become the
leitmotiv for many American military men who embraced this
view after their own failure in Vietnam.

In the late 1940s, Trinquier was assigned what Bernard
Fall calls "the difficult task of clearing Vietminh elements out
of the swamps and rice paddies surrounding Saigon." Trinquier was later put in charge of arming Vietnamese Montagnards and other tribal groups who would be parachuted
clandestinely behind enemy lines. Supplied by the Americans,
who greatly admired this industrious soldier and his secret operation, Major Trinquier had as many as thirty thousand men
under his command when "the regrettable Dien Bien Phu incident," as he calls it, put an end to the First Indochina War. The
Americans pulled the plug on Trinquier's clandestine forces, and
many of his twenty thousand troops were ferreted out by the
Communists and killed.

During the Vietnam fighting, Trinquier developed his theory of modern warfare. According to him, Vietnam's revolutionary conflict was the world's first modern war because it
involved a battle for the "hearts and minds" of the Vietnamese
people. Winning the allegiance of the civilian population was a
military objective as great as winning set-piece battles. A revolutionary force seeking to prevail in modern warfare will employ an "interlocking system of actions—political, economic,
psychological, military—that aims at the overthrow of the established authority in a country and its replacement by another
regime." Given the totality of these methods, an army trying to
suppress a revolutionary force must adopt its own panoply of
modern techniques. It will operate with small, mobile teams
of commandos and clandestine forces. It will employ torture. It
will force the relocation of civilian populations into armed

camps and employ terror and other techniques developed in the increasingly effective domain known as psychological warfare.

When they arrived in Vietnam to take over the French war, the Americans, often unknowingly, reinvented all of Trinquier's methods. Thinking themselves great innovators in fighting the Vietnamese revolutionaries, they were actually latter-day Trinquiers duplicating all of his methods for fighting a modern war—with no better luck. The Americans developed the Green Berets and other special forces operating with small, mobile teams of commandos. They employed torture and terror, most notably the Phoenix Program, which cultivated informants and assassinated fifty thousand suspected Communist sympathizers. They adopted wholesale the forced relocation of the Vietnamese population into armed camps, first known as *agrovilles* and then called strategic hamlets. Finally, they employed with gusto the psychological warfare methods designed to win the hearts and minds of the civilian population, whose allegiance would be the ultimate weapon in this people's war.

When asked to comment on his wartime reporting in Vietnam, David Halberstam remarked to British journalist Phillip Knightley, "The problem was trying to cover something every day as news when in fact the real key was that it was all derivative of the French Indo-China war, which is history. So you really should have had a third paragraph in each story which should have said, 'All of this is shit and none of this means anything because we are in the same footsteps as the French and we are prisoners of their experience.'"

In the spring of 1971, historian Alfred McCoy interviewed Trinquier and his superior officer, General Maurice Belleux, former chief of French intelligence for Indochina. McCoy at the time was traveling around the world researching his classic text *The Politics of Heroin in Southeast Asia* (published in 1972, with a revised edition, *The Politics of Heroin: CIA Complicity in the Global Drug Trade*, published in 1991). "By 1950–1951

younger, innovative French officers had abandoned the conventional war tactics that essentially visualized Indochina as a
depopulated staging ground for fortified lines, massive sweeps,
and flanking maneuvers," writes McCoy. "Instead, Indochina
became a vast chessboard where hill tribes, bandits, and religious minorities could be used as pawns to hold strategic territories and prevent Viet Minh infiltration."

Trinquier was given a large expanse of territory in which to
experiment with these new ideas. Operating along the Annamite
Cordillera, mountains which stretch from central Vietnam to the
Chinese border, Trinquier recruited and trained more than
thirty thousand tribal mercenaries, who busied themselves attacking Viet Minh supply lines and aiding the French military
effort. This included cultivating poppies in Laos and converting
them into heroin—the lucrative business French intelligence
services used to support themselves. Since it had no strategic
value, save as a way station between the coast and Trinquier's
inland empire, Dien Bien Phu was another component in Trinquier's strategy. Hmong opium cultivators produced a substantial crop of raw opium in the hills around Dien Bien Phu,
and the fort was supposed to keep Laos from falling into the
hands of the Viet Minh.

As recounted by Belleux and Trinquier in their interviews
with McCoy, Trinquier financed his operation by having French
paratroopers fly raw poppy sap from Laos to Vung Tau (then
known as Cap Saint Jacques), where it was transported to
Saigon. Here the Binh Xuyen river pirates, who controlled the
city's police department and opium dens, transformed the raw
poppy sap into a smokeable product. The proceeds from this operation were split between the pirates, France's Deuxième Bureau, and Trinquier's "supplementary forces" in the mountains.

Graham Greene wrote extensively about Dien Bien Phu because he considered it the most decisive battle in modern history, but there was one thing about the battle he never
understood. "What remains a mystery to this day," Greene

wrote in 1980, "is why the battle was ever fought at all, why twelve battalions of the French Army were committed to the defense of an armed camp situated in a hopeless geographical terrain—hopeless for defense and hopeless for the second objective, since the camp was intended to be the base of offensive operations. (For this purpose a squadron of ten tanks was assembled there, the components dropped by parachute.) A commission of inquiry was appointed in Paris after the defeat, but no conclusion was ever reached."

The mystery was solved only when Trinquier and Belleux revealed the importance of the heroin trade in financing the French army in Indochina, which in turn dictated the position of Dien Bien Phu and its strategic significance. After Vietnam, Trinquier directed the French torture campaign during the battle of Algiers. He went on to organize mercenary armies in the Congo and then retired to write his widely read military manuals on counterinsurgency, which recommend "calculated acts of sabotage and terrorism." If Trinquier's use of drugs to finance military operations was one strategy later adopted by the CIA, his embrace of torture as an effective tool in counterinsurgency was another practice that came to be widely employed in Vietnam.

Pham Xuan An eventually found himself engaged in every aspect of Trinquier's program. While working for his cousin at G5, he became an expert in counterinsurgency. Later he got involved in laundering drug money for Vietnamese intelligence, and he faced throughout his life the constant fear of being unmasked and tortured. He would either be implementing Trinquier's program or falling victim to it.

# Brain Graft

After the French defeat at Dien Bien Phu, the task of turning the old colonial entities of Annam and Cochin China into a country called the Republic of Vietnam, or South Vietnam, as it was popularly known during the twenty years of its brief existence, fell to the creative genius of Edward Lansdale. This was a plum assignment for the harmonica-playing, homespun hero of American counterinsurgency. To create a nation where none had previously existed was like Picasso facing a blank canvas. Lansdale would have to employ all the skills of modern salesmanship he had learned while launching new products at his San Francisco ad agency.

Lansdale had been handling accounts for Wells Fargo Bank, Union Trust, Nescafé, Italian Swiss Colony Wine, and Levi Strauss (he designed their first national campaign to sell blue jeans across the United States) when the Japanese attacked Pearl Harbor on December 7, 1941. He enlisted, at the age of thirty-five, as a lieutenant in the army's Military Intelligence Service in San Francisco. Working for William J. "Wild Bill" Donovan's Office of Strategic Services (OSS), precursor to the

CIA, Lansdale began doing double duty as military officer and spy. A decade after enlisting, Lansdale was in the Philippines masterminding his first "regime change"—cultivating a CIA-friendly candidate, Ramon Magsaysay, and engineering his election to the presidency. Lansdale's management of this campaign was a public relations triumph. Nationalists (representing a wide spectrum of political beliefs) who opposed U.S. strategy were transformed into "Communist" rebels who could be hunted down and dispatched with impunity.

In Vietnam, which Lansdale visited perhaps as early as 1950, he was charged with working the same magic he had brought to the Philippines. Traveling undercover, he made a six-week investigative tour of Indochina in June and July 1953. A year later, he arrived officially in Vietnam as "assistant air attaché." Colonel Lansdale was nominally working for the Military Assistance Advisory Group (MAAG) under General John "Iron Mike" O'Daniel, who was helping the French create a Vietnamese army. Unhappy with the Americans who were moving into town, the French had given O'Daniel a former Japanese military whorehouse in Cholon as his headquarters. A shed in the courtyard with a dirt floor and folding chairs lit by two bare bulbs dangling from the ceiling served as Lansdale's office. Here he began creating the training relations instruction mission (TRIM), whose job was to rush loyalist troops into parts of the country that were being given up by the Viet Minh. (After the signing of the Geneva Accords, Vietnam was "temporarily" divided at the seventeenth parallel, with each side retreating north and south of the line, until national elections could be held to reunite the country. These elections, scheduled for 1956, never took place.)

"There was too little amity in TRIM for me," Lansdale writes in his autobiography, *In the Midst of Wars: An American Mission in Southeast Asia* (1972). TRIM's French chief of staff, who was nominally Lansdale's boss, refused to speak to him. The officer placed his adjutant between himself and Lansdale, and even when they were talking in English, he insisted on having their conversation "translated." They had a "psychotic suspicion of everything I did," Lansdale said of his French colleagues. Assembled "from various intelligence services," they spent their days eavesdropping on his telephone conversations and writing reports on his activities. Never afraid to play the village idiot, Lansdale took his revenge by poking fun at the French chief of staff. Whenever they met at a social event, Lansdale would drape his arm over the man's shoulder and drawl in a grating American twang, "This guy is my buddy. You treat him right, you hear?"

Forbidden by the French from getting involved in the important business of the general staff—G1, administration; G2, intelligence; G3, operations; and G4, quartermaster—Lansdale was left with G5, civil affairs. This involved both white and black operations, ranging from propaganda to covert activity, including sabotage and assassination. "There was a large headquarters staff, three armed propaganda companies in the field, a staff of artists and writers, a radio unit broadcasting daily programs to the troops from the government radio station in Saigon, access to major printing facilities, and combat psywar equipment, such as portable sets for voice amplification, of a quality far superior to anything I had known," Lansdale writes in his autobiography. "What was lacking, fundamentally, was a real purpose to which all this talented manpower and fine equipment could be directed."

G5 "had a heavy political handicap," says Lansdale, owing to the fact that "Vietnamese in uniform were teamed with the soldiers of French colonial forces, fighting a Communist enemy amongst a population yearning for independence from France." In other words, South Vietnam's psywar operations were directed toward maintaining France's colonial power in Indochina.

"I started an educational effort with the French staff officers I had met," Lansdale says. "They found my ideas alien and suggested laughingly that I take up smoking opium instead." This suggestion was only half in jest. During his undercover tour of Indochina, Lansdale had discovered that General Salan, commander in chief of the Expeditionary Corps, was financing French military operations by selling opium from the Laotian highlands. "We don't want you to open up this keg of worms since it will be a major embarrassment to a friendly government. So drop your investigation," Lansdale was told, when he reported the news to Washington.

"As 1954 ended, the rhetoric said that Vietnam was an independent nation," writes Lansdale in his autobiography. "There still was a large French Expeditionary Corps present in the country, however, and there still were many Frenchmen throughout the Vietnamese civil and military establishments, although most of them were stepping down from positions of executive authority to assume the role of advisers. The French presence was evident and heavy. At most, Vietnamese officials were getting sniffs, not deep breaths, of the air of freedom and independence."

Lansdale, in a rather poetic passage, tries to describe the true Vietnam behind the colonial facade. I am not certain if he ever visited the house of psywar officer Pham Xuan An, but the description sounds remarkably like the neighborhood where An lived in a two-room house located between Chinatown and Saigon's central market. "Behind the façade of French provincial buildings and colonial life on the main thoroughfares of the Saigon-Cholon metropolitan area lay the real city, a densely-packed complex of Vietnamese hamlets. It was almost like a conjuring trick. Down alleys and byways past the concrete and stucco office buildings, shops, and villas there were the hidden hamlets, throbbing with an intense life of their own, with thousands of people crowded into wooden dwellings along a block or two of dirt lanes. A total of perhaps a million people inhabited these hamlets in Saigon-Cholon, out of the sight and ken of those on the paved thoroughfares. Few foreigners, except for groups of police, ever visited these hamlets. They made up a nearly secret city of timeless Vietnamese ways within a surface city that had taken to foreign modes."

America's first glimpse of the real nature of Lansdale's activities in Vietnam came when his former deputy, Daniel Ellsberg, released the Pentagon Papers—the top-secret *History of United States Decisionmaking on Vietnam*, completed in 1969. Ellsberg copied forty-three of its forty-seven volumes and leaked them to the *New York Times* and other newspapers in 1971. (Lansdale had two official postings to Vietnam, a two-year tour beginning in 1954, and another two-year stint from 1965 to 1967. In between, he directed the CIA's effort to assassinate Cuban president Fidel Castro. Ellsberg served as Lansdale's assistant in Vietnam for a year and a half, beginning in the summer of 1965. A swashbuckling hawk with a death wish, Ellsberg loved to carry a machine gun into the field and play weekend warrior. His transformation into an antiwar activist came later.)

Included in the Pentagon Papers is a document entitled *Lansdale Team's Report on Covert Saigon Mission in 1954 and 1955*. This anonymously authored report on Lansdale's Saigon military mission (SMM) presents itself as "the condensed account of one year in the operation of a 'cold war' combat team."

"The SMM was to enter into Vietnam quietly and assist the Vietnamese, rather than the French, in unconventional warfare. The French were to be kept as friendly allies in the process, as far as possible. The broad mission for the team was to undertake paramilitary operations against the enemy and to wage political-psychological warfare."

The report goes on to describe the covert acts of sabotage and terror that Lansdale launched against North Vietnam before his agents were evacuated from Hanoi in April 1954. The team "spent the last days of Hanoi in contaminating the oil supply of the bus company for a gradual wreckage of engines in the buses, in taking actions for delayed sabotage of the railroad (which required teamwork with a CIA special technical team in

Japan who performed their part brilliantly), and in writing detailed notes of potential targets for future paramilitary operations." These plans to blow up power plants, oil storage facilities, harbors, and bridges were unfortunately curtailed, laments Lansdale, because of "U.S. adherence to the Geneva Agreement," which ended the First Indochina War.

With an attempt at James Bondian flair, the Lansdale report describes the exploits of Lucien "Black Luigi" Conein and his SMM operatives in Hanoi, who "had a bad moment when contaminating the oil" used to run the city's buses. "They had to work quickly at night, in an enclosed storage room. Fumes from the contaminant came close to knocking them out. Dizzy and weak-kneed, they masked their faces with handkerchiefs and completed the job."

By 1955, Lou Conein was training paramilitary saboteurs in the Philippines and landing them on the shores of North Vietnam. The CIA launched a parallel effort with agents trained on Saipan Island. The infiltrators carried weapons, radios, and gold—a lot of gold—with an estimated value of close to a million dollars. With only a handful of exceptions, every agent who landed in the north was captured immediately on hitting the ground. Worse yet, many captured agents, without Lansdale or the CIA knowing that they had been captured, started broadcasting disinformation back to the south.

What Lansdale had begun as part of his cold war combat mission was taken over in 1964 by the U.S. military and expanded. When the Vietnam war ended in 1975, five hundred captured agents were incarcerated in North Vietnamese prisons, where they were left to rot for the next decade. "They must have had someone on the inside to roll up the entire network the way they did, all at one time," Conein told an interviewer in 1995. He wondered if a mole or spy had tipped them off, with the most likely candidate being Conein's "good friend" Pham Xuan An.

Among Lansdale's less heroic feats was the organization of "a small English-language class conducted for mistresses of important personages." His students included the "favorite mistress" of the army chief of staff. Lansdale tried to destroy Vietnam's largest printing press, which had fallen into the hands of the Communists in the north, and he conducted "black psy-war strikes," which included printing fake government decrees to be distributed in the north. He was particularly proud of the work done by Vietnamese astrologers, who were hired to predict disasters for the Communists and good omens for the south.

When his work as a wrecker became hampered by political constraints, Lansdale engineered another covert operation in which he blanketed the north with propaganda saying "Christ has gone to the south" and "the Virgin Mary has departed from the north." One leaflet showed Hanoi at the center of three concentric rings of nuclear destruction. Operation Passage to Freedom worked so well in convincing Catholics that they were in imminent danger that eight hundred thousand refugees fled from North to South Vietnam on American ships and airplanes. The south had a population at the time of seventeen million people, mainly peasant rice farmers and plantation workers. This huge influx of Catholic refugees provided the newly formed government of South Vietnam—which was run by a Catholic—with apparatchiks who quickly installed themselves as overseers and informants in the predominantly Buddhist south. Over half the high officials in the Diem government were Catholic, in a country that was ninety percent Buddhist. Loyal to the Americans who had "saved" them from the Communists, these refugees from the north were the perfect material for shaping into the new citizens of a new country. Lansdale had finally found his "third force," and it was not Cao Dai but Catholic.

The refugees flowing out of North Vietnam were also useful for highlighting Communist perfidy. Aiding Lansdale in this

task was navy medical officer Tom Dooley, who was assigned to
one of the U.S. military ships that ferried refugees from the Gulf
of Tonkin south to Danang. Dooley's book about the Catholic
exodus, *Deliver Us from Evil* (1956), was a bestseller. The dash-
ing doctor and his humanitarian exploits "located Vietnam on
the new world map for millions of Americans," says James
Fisher, Dooley's biographer. With Lansdale's assistance, Dooley went on to write other bestsellers about life in Indochina,
which paved the way for America's military engagement in
Southeast Asia. (Later, when Dooley was being vetted for
Catholic sainthood, it was discovered that he was a closeted ho-
mosexual and literary fraud whose books were heavily edited,
if not ghostwritten, by the CIA.)

    After his success in generating Catholic refugees, Lansdale
turned to consolidating the power of Ngo Dinh Diem, the roly-
poly, fifty-three-year-old bachelor who had been named prime
minister in the postwar government of Emperor Bao Dai. Born
in 1901, Jean Baptiste Ngo Dinh Diem was a Catholic mandarin
who had become a provincial governor at the age of twenty-five.
After brief service as interior minister in one of Bao Dai's pro-
French cabinets, he resigned from the government, accusing
the emperor of being a "tool" of the French. He collaborated
with the Japanese during World War II and was imprisoned by
Ho Chi Minh for six months before going into exile. In 1950 he
traveled to the United States, where he spent two years living in
Maryknoll seminaries in Lakewood, New Jersey, and Ossining,
New York. Diem was residing in a Benedictine monastery in
Belgium when the United States pressured Bao Dai to call
him back to Vietnam.

    Lansdale protected Diem from two coup attempts before
organizing his first successful military campaign, the "battle of
the sects," an attack on the Hoa Hao, Cao Dai, and Binh Xuyen
private armies. Since the Binh Xuyen river pirates were financing the French colonial administration, which included
a monthly check to Bao Dai, the battle of the sects was in fact

a battle against the French. The French had struck their deal with Bay Vien, the Binh Xuyen chief, out of necessity because without him they had neither the money nor the men to regain control of Vietnam after World War II. Bay Vien was indifferent to whether he supported the French or the Viet Minh, and he was a Communist before he was a capitalist, but the latter cut him a better deal.

While collecting "insurance" payments of two thousand six hundred dollars a day from Saigon's Grand Monde casino, the Binh Xuyen by 1947 had an army of ten thousand men organized into seven full regiments, making it the largest Viet Minh force in Cochin China. This same year the Viet Minh launched a wave of terror attacks against the French. Although Bay Vien initially supported the Viet Minh, by 1948 he had swung over to the French side, which allowed him to expand his lucrative hold on Saigon's drug traffic, gambling dens, and houses of prostitution. Bay Vien's link with the Deuxième Bureau was more than financial. The Binh Xuyen was so adept at gathering intelligence through a block-by-block network of informants that Diem's secret police later adopted this system themselves. To root the Viet Minh out of Saigon and secure the city from terrorist attacks, the French were obliged to turn over more and more territory and an increasing number of government functions to the Binh Xuyen.

Saigon became Bay Vien's personal fiefdom. Elevated by Bao Dai to the rank of general, he opened the Hall of Mirrors, the largest brothel in Asia, with twelve hundred employees. He ran the Grand Monde casino in Cholon and the equally profitable Cloche d'Or in Saigon, and he controlled hundreds of opium dens in Saigon and Cholon, with a percentage of their profits being paid yearly to Emperor Bao Dai. Vien's lieutenant was named director-general of the police in the capital region, which stretched sixty miles from Saigon out to the coastal resort at Cap Saint Jacques. Bay Vien's commercial contacts in France were key to his success. "The unchallenged leader of Saigon's Corsican underworld was the respected merchant Mathieu Franchini," says historian Alfred McCoy. "Owner of the exclusive Continental Palace Hotel, Franchini . . . controlled most of Saigon's opium exports to Marseille." He also managed the opium and gambling profits of the Binh Xuyen as their "investment counselor."

The Binh Xuyen remained in power until Lansdale and Diem succeeded in chasing them back to the Forest of the Assassins. From April 28 to May 3, 1955, the Vietnamese army fought the pirate forces house to house for control of Saigon. "More troops were involved in this battle than in the Têt Offensive of 1968, and the fighting was almost as destructive," says McCoy. Five hundred people were killed, two thousand wounded, and another twenty thousand were left homeless. "This battle was a war by proxy; the Binh Xuyen and Diem's army were stand-ins, mere pawns, in a power struggle between the French Deuxième Bureau and the American CIA," writes McCoy. One client army was fighting another, as the First Indochina War shaded into the Second.

In the official version of the story, a valiant Diem—whom Dwight Eisenhower called the "George Washington of Vietnam"—fought a heroic battle against the sects and vanquished them in combat. Later it was revealed that Lansdale had bought off the sects with more than twelve million dollars in CIA money, which allowed their leaders to retire happily to the French Riviera. (Lansdale, when asked about these funds, called them "back pay.") One of Lansdale's former assistants, Colonel L. Fletcher Prouty, maintains that the money also bought a lot of political theater, with Lansdale scripting battles to produce fake combat scenes.

Philippe Franchini, son of Mathieu, former investment counselor to the Binh Xuyen, remembers meeting Bay Vien in Paris several years after Diem's war against the sects. The young Philippe accompanied his father to Fouquet's on the Champs Elysées for an afternoon aperitif with Vien, who showed up at this fancy café with a tiger on a leash. "He was a bit of a clown," says Philippe. "But while you were laughing at his jokes and amused by his fabulous stories, you still knew that he was capable of killing you if he wanted to."

Lansdale's next move was to engineer an election victory for Diem. Supposedly a puppet for American interests, Diem never moved his arms the way the Americans intended. In this important psyops lesson on how to rig an election, he got carried away. In October 1955, the South Vietnamese were supposed to vote for Bao Dai or Diem. Lansdale arranged for the election to be conducted with colored ballots—red, which in Vietnam signifies good luck, for Diem, and green, which signifies bad fortune, for Bao Dai. After adding a stiff dose of vote rigging and intimidation, Diem announced that he had "won" the election with 98.2 percent of the vote. So began the history of the democratic, freedom-loving country of South Vietnam, whose interests the United States would selflessly defend during the next twenty years of its stillborn existence.

Diem set up a dynastic dictatorship oriented toward enriching his family and rewarding fellow Catholics with jobs. His younger brother, Ngo Dinh Can, ruled central Vietnam as a feudal warlord. Ngo Dinh Thuc, a Catholic archbishop, ran the family's rubber and timber estates. Ngo Dinh Luyen was appointed ambassador to Great Britain, while Diem's fourth brother, Ngo Dinh Nhu, controlled the secret police and Diem's private political party. Nhu's wife, Tran Le Xuan, served as South Vietnam's First Lady, and under her beautiful but austere gaze the country outlawed divorce and abortion and made the wearing of *ao dais*, the traditional Vietnamese costume, mandatory. The 1954 Geneva Conference, which had temporarily divided Vietnam along the seventeenth parallel, called for a general election to reunite the country in 1956. With Ho Chi Minh set to win this election, Diem invented reasons for canceling the vote and set about arresting his opponents. Communists and socialists were scooped up along with journalists, trade unionists, and Buddhists, until a hundred thousand people were thrown in prison camps.

"Without U.S. support, Diem almost certainly could not have consolidated his hold on the South during 1955 and 1956," wrote an unnamed analyst in the Pentagon Papers. "Without the threat of U.S. intervention, South Vietnam could not have refused to even discuss the elections called for in 1956 under the Geneva settlement without being immediately overrun by the Vietminh armies. Without U.S. aid in the years following, the Diem regime certainly, and an independent South Vietnam almost as certainly, could not have survived. . . . In brief, South Vietnam was essentially the creation of the United States."

"Lansdale was very successful in the beginning, but the Americans made a mistake," An says. "They set up Ngo Dinh Diem and a centralized government. They got rid of all the private armies which had been created by the French to help them, the Hoa Hao, the Cao Dai, the Binh Xuyen. Lansdale eliminated all of them in a very short period, from 1955 to 1956. Diem turned himself from a prime minister into a president and continued building up a symbolic government, a supposedly democratic government, patterned on the American government. This is when they considered that Lansdale's job was over. Unfortunately for the Americans, they didn't allow Lansdale's people to continue their work. When Diem and his family veered toward nepotism, the Americans found out too late."

What the Americans also failed to realize was the way Diem played into the hands of the Communists. This is why Pham Xuan An advised his colleagues not to topple Diem or work too hard at destabilizing his government. Having grown up in colonial Vietnam, An realized the effectiveness of the French administration. It was corrupt, but it worked. It spread a fine-grained network of spies over South Vietnam. It played to people's foibles and self-interest. It was lascivious and cynical, but it was also attuned to the social mores of Vietnamese society. By dispersing power from the central government to the sects, the French had created fiefdoms which the Communists would have had a hard time dislodging.

Opposed to this was the American approach to ruling South Vietnam. It consolidated power in a presidential dictator. It created an authoritarian regime which was so tone deaf to the mores of Vietnamese society that it worked as a huge recruiting program for the Communists. It generated revolutionaries by the thousands, as Vietnamese peasants were uprooted from their native villages and thrown into forced-labor camps. It laid down roads and built up a magnificent network of centralized state control, which the North Vietnamese, if they bided their time, could incorporate into their own authoritarian regime.

"The Communists were not ready to take over," An says. "We needed Diem to push people into the revolution."

From this perspective, Lansdale was a great, if unwitting, friend to the Communists. "Lansdale came to Asia as the mastermind of America's strategy of unconventional warfare," An says. "He was the kingmaker. He made Diem president of Vietnam. He was in charge not only of American counterinsurgency, but of everything in Vietnam: military affairs, politics, intelligence—they were all run by Lansdale's Saigon mission. He had a lot of experts to help him, like Lou Conein and Rufus Phillips. He recruited World War II veterans and young people. They knew how to do it. Lansdale was excellent, really excellent."

When asked to evaluate the world's most successful spies, An would never rank himself as high as Lansdale. An distinguished between "offensive" and "defensive" spies. Offensive spies work in enemy territory. They form strategic alliances and reconfigure world maps. Defensive spies operate in a narrower field. Even if they cross enemy lines, their goals are conservative and limited. An had a keen appreciation for Lansdale's brilliance. He felt as if he were studying at the feet of a master,

but the two men also shared jokes and stories and got on famously well with each other. "I met Lansdale quite often," An
says. "Those were very cheerful days."

As he traveled around Saigon, Lansdale was accompanied
by a large black poodle, but it was the German shepherd breed
that came to be associated with him. "Lansdale explained to me
about dogs," An says. "You have to watch the behavior of your
dog. They live by instinct. You have to learn to observe what
your dog is telling you. He will show you if you have to be vigilant of your guest. Your dog can protect you. Lansdale gave me
good advice."

Alden Pyle, the CIA protagonist in *The Quiet American,* also
travels around Saigon with a dog at his side. The footprints of
Pyle's dog, imprinted in the wet cement in front of British journalist Thomas Fowler's apartment, implicate the journalist in
Pyle's death. In this case, the dog fails to save his master but he
fingers his murderer.

"Soon after Lansdale left Vietnam, I went to the dog market," An says. "I saw a beautiful German shepherd for sale.
The man who was selling it said, 'This is the dog of Mr. Lansdale, chief of intelligence, who has just left the country. This is
a very intelligent dog.'

"I walked around the corner and saw another German shepherd for sale. 'This is Lansdale's dog,' said the owner. That day
every German shepherd in the market was 'Lansdale's dog,'
and you were supposed to pay more, because it was so intelligent. After that, there wasn't a German shepherd in Vietnam
that hadn't formerly belonged to Lansdale."

From Lansdale An acquired the practice of traveling around
Saigon accompanied by a dog. He kept a German shepherd nes-
tled at his feet in café Givral or heeling on the terrace at the
Continental Hotel. As An drove through town in his little green
Renault, his dog sat upright in the passenger seat looking out
on the road. Most importantly, his dog guarded his house at
night while An worked in his darkroom copying documents and

writing reports in secret ink. "He would growl softly when he heard a patrol moving through the neighborhood. He was very good at warning me in advance when danger was approaching."

One day when their paths crossed, Lansdale mentioned to An that he was headed to California on leave and asked if he wanted anything from the United States. An mentioned one gift that would be very special but also very hard to obtain. It would require Lansdale's swimming with the seals off the California coast.

"Oh, yeah?" Lansdale said, beginning to smile.

"You cut off the testicles of a male seal and put them in a jar full of whiskey," said An. "I need an aphrodisiac. I am weak in this area, and this is a very good one."

An guffaws on remembering his conversation with Lansdale about seal testicles. An was versed in astrology and folk medicine, the training of dogs and fighting cocks, the breeding of birds and fish. His knowledge of aphrodisiacs and domestic lore provided the subject matter for his jokes. It made him intimate with everyone. These were the amusing diversions of his life, while at the same time they were his methodology. He had mastered the art of putting someone like Lansdale at ease while joking about his personal foibles.

Daniel Ellsberg used to say that there were "three Lansdales," different personas he donned for different audiences. "The first was the Lansdale who was reputed to have a magical touch with foreigners. . . . What I saw him do with the Vietnamese—and I learned from him—was to listen to them instead of lecturing or talking down to them, as most Americans did. He treated them respectfully, as though they were adults worthy of his attention." Lansdale coached his Asian clients through public appearances; he wrote their speeches and organized their schedules. When President Diem presented Tom Dooley with Vietnam's highest civilian award, the event was scripted by Lansdale, with Diem doing nothing more than toeing the line for a photo opportunity.

"The second Lansdale who dealt with American bureaucrats often came across as a kind of idiot—a guy with crazy ideas, naive, and simplistic. He was not at all afraid to appear simpleminded to anyone he did not want to reveal himself to, which was ninety-nine out of a hundred people. To journalists, other than a couple he was close to like Robert Shaplen of *The New Yorker,* he was very guarded and careful about what he told them. To put them off, he spoke in the most basic terms about democracy and Vietnamese traditions.

"Then there was the third Lansdale you saw only if you were on his team or worked with him closely. After giving a journalist his hayseed routine, he would join us and his mood would change immediately. He would present an analysis of a situation that was filled with shrewd and perceptive, even cynical, detail about who was doing what to whom."

A less flattering view of Lansdale is provided by another former aide, air force Colonel L. Fletcher Prouty. As chief of special operations at the Pentagon from 1955 to 1964, Prouty was the Defense Department official who provided military support for CIA covert operations around the world. This included the counterinsurgency warfare that Lansdale was conducting in Vietnam. When Lansdale moved from Vietnam back to Washington, Prouty served on his staff. Prouty ended his career with a dark view of CIA malevolence, which he saw as a corrupting influence in American life. (Prouty was adviser to Oliver Stone when he filmed his conspiracy-laden movie *JFK,* and he makes a fictional appearance in the film as Man X—the military insider who knows where the bodies are buried.)

According to Prouty, the Vietnam war was a clandestine CIA operation run out of the Agency's black budget, until it got too big and the marines were forced to hit the beach in 1965. "From 1945 through the crucial years of 1954 and 1955 and on to 1964, almost everything that was done in South Vietnam, including even a strong role in the selection of generals and ambassadors, was the action of the CIA, with the DOD playing a supporting role and the Department of State almost in total eclipse." Prouty describes how Lansdale met with the Cao Dai warlord Trinh Minh Thé in his mountain hideout. He enlisted Thé's support by making him a brigadier general in the Vietnamese army and depositing in his church collection box a cool three million, six hundred thousand dollars. Prouty ends by characterizing his former boss as the leader of "a band of superterrorists."

Lansdale was the model for Colonel Edwin Barnum Hillandale in *The Ugly American* (1958) and for Colonel Lionel Teryman in Jean Larteguy's *Le Mal Jaune* (*Yellow Fever*) (1965). Most people mistake Lansdale as the model for another fictional character, Alden Pyle in *The Quiet American*. Graham Greene steadfastly maintained that Pyle was *not* based on Lansdale, but Lansdale, with the flair of an advertising man who knows that there is no such thing as bad publicity, succeeded in claiming the role as his own. He wrote himself into Hollywood director Joseph Mankiewicz's film script of *The Quiet American*, and he helped produce what Greene considered an act of cinematic treachery.

After buying film rights to *The Quiet American*, Mankiewicz visited Vietnam in 1956 to scout locations. He met Lansdale in Saigon and solicited his advice on the script. The U.S. State Department denied Mankiewicz permission to film in Vietnam on the grounds that Graham Greene was a suspected Communist, and only after Lansdale intervened and began shaping the movie to his own ends did the project get approved.

As the script progressed, Mankiewicz wrote to Lansdale, inquiring about the explosion in front of the Continental Hotel on January 9, 1952. Lansdale said the blast was caused by twenty kilos of French melenite (*plastique*) placed in the trunk of a Citroen 15 CV and detonated by a timing device. The bomb killed a dozen people and wounded twice that many. It would have killed scores more, but its intended target, a parade of French troops being rotated back to France, had been canceled.

Lansdale confirmed that the bombing was the work of General Thé, the Cao Dai commander. Thé got his melenite from the French Expeditionary Corps, which organized and equipped Vietnam's private armies, said Lansdale. (Greene maintained that Thé got his explosives from the Americans, which seems a more likely story, since his intended target was a parade of French soldiers.) In another version of the story, which Lansdale tells Mankiewicz in a postscript to his letter, General Thé had picked up a couple of dud bombs dropped on him by the French and wired them into the gas tanks of two stolen cars.

Although General Thé claimed credit for the bombing in a radio broadcast, the Communists were blamed for it. "I doubt if more than one or two Vietnamese now alive know the real truth of the matter, and they certainly aren't going to tell it to anyone, even a 'quiet' American," Lansdale wrote to Mankiewicz. "The French and others have put reports together and have concluded that Thé did it. Since General Thé is quite a national hero for his fight against the Binh Xuyen in 1955, and in keeping with your treatment of this actually having been a Communist action, I'd suggest that you just go right ahead and let it be finally revealed that the Communists did it after all, even to faking the radio broadcast (which would have been easy to do)."

With its American protagonist—played by war hero Audie Murphy—portrayed as a good guy fighting Communist per-fidy, Mankiewicz's film had one huge fan: Edward Lansdale. On the day he saw it, Lansdale dashed off a note to President Diem, telling him that the movie offered "an excellent change from Mr. Greene's novel of despair," one that would "win more friends for you and Vietnam in many places in the world where it is shown." In spite of the CIA's efforts to promote it, the film was a com-mercial and critical flop. It did succeed, though, in associating Lansdale with Greene's novel—a confusion he was glad to cul-tivate, or *reveal,* as Lansdale would say.

Greene called the movie "a complete travesty" and "a real piece of political dishonesty." He later wrote, "One could believe that the film was made deliberately to attack the book and its author. But the book was based on a closer knowledge of the Indo-China war than the American possessed and I am vain enough to believe that the book will survive a few years longer than Mr. Mankiewicz's incoherent picture."

Greene and Lansdale met only once. As recounted by Lansdale in a conversation with his biographer Cecil Currey, Greene and a group of French military officers were installed on the terrace of the Continental Hotel, sipping their afternoon cocktails, when Lansdale drove up and parked in front of the hotel. As Lansdale entered the Continental, Greene and the Frenchmen seated around him—estimated by Lansdale to number between thirty and fifty—began booing him. Greene leaned over to make a remark to Peg Durdin, the *New York Times* correspondent who was seated next to him. According to Lansdale, "Peg stuck out her tongue at him and said to him, 'But we love him [Lansdale].' Then she turned around and gave me a big hug and kiss. I said, 'Well, I'm going to get written up someplace as a dirty dog.' So I guess I made his book. I had a French poodle at the time and he was with me, in the car with me, and they commented about the dog."

Greene said the dog he had in mind belonged to René de Berval, editor of *France-Asie* in Saigon. (*The Quiet American* is dedicated to Berval and his girlfriend Phuong.) As Greene wrote in a letter to the *British Sunday Telegraph* in 1966, "Just for the record, your correspondent . . . is completely wrong in thinking that I took General Lansdale as the model for *The Quiet American*. Pyle was a younger, more innocent and more idealistic member of the CIA. I would never have chosen Colonel Lansdale, as he then was, to represent the danger of innocence."

An worked for Lansdale on psyops material and rumor campaigns for the Catholic exodus from the north, the battle of the sects, and Diem's rigged presidential election. Soon he began learning the master's tricks. Other able teachers arrived in Saigon as Lansdale staffed his Saigon military mission with the best spooks in the business. Some of these people became An's lifelong "friends," although a friendship in which you neglect to mention that you are your friend's sworn opponent is a curious thing to contemplate.

"When the Americans came to our office with their bad French, there was only one person they could talk to. And when he was away, *I* was the only one they could talk to," An says. "Soon I was the liaison officer between the Americans and the Vietnamese. First there was Lansdale and then Lansdale's people and then other military officers. I made friends with all sorts of Americans and even their families."

Fifty years later, An remembers every detail about these encounters with his American friends and their children, for whom he had a real fondness. "I became friends with a master sergeant named Frank C. Long and his wife, Mary, and their three children, Kathy age six, Peter age four, and three-year-old Amanda. I was working at the American military headquarters. He was the officer in charge of setting up the training program for the Vietnamese. I saw him every day at the office, and then on weekends we would go to the swimming pool. I practiced my English with his wife, who was a legal secretary. She taught me shorthand and American culture, and I played with the children. Actually, they were my teachers when I was learning about American culture.

"I was impressed that the Americans taught their children to behave so well. They knew how to be friends with the Vietnamese children and play with them at school. I was so impressed by these children that I took them to meet my family. 'They are very beautiful children,' my father admitted. 'But they are not as well groomed as French children.' This was his prejudice. He always thought the French were the most beautiful. I disagreed. 'They are not like French children,' I said. 'They are polite. They know how to behave.' The French children used to beat me when I was young. They would come up and punch me for no reason at all. I wanted to fight back but my father wouldn't let me."

An made friends with another military man, Mills C. Brandes, one of Lansdale's intelligence officers, who also had three children. The Americans were not encumbered by the racism and arrogance of the *petits blancs colons*. They were vehemently anti-Communist, and they organized the world along an axis that flipped from white to black. But at this early stage in the war, they acted like deferential guests who were pleased to be visiting the land of their Vietnamese hosts. "They taught me all kinds of things, and their children taught me," An says. "I learned from them, preparing myself before going to the United States."

The three Lansdale team members closest to An were Lucien "Black Luigi" Conein, the "indispensable man" who directed Lansdale's black operations; former OSS officer Mills C. Brandes; and Rufus Phillips, who later ran CIA operations in Laos and then directed Vietnam's strategic hamlet program.

When I ask An if any of these men suspected him of being a Communist, he says, "No, no one knew, not even Lou Conein, and he knew everything. He was a very good friend. He came here first as a major, working for Lansdale. He had been a French soldier. He swore like a trooper. Whenever we got together for a drink at the Continental, Lou Conein and Bob Shaplen and I, Conein would be swearing in French, Shaplen in English, and I in Vietnamese. It was like hell in a very small place."

"Lou Conein was always the man the Vietnamese trusted," An says. "When they pulled a coup in 1963, he was the only outsider invited by the generals to watch the operation. They allowed him to phone the embassy and keep them posted on the progress of the coup." Thanks to Giai, his cousin, An also knew that Conein had fallen into a "woman trap" set for him by the Deuxième Bureau. "They used lots of pretty girls for gathering information. They succeeded in fooling many people. They failed to trap Lansdale and his other men, like Rufus Phillips, who was very handsome, but the French were successful in fooling Lou Conein."

Mills Brandes, who was working under MAAG cover as an "engineer," became a kind of surrogate father figure for An, whose own father was an engineer. "He was very quick, very agile with the punching bag. He worked out every day," says An, who makes the sound of someone hitting a punching bag *rat-tattattatta.* "He was husky, very strong, very friendly. He helped me learn English. When he was busy, his wife did it at home. Anytime I was free, I would give him a ring and come over. I would write stories, and they would correct my writing." Brandes was the man who gave An a copy of *The Quiet American,* perhaps without realizing how poorly Americans are depicted in Greene's novel.

Another of Lansdale's energetic spies was Rufus Phillips, a strapping, six-foot football player from rural Virginia who graduated from Yale in 1951 and joined the army. After being reassigned from Korea to Vietnam in 1954, he worked on Lansdale's team for a year and then moved to Laos. He returned to Vietnam in 1962 with the Agency for International Development and continued working in Vietnam as a consultant from 1965 to 1968.

"The South Vietnamese government existed in name only, a collection of French-trained civil servants who didn't have a clue what to do without the French giving them orders," Phillips said in an interview with Christian Appy. "We didn't know if Diem would survive or even if South Vietnam would survive. I think most of the Americans on the spot had pretty well written it off. They were extremely pessimistic.

"When I was in Laos I knew the Diem government was beginning to go off the rails. . . . Instead of insisting on democracy when Diem was still open to advice, the U.S. supported the creation and development of a secret, elite political party called the Can Lao. It was controlled by Diem's brother, Ngo Dinh Nhu. It was almost a carbon copy of the Communist Party as an organizational weapon. The idea was to build up a kind of personality cult around Diem and to have one party that would, in effect, swear people to loyalty. When Lansdale argued against it with Allen and Foster Dulles, he was told he was being naive. So we aided and abetted the worst side, not just of Diem but of the Vietnamese who had no experience in democratic politics."

An and Phillips became close friends. Phillips respected An's knowledge of Vietnamese history and his political acumen. An respected Phillips's intelligence and sincerity. "Vietnamese women were crazy about him, but he avoided the woman trap," An says. "He remained formal, aloof. He learned French and played the game very well."

Something curious happens when the two men speak of each other. They don't sound like enemies on opposite sides of a war. They sound like teammates rooting for the same side. "The Americans should have listened to him," An says of Phillips. "He wanted to put pressure on Diem to correct his mistakes." But Phillips failed to realize that An was thinking ten moves ahead on the chessboard of Vietnamese politics. He wanted Diem to succeed, but only as a way station to Communist rule. Diem was their unwitting agent, fighting off river pirates and crazy religious sects to unify southern Vietnam in advance of the day when the Communist Party would replace the Can Lao Party with its own police network. How simple it would be to swap the real thing for the carbon copy.

An's career as a spy was inadvertently advanced when his cousin, Pham Xuan Giai, was forced to flee the country after a failed coup attempt. "The French gave him money to pull off a coup against Diem in December 1954, but the coup failed. The Americans found out about it and spoiled it, so he had to go into exile in Laos."

"While he was there, the CIA people used him to work for the Americans, and the Deuxième Bureau used him to work for the French. He got involved in cooking another coup in Indonesia. It was all very complicated," An says, waving his hands in front of his face. "These people had too many brains. I was one of the stupid men."

From being an elf in Giai's shop producing psywar pamphlets and rumor campaigns, An moved up to being the point man at TRIM responsible for sending Vietnam's military officers for training in the United States. This is when he began accumulating the skein of contacts and favors that made him the best-connected man in Vietnam. "I picked out the likely candidates, assembled their CVs, and arranged their security clearances with Vietnamese intelligence and the U.S. embassy. The Vietnamese were sent to schools in the U.S. to learn about counterinsurgency, like Nguyen Van Thieu, who later became South Vietnam's president. He was sent to Fort Leavenworth in Kansas. I filled out his paperwork and followed the reports that were sent back to MAAG."

Although he had yet to set foot in America, An lectured the Vietnamese on what to expect when they got there. "Americans shake hands when they greet each other. They look you in the eye when they talk and smile a lot." An also told them that Americans were sticklers for rules, even rules that if strictly applied would prevent any Vietnamese from ever getting to the United States. For example, Vietnam's military officers always failed their medical exams. Many of them had been exposed to tuberculosis or recovered from earlier infections. "I spent a lot of time arguing with the American doctors about these exams," An remembers. "I had to explain to them the difference between scars from previous infections and active cases of tuberculosis." Worms were another touchy subject. In a country that fertilized its fields with human excrement, few people in Vietnam were free of parasites. "There were hookworms and tapeworms, all kinds of worms," An says.

The last time An had shot a gun was when he fired on a platoon of French soldiers moving through the Mekong delta in April 1946, but he was armed again when he went into the field with two American soldiers in January 1956. He was carrying the pistol given to him by his cousin before he fled into exile. "It was a Walther 7.65 millimeter, with a brown handle and a shiny, blue-green barrel. This is what we call a 'love pistol.' It is designed to be carried in your handbag or in your pocket and removed when it is required to shoot your spouse or her lover."

"I had never used it, and I didn't even know how it worked, until I went into the field one day as liaison officer for Colonel Glenn and Colonel Hicks, two American advisers. We were going into the delta to watch Diem's troops fight the last Communist forces which had been left behind. We drove to Long Ha by jeep and then took boats from there to Moc Hoa, in the Plain of Reeds, near the Cambodian border. While out in the field with Lansdale's men, I tied the pistol with a string to my belt loop, so if it fell out of my pocket, I wouldn't lose it."

When they demanded to see what was in An's pocket, Colonel Hicks and Colonel Glenn laughed at his little pistol. Like all American advisers, they carried big Colts. They asked if An had ever fired his gun and then shook their heads in disbelief.

"An, you are the worst soldier we have ever seen in our lives," they said. "You are smart, but you have no initiative. What you need is a brain transplant. You need an American brain grafted onto your Vietnamese brain. Then you might be able to go out in the world and accomplish something.'"

After a crash course in the field, An knew how to break down his pistol and clean it. He also knew the correct way to smoke cigarettes. The advisers noticed that An was puffing Lucky Strikes without inhaling. He had the profligate habits of a customs inspector who got his cigarettes and other contraband for free. "They taught me how to get the smoke into my lungs and blow one part out through my mouth and the other part out through my nose, and then they taught me how to smoke cigars. It was great, really good," says An, laughing. "That's how I got addicted, more than fifty years ago, and this is why I have lung problems today. Every time I smoked, I thought of my two advisers, Colonel Glenn and Colonel Hicks."

An also succeeded in grafting an American brain onto his Vietnamese brain. He learned the skills of Western journalism—its analytical methods and repertoire of investigative techniques—and applied them to becoming Vietnam's greatest spy. An had good teachers. He used them.

In one of our last conversations in 2006, An spoke again about his conflicted cultural inheritance. "I spent so many years working with the Americans that as time went on, my brain became resistant to the training and intoxication of the Communists."

He corrects himself. "I mean to say *indoctrination* of the Communists. Unfortunately, an American brain got grafted onto my Vietnamese brain. It became in the process a kind of composite substance, very hard and very difficult to break. At this point nothing can be done about it. It's best just to leave it there. I'll soon be dead anyway, and then no one will have to worry about what I think." An laughs, one of the long, hearty laughs he reserves for life's good jokes.

Then he tells me a story about a king and his adviser. "One day the king is invited to dine at the house of his adviser. This mandarin has an excellent cook and domestic staff, but they hate him because he is a tough bastard. So they decide to get their revenge. At lunch they serve their master the stone of a jackfruit, cooked in a special way, so that he doesn't recognize what he is eating. By evening, as the jackfruit ferments in his stomach, the mandarin begins farting."

Here An makes the *pfftt, pfftt* popping sounds of a farting mandarin. "By the time the king comes to dinner, the mandarin is farting one fart after another, *pfftt, pfftt, pfftt*."

"'What is that noise?' demands the king.

"'It is the noise of a toad in my garden,' says the mandarin.

"'But why, if a toad is making this noise, does it smell so bad?'

"'It is a dead toad.'

"'How does a dead toad make this noise?' asks the king.

"'There are *two* toads,' says the mandarin. 'One is alive. One is dead. The noise comes from the living one. The smell comes from the dead one.'

"The king is happy. He thinks he knows the truth of the situation because he has a coherent explanation for what is happening. But really all he is getting is a ridiculous story. This is how we describe the job of the adviser. It is the work of toads."

# Travels
# in America

In 1956, An's Communist handlers ordered him to quit the Vietnamese army and start a new career. They wanted him to go to the United States and study the country that was waging war on them from halfway around the world.

An was the first Communist spy at Vietnamese military headquarters, but when another officer was recruited from the general staff, it was time for him to move on.

"After being demobilized I was supposed to go back to the customs house. But I didn't like being a *fonctionnaire*. I wanted a free profession. This was my problem, always my problem. I refused to go back. I submitted a letter of resignation, which had to be approved by the minister of finance, and I took all the money out of my pension. People were surprised. 'You have a lifetime job. Why would you leave that?'"

An thought of becoming a doctor or studying economics, a subject that had interested him ever since he read *Economie Politique*, a book based on Karl Marx's *Capital*. "I thought, maybe I'll go to America and study economics or political theory.

I would go for four to six years and get an M.A. degree or, if possible, a Ph.D. while learning about American culture."

But An had a hard time getting to the United States. "The U.S. military attaché took me to visit the Asia Foundation. They offered me a scholarship, but the Vietnamese authorities refused to allow me to accept it because I didn't have a high school diploma. This was their excuse for giving the scholarship to their family members and relatives." His plan hit another roadblock when he was told that he could not study subjects such as politics or economics that were taught in Vietnam, no matter who paid his way to America.

It was Mai Chi Tho, head of North Vietnamese intelligence, and Muoi Huong, An's case officer, who decided to send him to the United States to be trained as a journalist. Muoi Huong got the idea from Ho Chi Minh, who had worked as a reporter. It was the perfect cover for a spy, granting access to obscure places and elevated people. The plan was approved at the highest levels of the Vietnamese Politburo, but it would take several years to execute. An's father was dying. French-trained administrators, who did not like the idea of sending a Vietnamese to study in the United States, blocked An's exit visa. The Communist Party had a hard time finding enough money. Finally Mai Chi Tho scraped together eighty thousand dong, which at the time was worth about two thousand dollars. This was sufficient to buy An's airplane ticket to America and four new suits—if only he could find a way to get out of Vietnam.

"The idea of becoming a journalist was all right, but I didn't know much about it," An says. "'Journalism is very important but very dangerous,' Muoi Huong told me. 'Everyone is suspicious of journalists, thinking that they are carrying out intelligence activities.'

"I had to ask the people of the revolution to borrow money for me," An says. "The Communist Party paid for my travel to the U.S. I had six years of pension, but that wasn't enough. I didn't even own a suitcase. Luckily, Mills C. Brandes gave me his old World War II Samsonite, made out of cardboard."

An's last hurdle lay in getting his visa. This time he was aided by Diem's secret police. He began by contacting his cousin, the same one who had hired him to work in the psychological warfare department. Pham Xuan Giai's sister was married to Le Khac Duyet, who was head of security and ran the police in central Vietnam for Ngo Dinh Can, the youngest brother in the ruling family. Can, on Duyet's recommendation, sent a message to Tran Kim Tuyen, the diminutive genius who ran Ngo Dinh Diem's family affairs. "He was in charge of political, cultural, and social affairs at the Presidential Palace," An says. "Actually he was the front man of the secret police. Everything was under his authority."

With a Hanoi law degree and training as a military medic, Tuyen was one of the Catholic refugees who had come south in 1954. He hailed from Phat Diem, which is described in *The Quiet American* as a medieval town "under the shadow and protection of the Prince Bishop," who had his own private army. Greene, a Catholic convert, describes Phat Diem as "the most living town in all the country." By *living* he means *faithful* or *religious*. Phat Diem, like other Catholic enclaves in North Vietnam, was destroyed during a pitched battle between the Viet Minh and the French colonial forces. (Greene visited the battlefield and overheard soldiers, "most of them Germans," exclaim *Gott sei dank* when they saw more dead Vietnamese than Legionnaires floating in the city's canals.)

As An would say of the way he obtained his visa, "This is the Vietnamese way, pure Vietnamese." You ask a cousin to ask his sister's husband in central Vietnam to intervene with his boss, who in turn sends a message back to Saigon via your cousin's sister's husband, who actually travels there in person, that you should be given an exit visa, and *voilà*, the visa that yesterday was impossible to obtain suddenly appears on the desk of

Dr. Tuyen, as he was called. This means, of course, that you are beholden to every family member who aided you in this project, and you are particularly indebted to Dr. Tuyen, who delivered the document.

There was one final hurdle before An could leave. He was keeping a death watch at his father's bedside. Tuberculosis had claimed one of his lungs and weakened his heart. He was gasping for breath and visibly failing. "One day I had to take my niece to Cholon on my scooter," An remembers. "While we were waiting for the rain to stop, my father said, 'Hurry home. I have something important to say to you.' He ordered my mother to bring him warm water to wash his face. He changed his clothes and lay down to rest. On my return from Cholon I gave him another shot of medicine to help his heart."

"He started breathing heavily, a labored, hissing kind of breath, *hssssssss.* He was having such a hard time breathing that I held him upright in my arms. 'Bring me a piece of blank paper,' he ordered. I brought him the paper. He signed it. 'You can type in the date later,' he said. He signed ten more sheets like this. 'You can use these when I am gone,' he said." An's inheritance now included his father's signature, if needed, on ten forged documents.

"He was expiring. I knew he was dying. The black butterfly of death, the *papillon nocturne,* flew in the window. Normally they fly only at night. It settled on the mosquito net over my father's bed. The death throes began, the agony that comes before you die. My father breathed his last breath. The butterfly fanned his wings. I knew it was the end. My father's heart stopped beating."

His father died on September 24, 1957, and two weeks later An arrived in Costa Mesa, California, to enroll as a freshman at the local community college. An was a thirty-one-year-old Communist spy, a retired customs officer and psywar specialist when he began studying at Orange Coast College, which had been recommended to him by an American adviser in Vietnam. He was possibly the first Vietnamese to live in Orange County. (It is now home to one hundred and fifty thousand Vietnamese refugees and their descendants.) Called Confucius by his classmates, An studied political science, American government, economics, sociology, psychology, Spanish, and journalism. He chaperoned eighteen-year-old coeds to the beach and spent a lot of time working on the *Barnacle,* the school newspaper, for which he wrote occasional articles, such as a movie review of *The Quiet American.* Finding the movie potentially confusing, An recommended that it "not be shown in Vietnam."

An describes his two years in the United States, which included internships at the *Sacramento Bee* and the United Nations, as "the only time in my life when I wasn't anxious." (His travels across America were financed by the Asia Foundation, which was later revealed to be a CIA front.) He fell in love with America and with an American, Lee Meyer, a lithe blonde who was his editor and writing coach at the *Barnacle.* "She knew I loved her, but I never told her," An says. "We Vietnamese never tell what we really feel."

An arrived at OCC on a Saturday, when the commuter school was empty of students and his dormitory was locked. "It was lunchtime, and I had no idea where to go," he remembers. "Suddenly one of the students arrived back at the dorm. I told him I was a new student and had just arrived in America. He offered me some red beans."

"Then Mr. Henry Ledger, the building manager, arrived. 'We were waiting for you,' he said. 'We kept your room empty for a month, but we finally had to put somebody in it.' He had another room for storing sheets and towels. He emptied it out and put me in it. It was a nice room with a good view, and I was alone here, while all the other rooms had two people in them. He went out and got me a chair and table and a bookshelf for my books. The room had no dresser, but I didn't have much clothing anyway. All I had was my cardboard suitcase borrowed from Mr. Brandes and a new bag for carrying my books to school."

An's dormitory had originally served as a barracks for the Santa Ana army air base. This boot camp for soldiers inducted into the army air forces also served briefly, at the end of World War II, as a prisoner of war camp for soldiers captured from Rommel's Afrikakorps and as a Japanese-American internment camp, where enemy aliens were held before being deported to Japan. When the base was converted into a community college in 1948, courses in subjects ranging from cosmetology to petroleum technology were taught in sixty-eight Quonset huts and barracks inherited from the military. Many of the teachers were also inherited from the military. The air base band master became head of the OCC art department, and a former mess captain became a professor of social science.

"The night I arrived in California the students had organized a big square dance at the cafeteria," An says. "The school band was playing. Two teachers, a lady and a man, had been brought in to show the students how to square dance. A student took me to the dance so I wouldn't feel homesick. I sat on the side like a wallflower. Then a young lady came over and took me out on the floor. Everyone was dressed like hillbillies and cowgirls. They were hopping up and down like turkeys. They ordered me back and forth. This was the first time in my life that I held a girl in my arms like this. I was hot and cold all at once. I realized I was going to make many, many mistakes.

"They would take me to the beach, five or six girls at a time. I had no money for going out and no family to visit. I was always in my dorm room studying, but no one else stayed in the dorms. Everyone else was always out doing things. So the girls would come and ask me to go to the beach with them. I never swam. The water was too cold, but the girls swam. They were strong and powerful. I was thirty-one years old. They were seventeen or eighteen. They took me along as their 'life saver.'"

These were happy years for An. He loved the migrating swallows that nested under the eves of his dormitory, the sunny California students with their homecoming dances and beach parties, the taskmaster professors who at the same time were friendly and accessible. As An reported in the *Barnacle,* he learned how to write "the American language of H. L. Mencken, to enjoy the hi-fi, to rock and roll, to do my homework with the radio and the familiar heater noise, and to fill my lungs with the air of the humorous jokes of my dorm mates."

"I did many things the way we do them in Vietnam, which my classmates thought was hilarious," An says. "One day, for example, I was in the men's toilet, urinating. I noticed that every time I went into the bathroom, students would run down the hall to look at me. When I had finished, they would run out of the room laughing. Finally, one of the students, a former marine in the Korean war who was studying on the GI bill, told me what was happening. 'An, no one wants to embarrass you, but we think the way you urinate is very funny. You roll up your pant leg. Here in America, we pull our pants down.' This was another lesson I had to learn, how to unzip my trousers."

The most important lesson for An was how to disguise the fact that he was a Communist agent. He had some near misses, and perhaps his time in California was not as carefree as he pretends. "My speech class was taught by a former colonel, an artillery officer in the military reserve. He always gave me a C minus. 'In your speeches, you use too many revolutionary terms,' he told me. 'You must change this.' I tried to explain that I had learned English from the magazines that were sent to Vietnam by the French Communist Party. Fortunately, one of my fellow students was a Canadian, an older woman who was returning to school to finish her degree. She became my *déesse,* one of my female protectors. She began correcting my speeches, and after that I got a C plus."

"I also got into trouble with Miss Fowler, my freshman English teacher. She was a former intelligence officer in World

War II and an expert, during the McCarthy era, in hunting out pro-Communist elements. One day she asked me, 'Have you come here to learn or to do something else?'

"'To learn,' I assured her. 'I have worked with American soldiers; that's why they sent me here.'

"'I am suspicious that you have come to do something else.'

"What she told me made me more vigilant. I Americanized myself. There was no more revolutionary talk. No more French, either."

That An became a great journalist as well as a great spy is a testament to the American method of training reporters by having them spend long hours producing student newspapers. While working as a subeditor and writer for the *Barnacle*, An penned stories on campus food, dorm life, and the special needs of foreign students, which included a large contingent of Persians who had come to California to study the state's offshore oil wells. There were sixteen students on the *Barnacle* staff, all of them enrolled in Journalism 101 and 102. The year An was listed as "Page 2 Editor," the paper placed second among Southland junior college newspapers in a competition at the University of Southern California.

The long hours An spent at the student newspaper may also have been motivated by falling in love with his editor, Lee Meyer, who combined a winning smile with serious, black-framed spectacles. Lots of people fell in love with Meyer, judging from the affectionate messages inscribed in her yearbook. An calls her "an ideal friend" in his inscription and writes of his hope that "our friendly relationship would be closer and closer in spite of improper situations." An is referring to the fact that Meyer was engaged at the time to a medical student she would later marry—unhappily and briefly. "She was the girl I would have married if I'd had the chance," An says.

That An and Lee's affection was mutual is evident from letters they exchanged late in life. Lee contacted An after reading about him in an article published in *Newsweek* on the twenty-fifth anniversary of the end of the Vietnam war. She was pleased to be back in touch after so many years, and they struck up a correspondence that lasted until her death in 2003. An was "very, very dear to Lee," says Janet Simms, Lee's domestic partner when she was a practicing psychologist in Los Angeles. An wrote in return, "You have often been in my heart and thoughts."

After his first year at OCC, An attended summer school to finish more credits, and then he traveled up the coast to visit a Vietnamese friend who was teaching at the army language school in Monterey. His plans had changed and he would be heading home as soon as possible, if he could get there. An's sunny year in California was the darkest time in history for the southern Viet Minh, the sixty thousand Communists who had remained below the seventeenth parallel when Vietnam was divided in 1954. "The Diem administration dragged a guillotine around the countryside, decapitating Communists, and by the end of the campaign in 1958, eighty-five percent of the Party members had been wiped out, either killed or jailed," An says. He learned in a coded letter from his younger brother, Pham Xuan Dinh, that Muoi Huong, his case officer, had been arrested. He also learned that he was being summoned home because the Viet Minh—soon to be reborn as the Vietcong— were finally embarking on the armed struggle that would launch the Second Indochina War.

"My brother was arrested while I was in America," An says. "They asked him about Muoi Huong and why he had come to visit me at my house. My brother was detained by the Saigon police until after Tết in 1958. My cousin got him out of jail— the one who worked for Ngo Dinh Can as chief of security and head of the police in central Vietnam. He came to Saigon to see the chief of police. My brother was released directly into his custody.

"My brother wrote me a letter implying that my two direct superiors had been captured. He gave me enough hints so that

I understood." As An tells me this story, one of his birds starts screaming in the background like a police cruiser with its whoopee siren going full blast. If his younger brother Dinh got off relatively easily, the same was not true for Muoi Huong. He was tortured in the Nine Caves prison in central Vietnam for six years. He did not reveal An's name, but it was a perilous moment for all the agents in his network.

An's friend Cao Giao was also serving a term in Ngo Dinh Can's infamous prison. "He knew Muoi Huong, that he was a high official in the Communist Party and chief of intelligence in the south. The two had worked together when Cao Giao was passing information to the Communists, giving them advance warning of the Japanese coup d'état. He stood to gain his freedom by denouncing Muoi Huong, but Cao Giao never denounced anyone, even under torture. He walked by him with a stone face that revealed nothing of their past association. He was one of the brave ones who never lost their morale."

"How can I get in touch with my leaders who have been captured, I wondered. I wasn't supposed to look for them or contact them. It was their job to contact me, but if I stay in America how will they find me? If I don't return to Vietnam, I'll be abandoning the fight for independence, but if I return now that my leaders are in jail, I risk being arrested and going to jail myself. If Muoi Huong had informed, I would have been finished. I strongly believed he would confess. He was a human being. I had already seen many cases like this. But he didn't confess. Others did, but not Muoi Huong."

After An learned that he was being summoned back to Vietnam, he started studying Spanish. If his cover were blown, maybe he could slip over the border and travel home via Cuba, where Fidel Castro was coming to power. An also learned, while visiting his friend at the foreign language school in Monterey, that the Communists, after holding them back for several years, were finally allowing the revolutionaries in the south to resume guerrilla warfare. "That's why I decided to go back," An says.

In the spring of 1959 he graduated from Orange Coast College with an associate's degree in journalism. He drove up the coast to Monterey and on from there to Sacramento, where he stayed for two months, working at the *Sacramento Bee* in an internship arranged for him by Eleanor McClatchy, a member of the newspaper's founding family. An's stipend was paid by the Asia Foundation, which had also arranged for him to fly to New York at the end of the summer for another internship, this one at the United Nations.

"Mrs. McClatchy was a very nice lady," An says. She in turn thought he was a very nice man, and with introductions from the CIA and Edward Lansdale and An's other good friends in U.S. intelligence, she was glad to welcome this young Vietnamese gentleman to Sacramento. There was a slight problem when he was denied lodgings because the landlord didn't accept "mongoloids," but An shrugged off this racist slight. "This is normal in America," he says. "Even Henry Kissinger wasn't allowed to stay in certain hotels because he was Jewish."

McClatchy took him to meet the governor, Edmund G. Brown, who was hosting a state visit from the prime minister of the Soviet Union. "I was allowed to tag along, to see how they covered the story of a big shot paying a visit to the governor of California." An had already met the governor and had his photo snapped while standing next to him at a conference of student newspaper editors, but it wouldn't hurt to meet him again. An was assuming the professional demeanor that would serve him so well as a spy. He was compiling a résumé of CIA recommendations and McClatchy service that suggested he might be working for the Agency. Soon after his arrival in Sacramento, the *Bee* ran a story on its new summer intern headlined, "Vietnam Journalist Aims to Fight Red Propaganda." As An wryly remarked to an interviewer in 2005, "I used everything Lansdale taught me for this article. He was an excellent teacher."

An paid a visit to the Asia Foundation headquarters in San Francisco, hoping to convince them to allow him to drive across

America instead of flying. "I had bought a ten-year-old Mercury from an old lady for two hundred and fifty dollars," An says. "It had an eight-cylinder engine and consumed gas like it was drinking water. It had a heater but no air-conditioning. The director of the foundation advised me to stay in YMCAs, which cost only five dollars a night, or cheap motels. 'Don't pick up any hitchhikers. They're dangerous. They will know that you are alone and a foreigner. They can take your money and kill you.'"

Although he possessed two Vietnamese driver's licenses, one military and one civilian, An had never actually driven a car before coming to the United States. The *Sacramento Bee* had kindly provided its interns with a driver's education course, and, promising not to "drive like a hot rodder," An started traveling at the end of August. "It was because my French teacher had taught me about Chicago gangsters and the city's humane, modern methods for killing animals that I wanted to drive across America." An saw a summer windstorm race across the Nevada desert like a big tornado. Amazed to see branches and tree limbs and entire trees swirling up into the sky, he stopped to record the event with a camera shooting Ektachrome slides.

"I drove very slowly. I would often stop to drink a Coke and rest. I took the middle route from California to the East Coast. Whenever there was a beautiful landscape, I would stop and watch it. I would pull over to the side of the road and get out of my car. I would lie down and stare up at the sky until I was ready to start driving again. I was lucky. I met more nice people than naughty people. Maybe they were naughty among themselves, but not to me, like when I was in San Francisco. One evening, I was walking toward the wharf to have dinner when I ran into a band of guys with knives drawn. They were chasing another band of guys, but they were too busy trying to kill each other to bother me."

An drove down the Strip and visited the gambling casinos in Las Vegas. Outside the city, he saw a long line of freight cars rolling across the mountains and disappearing into a tunnel. "I asked a man who was standing near me, watching the train, 'Is it carrying people from the West Coast to the East Coast?' 'No,' he said. 'This is a special train. It doesn't take any passengers. It is carrying scientists into a tunnel in the mountain, where they do atomic research.' Then he showed me on a map where America makes its atomic bombs. 'Don't go here,' he said. 'They will arrest you.'" An chuckles on remembering the friendly American who told him these military secrets. Communist intelligence agent Pham Xuan An now knew where the Vietnamese army should attack if it ever invaded the United States.

An visited the Mormon Tabernacle in Salt Lake City and watched cowboys herding cattle in Wyoming. He drove only during the day, and when the sun went down he stopped at the YMCA or a cheap motel. He would start driving again the next day at sunrise. "The country was big and beautiful, with enormous variety. I had never realized how big America is. This is not something I imagined from hearing it described."

After crossing the Rocky Mountains and the Great Plains, An was amazed by the rich farmland in Iowa. "I saw mile after mile of corn. It took me almost a whole day of driving to get through the corn. I stopped to look at the turkeys they raise there, huge, chocolate-colored turkeys. They stretched all the way to the horizon."

By the time he reached Chicago, he was having trouble with his carburetor. He was surprised when a new one was installed quickly instead of the old one being taken out and repaired. He started driving around town, looking for the miraculous machine his French teacher had told him about. "I drove to the stockyards, but I couldn't find the machine anywhere." An laughs, "I would have to create this machine if I wanted it to exist."

Except for the speedy car repair, An was disappointed by Chicago. "I thought I would find something in Chicago that made it more modern than Vietnam." But even the gangsters were less colorful than Bay Vien and his river pirates. An drove to Niagara Falls, where he spent a week attending a seminar for Vietnamese Catholic students organized by Emmanuel Jacques, a Belgian Jesuit missionary. An never pretended to be anything but Buddhist. He must have thought it a good idea, though, to add Father Jacques, who had lived in Vietnam and "spoke Vietnamese like a Vietnamese," to his list of references.

An drove next to Washington, where he stayed in Arlington, Virginia, for ten days with his CIA friend Mills Brandes and his family. "After seeing Capitol Hill, the White House, the Pentagon, they took me on a tour of the FBI, where I saw agents shooting at targets on the firing range with live ammunition," An says. "They pushed a button and up popped a shooter. We were supposed to admire how many bull's-eyes they got. Most people got bull's-eyes."

"I asked them, 'What is this used for?' 'It's a warning to people: *don't commit crimes, or the FBI will put a bullet in you very easily.*' I thought to myself, 'This is good psychological warfare, meant to reduce the number of criminals.'"

An drove back to New York in time to watch the opening of the United Nations. The Asia Foundation introduced him to the U.N. correspondent from India, who took him to get a press pass and showed him around. "This was the session where Nikita Khrushchev made his first visit to the United States. The streets were lined with mounted policemen, riding huge horses and looking very handsome in the autumn light. Crowds filled the sidewalks to watch Khrushchev drive by in a black limousine, with the Soviet flag flying on the hood of his car. I watched his motorcade pass by. Then I went to the press gallery to watch Khrushchev deliver his speech."

I ask An if he was excited to see Khrushchev in New York, as a fellow Communist, and if he believed him when Khrushchev said to the United States, "We will bury you!"

An gives me a rousing yes, a long, drawn-out note of agreement, accompanied by a hand wave of assent, fingers mounting skyward. "It was the Soviet policy at the time to support wars of liberation. The Chinese under Mao Tse Tung were doing the same thing. To meet this challenge, the Americans were developing the doctrine of counterinsurgency to fight against wars of liberation. The strategy was the same in Vietnam and elsewhere around the world. Liberate the former colonies. Pretend to launch them on the road to self-determination, while introducing special forces and using unconventional warfare to fight the revolutionary forces. This policy actually goes back as far as 1950, when the United States signed the agreement supporting the French in Indochina and setting up Lansdale's Saigon mission."

"I wasn't opposed to Americans. I was opposed to their strategy. I had no choice. They were fighting a war. We had to counter it. We on the Communist side had to understand this strategy. We had to pull together all the information we could get and analyze it. This is not an easy thing to do, but without it, you are fighting a war in the dark. You may win the war by accident, but it is more likely that you will lose it by ignorance."

I ask An if it was hard for him to live his double life of intrigue and subterfuge. "It is hard," he says, repeating the statement three times. Then he mentions a former lieutenant colonel in the U.S. army who had befriended him while he was a student in California. An was returning from his first visit to Monterey when he missed the bus stop for Orange Coast College. He got off down the coast in Laguna Beach. It was New Year's Eve, and no more buses were running. The colonel, coming to pick up his daughter who was visiting for the holidays, offered him a lift to the college and later invited him to his house, where An became a regular visitor.

After An had returned to Vietnam and started working as a reporter, the colonel wrote to him, asking if he would look after his son, who was being sent to Vietnam as a lieutenant in the air force. "After thinking about it, I refused to get in touch with his son," An says. "I was working for the other side, in intelligence. If I met him I might take advantage of him re-flexively. Because I know his father, I might get some infor-mation out of him. What if I were tortured? What if I broke and revealed that this man had given me information? It would be very bad. So to respect the man who had helped me and not by mistake, not voluntarily, not willingly to take advantage of his son, I refused to see him."

"This is why I don't want to write a memoir," An says. "I would have to name names, and that's not good. Some peo-ple have died already, but others are still alive. A lot of people helped me out of personal friendships. There is no reason to be-tray them now."

I ask An how he feels about the fact that his intelligence was responsible for getting Americans killed. "I hated to see this," he says. "When I saw young American soldiers being evacuated from battle, lying on top of personnel carriers, many of them dead or dying, it reminded me of my friends in junior college, young men eighteen or nineteen years old who might have been drafted and sent to Vietnam. This is why I prayed that the war wouldn't last long."

An's double life was filled with conflict and tragedy, but there was no fake sentimentality on his part. He had a choice to make, and he made it. Some of this I credit to the fact that he was a journalist. He faced reality and dealt with it. There was a war on. He was a soldier in this war. He did his duty. "That's all," he would say. "It was very simple." This was one of his fa-vorite expressions. Of course it was not simple. It was heart-wrenchingly complex, and the moral dilemmas were insoluble. A man less tough in mind and spirit would have been destroyed or would have given himself away. An reminded me of a great gambler, one of those Las Vegas professionals who has learned to disguise what are known as "tells"—the involuntary signs that reveal your hand, either good or bad. An the jokester, the prankster, the dog-loving man-about-town had displaced onto his quirks and personal habits all the emotion that otherwise

would have revealed in his face what he was feeling. *That's all.*
*It's very simple.*

"In New York, the Asia Foundation arranged for me to stay
with one of their men who lived in the Bronx. He took me
around and showed me Central Park, where I saw a lot of crazy
people making speeches. I took a sightseeing trip around New
York. I rode the ferry out into the harbor to see Lady Liberty.
I went to visit the offices of *Time* magazine. They said, 'Maybe
in the future you will work for *Time*.' I said yes, that would
be very nice. But for now, I prefer to go back home and work
for Vietnam Press. The Asia Foundation had already told me,
when I returned to Vietnam, that I should work for Vietnam
Press, to help them."

The ambiguity of An's statement only strikes me later, and
I never get to ask him about it. Why is the Asia Foundation advising him to work for Vietnam Press? Will An be helping the
cause of Vietnamese journalism or the CIA?

"I had briefed Vietnamese officers before sending them to
the United States, showing them pictures of life in America, but
I was amazed when I saw it with my own eyes. The only way
Vietnam could fight a war against the United States was to
hope that one day they would go away. Vietnam is a small, isolated country. We had relations with almost no one outside our
borders, and inside we were fighting day and night. We came
from zero. We had to sacrifice until we were reduced to zero.
No matter how long it took, we had to continue. We had already
fought for hundreds of years against the French and thousands
of years against the Chinese. There was no reason for us to
stop now."

Almost two years to the day after he left Vietnam, An sold
his car and flew from New York to San Francisco. This was his
last chance to change his mind. He had been offered a language
teaching job in Monterey for a salary of three hundred and
fifty dollars a month, a lot of money in those days. Lee Meyer
had sent him a postcard from San Francisco, showing the bay

and the famous island prison of Alcatraz. "I will see you before you go home," she wrote.

"When my plane landed in San Francisco, I went to the Golden Gate Bridge to look over the bay toward Alcatraz island. There it was, floating in the water, exactly as in the postcard Lee Meyer had sent me. I stood on the bridge thinking of her, and I almost changed my mind. I thought to myself, This is where I'm going to end up if I go back to Vietnam, in prison, but a prison not so beautiful as Alcatraz. For me, it will be Poulo Condore and a tiger cage. They are both islands, but Poulo Condore is far worse than Alcatraz."

It was October 1959, with a fall chill in the air. In An's pocket was an airplane ticket to Saigon, bought for him by the Asia Foundation. Rising below him in the harbor were the solitary smokestack and sun-raked walls of Alcatraz. He could stay in America and take a correspondence course to finish his college degree at Berkeley. He could marry an American and forget about the long war his country was fighting. Finally An the patriot, who had in his possession four suits that belonged to the Communist Party of Vietnam and should rightfully be returned to the people, boarded his plane and flew home to Saigon. Thus ended his first and only visit to the United States.

"I have two loves, like Josephine Baker," An says. "I love my country, and I love the United States. When the war was over, I wanted them to get back together."

# Confidence
# Game

On returning to Saigon, An was so frightened about of having been exposed as a spy that he hid in his house for a month before settling on a plan of action: rather than waiting for the police to come and arrest him, he would go to the police and learn what they knew about him. Using his family connections, he contacted Tran Kim Tuyen, the former military surgeon who ran South Vietnam's intelligence network for President Ngo Dinh Diem and his younger brother Ngo Dinh Nhu. This extensive, CIA-supported network of spies and clandestine military forces operated out of the president's cabinet under the anodyne name of the Office of Political, Cultural, and Social Research. If Tuyen hired him, An figured he would be safe from arrest, at least for the moment.

In short order, An became Tuyen's assistant, his factotum and confidant. At times, it looked as if An were the sole man Tuyen trusted in Saigon. An handled Tuyen's business and even laundered his money. "Tuyen controlled the shipment of opium from the high plateaus down to Saigon," An says. "Actually, it was the owner of Saigon's Floating Restaurant who owned the business, but he paid Tuyen the protection money that kept it going."

A number of sawmills in Cholon operated as fronts to Saigon's opium refineries. "They cut down trees in the mountains on the Laotian border and hollowed them out. These hollowed-out trees were filled with opium and trucked down to Saigon's 'lumber yard factories' in Cholon. Tuyen knew about it. His men took bribes, and he himself had funds deposited in foreign bank accounts. But he was a modest man," An assures me. "He never stole money hand over fist, which is the style of today's crooks."

Tuyen used An as his interpreter for foreign financial transactions, and he relied on him for other sensitive assignments, such as dealing with visiting Americans. On one such assignment An met Gerald Hickey, the expert on traditional Vietnamese culture who loaned his anthropological services to the U.S. government (and was subsequently blackballed by academia). An describes how he accompanied Hickey when he went out to examine Vietnam's *agrovilles*—Diem's first strategy for fighting the Communists.

If revolutionaries swim like fish in the sea of peasant life, the way to kill them is to dry up the sea. First, you remove the peasants from the countryside and relocate them into fortified enclaves known as *agrovilles*. The only people remaining in the countryside will be, by definition, revolutionaries, who can be bombed or gassed out of existence. In practice, Diem's *agrovilles* were forced labor camps full of alienated peasants. They flew the Republican flag by day and nurtured the revolutionaries by night. Diem was forced to abandon this initial experiment in counterterrorism after a year, but he and his American advisers refloated the scheme again in the 1960s, when *agrovilles* were renamed "strategic hamlets."

"I liked Gerry Hickey," An says. "He was very intelligent and always cheerful. He wanted to find a political solution for the war. Unfortunately, people didn't listen to him." It was Hickey's

long-held belief that Vietnam's warring parties should negotiate their own settlement.

When Hickey and other Americans came to visit the president's office, An was tasked with showing them the *agrovilles*.
"I took them across the Mekong River into Kien Hoa province
(the old Ben Tre province). They were pacifying that area. It was
infested with Viet Minh after the First Indochina War. A year
after it was started, the program failed. Dr. Tuyen gave me a car
and asked me to visit the *agrovilles* and report to him on what
I found. He knew that people were lying to him, the district
chiefs and province chiefs. He needed someone he could trust,
who could go out in the field and give him a secret report on what
was really happening. I drove all the way to Rach Gia, on the
Gulf of Thailand in the south. Then from there I drove through
central Vietnam to Hué in the north. I came back and reported
to Dr. Tuyen, 'The *agrovilles* program is finished. Forget about
it. You have to do something new.' That's why he dropped the
*agrovilles* and switched, with the help of the Americans, to
building strategic hamlets."

An's handling of this assignment reveals how he became a
trusted adviser to so many South Vietnamese and American officials. When asked to study a sensitive military issue, he examines the matter firsthand, like an investigative journalist,
and returns with a blunt report: "Your strategy is not working.
Find a new strategy." At the end of the day, he looks like the one
honest man in Vietnam, the person to consult for confidential
evaluation of what is really happening. He tells the truth to
Dr. Tuyen. He tells the truth to his Communist handlers. It is
the same truth but it has different meanings, depending on
who is hearing it. Tuyen confronts a strategic weakness that
needs fixing. The Communists learn about a strategic weakness
that can be exploited.

An protected his cover by telling his Western bosses the
same truth he told to his Communist comrades. But what
happens when this "truth" is converted into a chess piece and

projected forward on the board, five or six moves ahead? What does it mean that a Communist spy advised the South Vietnamese government on how to build more effective fortifications in the countryside? After all, the move from *agrovilles* to strategic hamlets entailed an increased military presence, beefed up armaments, and more coercion and brutality directed at Vietnam's peasants. Is An's advice an example of compartmentalization? Was he thinking like a Westerner by day and a Communist by night? Or was there something deeper at work? If you immiserate the populace, uproot and brutalize them, will they become increasingly ardent in their support for the Communists? Was An offering "information" or "disinformation" or some third category of "truth"? In any case, he was now launched on the career that would make him at once the most trusted adviser and the most effective spy in twentieth-century Vietnamese history.

As we sit talking in his living room, An keeps himself positioned near the telephone and a pad of paper, and there is always a pen tucked in his breast pocket. Old colleagues call to ask him out for coffee. Foreign visitors request meetings. News arrives that old friends have died. An keeps these conversations brief. We always return to where we left off. In this case, I ask him what he means when he talks about an area being infested with Viet Minh in need of pacification.

"I use this language because I had to think like an American," he says. "I had to think like a nationalist. If I had thought like a Communist, I would have been finished, finished completely."

While working for Dr. Tuyen, An was once asked to interpret for a distinguished American professor. Tuyen, who had been detained by the Communists in 1945 in North Vietnam before he escaped to the south, was fiercely anti-Communist and highly suspicious of anyone sympathetic to their cause.

After a three-hour interview, the American professor invited An to lunch. An was surprised when the professor announced that Tuyen was either a Vietnamese Communist or a member of the KGB. "His way of reasoning and explaining things and arriving at conclusions—they are all Communist," said the professor. "Today, as he narrated one story after another, they were all presented with Communist logic.'"

"I don't really know how the Communists think," An said, "but the Vietnamese welcome Dr. Tuyen's logic. They consider him brilliant. He examines everything from A to Z, before arriving at sound conclusions. We think he is an excellent analyst, and now you say that this way of explaining things is 'Communist.' I am shocked to think that what you say might be true.'"

"I am just letting you know that you have to be very careful with this man. I don't want you to come to grief in the future," said the professor.

"May I tell him your opinion?"

"It is up to you. If you tell him what I think and he works for the Communists, then he will be more careful and you will have to be even more suspicious of him."

An narrates this story as if he is leading up to the punch line of a splendid joke. A grin hovers around the edge of his lips. He waves his hands through the air and sits bolt upright on the front of his chair.

"After lunch, I walked from the river up to Dr. Tuyen's office. 'Hey, Dr. Tuyen,' I said, finding him at his desk. 'Do you know what the American professor says about you? He says you are a Comm . . . u . . . nist! You are not working for the Vietnamese government. You are working for the KGB!'

"'An, are you joking?' Tuyen asked.

"He knew I liked to joke all the time. It's my way of talking, like I'm joking, but I'm serious," An says.

"I never lie," An told him, before explaining the professor's line of reasoning.

Tuyen looked surprised. Then he said, "The professor is right."

"Does this mean you are a Communist?" An asked.

"No! I am not a Communist," Tuyen reassured him. "But the professor's analysis is correct. The Communist way of reasoning is so logical, so appealing, so clear. It took me three years to learn how to imitate their way of thinking. Now I talk this way naturally. I didn't realize that one of these days an American professor would figure out what I was doing, and maybe I wasn't even aware of what I was doing, but this is a big mistake," Tuyen admitted.

"Lesson learned! You will have to correct your way of talking." An chided him in the singsong voice of a schoolboy teasing one of his classmates.

"I had to learn this lesson for myself," An says. "I had to learn how to talk like an American, think like an American. Actually, learning how to write balanced stories, like an American journalist, helps you a lot as a strategic intelligence officer. It makes you more objective."

When asked if he used this "objective" language in writing his reports to the Communists, An said he did. "I would talk about pacifying areas filled with Vietcong terrorists. They knew what I meant. This is why the government sent me to school in 1978 and 1979. They found after the fall of South Vietnam that I used a lot of foreign words. I tried using the new Communist words, but I didn't understand them. I speak an archaic Vietnamese. I learned the new words, but I've forgotten most of them by now." An laughs again, a deep guffaw at life's absurdities.

An was eventually moved into the job for which he had been groomed by the Asia Foundation when Tuyen sent him to work for the Viet Tan Xa (VTX), the official government news agency, which was affiliated with Reuters. Before An officially severed his ties as a South Vietnamese intelligence agent, he was getting paid simultaneously by Tuyen, VTX, and Reuters. At VTX, An was put in charge of the foreign correspondents. Many of them, with no training as journalists, had never filed a story. An ordered them to file at least one a week. They complained to Tuyen, saying that doing journalism would get in the way of their work as spies—their real job. Supporting An,

Tuyen instructed his foreign agents to get "serious in your work" and start filing stories like An the "professional pressman."

Tuyen was An's patron for three years, until he fell from power after an attempted coup in December 1962. "Whenever he cooked up something he discussed it with me," An says. "When he was planning to pull off a coup, he asked me to come to his office and help him." After his failed coup attempt, Tuyen spent the next thirteen years under house arrest, scheming to bring down one government after another. The bonds of friendship and obligation between An and Tuyen held fast up to the last day of the war, when An helped his friend escape the Communist forces advancing on Saigon. "I helped Dr. Tuyen get out of here. I knew I would be in trouble. This was the chief of intelligence, an important man to capture, but he was my friend. I owed him. He had been nice to me. He helped me with everything."

An's working method continued unchanged as he moved from Tuyen's office to VTX and on from there to a full-time position at Reuters. Recognized as one of the hardest-working journalists in town, always ready to help his colleagues with informed opinions or telling anecdotes, An gave information in order to get it. "Their food is information, documents," An says of the similarities between journalists and spies. "Just like birds, one has to keep feeding them so they'll sing."

"From the army, intelligence, secret police, I had all kinds of sources," An says. "The commanders of the military branches, officers of the special forces, the navy, the air force—they all helped me." In exchange for this steady stream of information, An gave his South Vietnamese informants the same thing he gave his Communist employers. "We discussed these documents. As the South Vietnamese tried to figure out what they meant, they had a problem. How were they going to deal with the Americans?" An then turned around and advised the Americans on how to deal with the Vietnamese. It was a high-level confidence game, with death hovering over him should he be discovered photographing the strategic plans and intelligence reports that were slipped to him by his South Vietnamese sources.

An was so well informed and well connected and so fluent in explaining Vietnam's political and military situation to visiting Westerners that Peter Smark, the Reuters bureau chief in Asia, hired him in 1960 as the agency's local Vietnamese correspondent. Founded in 1849 by German bank clerk Israel Beer Josaphat, Reuters originally employed carrier pigeons to deliver stock reports. The pigeons were soon carrying other kinds of news, and after Josaphat moved to England—where he christened himself Baron Paul Julius von Reuter—the Reuter Telegraph Company began building a worldwide network of news bureaus. Known for speed and brevity, Reuters employs a buttoned-down British style bleached of emotion. Scoop the competition and report the facts are its twin mantras. It was An's job to put his ear to the ground and work the back channels at the palace to come up with early warnings on coups and countercoups, palace intrigues, military campaigns, aerial bombardments, troop deployments, battlefield losses, and everything else that gets reported out of a war zone.

While working for Reuters in the 1960s Pham Xuan An became the irrepressible man about town who knew everything about everybody and was seen everywhere, in all the city's best restaurants and cafés, chatting and joking with everyone from generals and ambassadors down to the local cyclo drivers and dance hall girls. An established himself as the go-to man for newly arrived Americans who needed briefings and old-timers who needed a tip. He was always generous with his advice and stories, always a good source of local color. The news reports filed out of Vietnam that started with an anecdote provided by An must number in the thousands.

On January 25, 1962, An married Hoang Thi Thu Nhan, a young woman who sold embroidery and lacquer boxes in a store on the rue Catinat. Ten years his junior, Thu Nhan was not one of his *deésses,* the women who kept him out of harm's way throughout his life, nor was she a member of the Communist Party. It was not until a month after they were married that An told his wife a few things about his secret life. Thu Nhan was not the designated agent charged with destroying An's affairs were he to be captured. This role was reserved for two other female spies, Tam Thao and her sister, Chin Chi, who had previously declined An's offer of marriage. Le Duc Tho, founder of the Indochina Communist Party and Pham Xuan An's marriage counselor, played an unknown role in An's family life, but the wedding was undoubtedly discussed by the Party at the highest levels.

"My wife knew a little bit, but she thought I worked for the revolution. She didn't know anything about intelligence," An told an interviewer in 2004. According to An, everyone in his family was sympathetic to the revolutionary cause, but for security reasons they were kept in the dark about his work. His middle brother, Pham Xuan Hoa, four years younger than An, had been trained in France as a helicopter mechanic. He was flying on President Diem's helicopter during a stormy night flight in 1962 when the craft hit the mountains north of Saigon and all thirteen people on board were killed. Diem was not on the flight. An's youngest brother, Dinh, trained as a lawyer, got in trouble defending political prisoners and was himself imprisoned briefly. He was drafted into the army as a porter carrying munitions into battle until An used his family connections to get him reassigned to Diem's staff. "Everyone in the family knew I was working for the Communists," An says. "My brother Dinh wanted to join, but I said no."

Tam Thao, Chin Chi, and An were in the same political cell. He taught the girls English and visited their house to court the beautiful Chin Chi. They waved good-bye at the airport when he flew to America, and they welcomed him back to Saigon on his return. After An had lain low for several months, Tam Thao took him to the tunnels northwest of Saigon and reintroduced him to the intelligence network, which had been rebuilt after Muoi Huong was captured. She was An's original courier. She had a false wall built in her apartment for evading the police, and this hiding place was used by the head of their intelligence cell during his visits to Saigon. Tam Thao had her own career as a spy, working as secretary and confidante to a number of U.S. military officers. Chin Chi did similar work until she was summoned into the jungle in 1965. Four years later Tam Thao was also moved to the jungle, where she found a husband approved by the Party and was allowed to marry.

When I learn that Tam Thao and Chin Chi, now widows, are once again living in Saigon, I arrange to meet them for tea. I find them sitting on the ground floor of a three-story house on a quiet street in one of Saigon's nicer neighborhoods. After threading my way through the motorbikes parked in the court- yard and removing my shoes, I enter the downstairs living room, which is formally decorated with a large red upholstered couch and matching chairs covered with lace antimacassars. On top of a mahogany curio cabinet sits the family altar. Inside the cabinet, among other souvenirs, is a small Statue of Liberty which Tam Thao tells me she has recently bought on a trip to the United States.

Both women are trim and elegant, with carefully coiffed hair. A tall woman with a handsome, even-featured face, Chin Chi wears a white silk pants suit, embossed with flowers and decorated with bone buttons and black piping. I see that she was once a great beauty, with sensual lips, high cheekbones, and large brown eyes. Today she has frosted hair and the retiring manner of a younger sister who has always allowed her elders to speak for her. She and Tam Thao are the kind of meticulously assembled matrons who could be chatting with me about their bridge club, but are instead describing their lives as spies and jungle soldiers.

Born a year apart, the girls were teenagers studying English and French at Gia Long *lycée* in Saigon when they met An, who was four years older than Tam Thao. He tutored both girls in

English and fell in love with Chin Chi. After the girls joined the Tran Van On student protest movement in 1951, Chin Chi went into the jungle for a year of revolutionary training. When she returned to finish high school, she was hired as a translator by the U.S. operations mission, which directed Vietnam's strategic hamlet program. She traveled around the country by helicopter, accompanying doctors and nurses into the field. "I talked to An and told him everything I saw," she says. "I was a spy."

After resisting An's advances, Chin Chi worked as a spy until she slipped out of the city in 1965 to take up the life of a jungle soldier. She remained single until 1968, when she married a North Vietnamese colonel and gave birth to a daughter. When I ask Chin Chi if Pham Xuan An was ever in love with her and wanted to marry her, Tam Thao chuckles and Chin Chi smiles.

"He wanted to marry me after he came back from the United States," she says. "This was in 1959. My family agreed, but I said no. I turned him down. I wanted to travel abroad. I wanted to go to England to study, but Mr. Muoi Huong, our chief, did not approve of my leaving the country. I went into the jungle instead.

"His wife won't want to hear me say this," she adds. "It's an old love story. Mr. Muoi Huong supported the marriage, but I was too young. I wasn't thinking about love at the time."

Later in the afternoon, after many more cups of tea, Chin Chi offers another explanation for why she resisted An's advances. "There was a curfew, and everyone had to go home except for An, because he had a press card and could come and go whenever he wanted. So he would stay late into the night, talking, talking. There was no way to shut him up."

"Seven months after I turned him down, An married Thu Nhan," she says. "A spy must have what appears to be a normal family life and a wife to manage the family, in case he is captured. There was a problem, though, since Thu Nhan was not a member of the organization. If An was captured, the secret documents in his house were to be given to Tam Thao. She was the one who knew where they were hidden."

At the end of the afternoon, Tam Thao takes my notebook and draws a map of the neighborhood where they lived during the war, with directions on how to find Pham Xuan An's old house. Giving the old and new street names, she tells me that An's house was at the end of an alley off Ngo Tung Chau Street, which is now called Le Thi Rieng. His parents owned the house next door, where his mother lived until her death. An lived with his wife and four children in two rooms because, as Tam Thao explains, "he was saving his money for when he was arrested."

Only recently have we learned the identity of the man who directed Pham Xuan An's spying after he returned from America. On the day he and Tam Thao drove out to the Cu Chi tunnels, they went to see Cao Dang Chiem, a shadowy figure who long held a position at the top of Vietnam's intelligence services. Living in a safe area outside of town, Chiem was the Viet Minh police chief of Saigon by 1947. Earlier he had played an accidental role in America's decision to go to war in Indochina when, in September 1945, Lieutenant Colonel A. Peter Dewey became the first American killed in Vietnam. His death was a mistake for which the Vietnamese apologized, but it set in motion the next thirty years of warfare in Southeast Asia.

Colonel Dewey led the Office of Strategic Services (OSS) intelligence team that arrived in Saigon on September 4, 1945. Charged with recovering two hundred and fourteen Americans who had been taken prisoner by the Japanese, Dewey met with members of the Japanese high command and with Dr. Pham Ngoc Thach, who was serving as minister of foreign affairs for the Viet Minh. Dewey, who had studied French history at Yale and law at the University of Virginia, was the son of a prominent U.S. congressman and, at twenty-eight, a distinguished veteran of OSS operations in Europe. He and his seven-person team were the only Westerners in Saigon, until a

British Gurka division from Rangoon and some French paratroopers from Calcutta arrived in the city on September 12.

Ten days later, on September 23, after British General
Douglas Gracey had ordered French troops released from internment and rearmed, they rampaged through the city, killing
hundreds of Vietnamese and reclaiming Saigon as French territory. Dewey implored Gracey to intervene. As he wrote in a
prophetic report to his OSS colleagues in Hanoi, "Cochinchina
is burning, the French and British are finished here, and we
ought to clear out of Southeast Asia." Gracey declared Dewey
persona non grata and ordered him to leave Saigon. In a fateful move, he forbade him from flying an American flag on his
jeep. On September 26, Dewey left the Continental Hotel and
headed in his jeep to the airport. Mistaken for a French officer,
he was killed in a Viet Minh ambush: the first American casualty in what would become the Vietnam war and, since his
body was never recovered, the first MIA. Appalled by the mistake, Ho Chi Minh sent an apology and letter of condolence to
President Truman.

The day Dewey was killed, Cao Dang Chiem was commanding a troop of soldiers guarding the bridge to Dakao,
where Alden Pyle would later meet his demise. All we know of
Chiem's involvement in Dewey's death is that he was one of the
few people in Vietnam who knew where the body was buried.
Chiem rose quickly through the ranks to become Vietnam's
preeminent spymaster. After providing security for the Communist leadership in the south, he went on to direct the most
powerful of Vietnam's three intelligence agencies—the Office
of Strategic Intelligence, which was run from inside the Communist Party's Central Committee. (The other two agencies
were Public Security, run by the police, and Military Intelligence, attached to the army.)

Pham Xuan An always insisted that he worked in "strategic
intelligence." To his Western visitors, this sounded like a cerebral

activity removed from the dirty work of tactical intelligence. What An said was literally true, but the impact of his affiliation resonates clearly only when we understand the direct link between the Office of Strategic Intelligence and the Vietnamese Communist Party.

In May 1962, when New Zealander Nick Turner succeeded Peter Smark as the Reuters man in Saigon, he arrived to find the voluble Pham Xuan An holding court in the Reuters office, which was installed in a corner of an old French villa near the Presidential Palace. Reuters shared the space with its nominal ally Vietnam Press (VTX). A year later, when the Buddhist crisis erupted, Reuters was thrown out of the villa and cut its ties to VTX. Reuters was running stories critical of "the arrogance and incompetence of the Catholic Diem regime in handling the Buddhists," says Turner, which made relations dicey with this "government-controlled propaganda agency." Reuters moved its office downtown to a second-floor walkup on rue Catinat, which was good for An, since he was now a stone's throw from café Givral, the Continental terrace known as the "Shelf," and his other Saigon haunts.

Although they worked together productively in the office and traveled together in the field, garnering more than their fair share of scoops, Turner is one of the few people An does not remember fondly. An also tells me that he advised Turner to trim the emotion out of his prose, to make it more evenhanded and less sympathetic to the Communists.

In 1962, NLF soldiers launched an attack on the military outpost at An Lac village, thirty kilometers from Saigon on Highway 4. When Turner and An arrived on the scene, they found that local militiamen had been killed along with their family members, including women and children. Turner thought the local townspeople should be outraged by these "atrocities." Instead, they were happy with the gruesome outcome. "We hated these people," they told An. "The soldiers and their wives and children took advantage of us. They came to the market and stole food without paying. If you didn't bribe them, they would open fire and kill you."

An also learned that the militiamen stationed in the village were refugees from the north. Their outpost had been attacked from the outlying rice fields. The guerrillas had crawled through the plants, ducking under water to avoid the searchlights which raked the surface. This was their only possible approach, and the soldiers' family quarters happened to lie in the way. The women and children had died accidentally in the crossfire.

"Nick Turner wanted to report these details. I advised him to tone down the story. 'If you write it this way, Reuters will get in trouble with the government.' A journalist faces this kind of situation all the time. You don't dare write the story the way it happened.

"The same was true for the atrocities committed in Vietnam by the South Koreans. In one operation, the Koreans rounded up the women and children in a village and dropped them in a dry well to kill them. Anyone who tried to save them was shot. Fortunately an American soldier found them and intervened. I was working for an American journalist at the time. She wanted to write this story. I said, 'Please, this is too awful. The Koreans rely on the Americans, and you're an American too. Remember, an American saved the villagers, and no one was killed.'" The reporter dropped the story.

This was one of numerous incidents when An steered his fellow journalists away from stories about atrocities committed by the Republican side in the war—stories that would have made the Communists look good by comparison. To maintain his cover, An shied away from reporting anti-American news. The charge that he planted pro-Communist propaganda in the publications for which he worked is off the mark. An did not plant disinformation. At times, he even opposed planting information. He wanted to avoid standing out as a critic of the American war. "I was in a very bad position," he says. "On one

side, I had many American friends. On the other side—
my side—were the Communists. This is often the case for
human beings. They find themselves in complicated situations.
I had to solve the problem the most humane way I could. I didn't
want to create more animosity between Americans, Vietnamese,
and Koreans, and I didn't want to see innocent people getting
killed." I ask An if running the Korean story might have prevented similar atrocities from occurring in the future. "You
cannot prevent them from happening," he says, before repeating, "You cannot."

M y daily conversations with An fall into a pattern. I arrive
at his gate in the morning and pull the bell. An shuffles
down the driveway and shakes my hand with his bony fingers.
We stroll through the garden, admiring his cocks and singing
birds and greeting the little dogs he keeps tied near his front
door, before sitting for hours in his *salle de séjour.* His voice is
low, hardly a whisper over the sound of the traffic roaring outside his gate. As the hours advance, I move from the couch into
a chair next to him. Pretending to adjust the microphone at his
throat, I lean my ear toward his lips. Like a Vietnamese Jean-
Paul Sartre, who preferred to conduct his political battles over
a cup of coffee at the Café de Flore, An rarely claims to have
done anything more during the war than observe and analyze
events. But we know of several occasions when he reached behind the curtain to adjust the scene. One was the battle of Ap
Bac in 1963, which marked a turning point in the expanding
American war. For the first time the Vietcong fought at battalion strength and won a decisive victory against Vietnamese
army units supported by American helicopters, armored vehi-
cles, and artillery. Two Vietcong soldiers received North Vietnamese military exploit medals for winning this battle. One
was the commander of the Communist forces. The other was
Pham Xuan An, who devised the winning strategy.

How does a correspondent for Reuters win a combat medal? When asked, An always scurries behind his standard explanation: he did strategic analysis and provided background information on the commanders and troops involved. But An did far more. He was intimately involved in training the Vietcong troops who engaged in the battle, advising them on how to fight against helicopter gunships, armored personnel carriers, and other new weapons which were then being introduced into Vietnam. He mapped the battlefield strategy and helped lay the trap that led to the Communist victory, and then he went out and got the story reported.

The battle took place outside the hamlet of Ap Bac, forty miles southeast of Saigon, in January 1963. "Up till then Viet Cong activities had consisted of hit-and-run attacks, avoiding pitched battles," Nick Turner wrote in an article called "Media and War: Reflections on Vietnam," which was published in 2003. "The Americans said that if the Communists could be made to stand and fight they would get a bloody nose. Ap Bac was the first pitched battle between substantial Viet Cong and government forces, and it was a Viet Cong victory. And it could not be hidden because on the night of the battle I drove to the scene, taking Neil Sheehan of UPI with me, and at dawn we inspected the battlefield and got a clear picture of what had happened."

When I ask Turner how he knew to head to Ap Bac, he pointed to Pham Xuan An. "An was the first reporter to break the news. He fed me the initial story and details that got me to write it. He told me some American helicopters had been shot down and that I should go to Ap Bac. America was not directly involved in the war at this point; so the fact that American helicopters were getting shot down was big news. It was the first major battle of the war. The Communists stood and fought. They inflicted serious damage, shooting down five troop-carrying helicopters, and then they disappeared into the countryside. The story broke in the Western press and was written exactly the way the Communists wanted it written."

The battle pitted three hundred and fifty Vietcong soldiers against forces from South Vietnam's 7th Infantry Division, which was being advised by Lieutenant Colonel John Paul Vann. At the disposal of the Republicans were ten Shawnee helicopters, five Huey "flying shotgun" helicopters, thirteen M-113 "green dragon" armored personnel carriers, and fourteen hundred troops, supported by long-range artillery, thirteen fighter-bombers, and all the napalm they wanted. Within minutes of the attack on Ap Bac, fourteen of the fifteen helicopters had been hit. Four went down and three Americans were killed, with another eight wounded. A fifth helicopter was downed during a rescue attempt. At the end of the battle, the Communists slipped away with thirty-nine wounded soldiers and eighteen killed. The Saigon forces lost eighty killed and a hundred wounded, not counting the Americans.

"Emulate Ap Bac" became both a Communist slogan and method. Diagrams and descriptions of the battle were sent to all the Communist forces in the south. The engagement was studied as a classic model for how the Vietcong should fight their better-equipped opponent. Simply teaching marksmen to lead helicopters like ducks would result in five thousand of these expensive machines being destroyed in the course of the war.

Turner speculates that An might have played another role in the battle. "He would have had enough knowledge of the battlefield tactics, rules of engagement, logistics and battle-readiness of both the Vietnamese and Americans in that area at that time to give pretty good advice on the way to set up a trap for them. Certainly Ap Bac had the hallmarks of a trap. The Americans in particular (who at that time were still in an 'advisory' role but also providing helicopter support and air cover for ARVN troops) had been saying that they couldn't wait for the opportunity to engage a force of well-trained VC regulars who were prepared to stand and fight instead of melting away. The importance of Ap Bac was that this is exactly what the VC did, for the very first time. But they did it according to their own carefully laid plan, not through being cornered and forced to defend themselves."

Following Ap Bac, An busied himself covering the other big stories of 1963, including the Buddhist protest against Diem's increasingly repressive government. Monks began sitting in the lotus position in Saigon streets, dousing themselves with gasoline, and burning themselves to death. To amplify their protest, they needed a journalist who could broadcast word of impending immolations without tipping off the police. "Before they burned themselves, the monks would ring me and give me the story first," An says. "I knew that someone was going to die. If I reported it to the police, a life would be saved, but this was against the rules. The source had given me the story on condition that I shouldn't reveal it before it happened. These are the ethics of the press. You have to observe them, no matter how tough it may be." These are also the ethics of an intelligence agent who knows the propaganda value of burning monks.

On November 1, the Diem government was overthrown in an American-supported coup d'état. Ngo Dinh Diem and two of his brothers were killed. The CIA officer supervising the operation, with an open telephone line to the U.S. embassy and forty two thousand dollars in Vietnamese piastres stuffed in his pocket, was Pham Xuan An's friend Lou "Black Luigi" Conein. Three weeks later, President John F. Kennedy was assassinated in Dallas, Texas.

Technically, I may have fired him," says Turner, revealing by his choice of words that this is a complicated subject. "An was the best Vietnamese journalist in town. He had a sophisticated mind. He had the best contacts among the military and intelligence communities. The Americans trusted him. He had entrée to Colonel Lansdale's outfit. He was my intelligence officer. Things were extraordinarily devious in Saigon in those days. We assumed everyone was an agent of someone and that everything we said was reported somewhere. People worked as double agents and triple agents. This could be a lucrative business, but it might also have been a political requirement for staying alive."

An would tell Turner what the Communists were going to do, and "invariably that's what they did. His perception of events was uncannily well-informed," Turner says. Oddly, Reuters had no use for this information. The agency avoided analytical articles and think pieces, sticking to hard news, short and terse, to keep the cable costs down.

As far as Turner was concerned, An could be both a Communist and a good reporter so long as he did the job he was paid for, but his capitalist employer was getting short shrift compared to his Communist bosses. "An would disappear from the office for several days at a time. He wouldn't tell me where he was going, and when he returned he wouldn't tell me where he had been or what he had done. He just disappeared. People speculated he had a girlfriend, but I didn't believe it. I knew he was very fond of his wife, and I didn't think he was involved with anyone else. I suspected he was going off to talk to the Vietcong."

"'Look, An,' I told him, 'for all I know, you may be working for the Vietcong. That's fine, so long as you do your job for me.'" Actually, though, it wasn't fine, since Turner's sources, particularly his sources in the intelligence community, would have disappeared if they had known he had a Communist sympathizer in his office. "When I went to talk to intelligence sources, I used to tell An about it," Turner says. "Then I stopped doing this. He sensed I was withholding information from him. As his sources dried up, this made him less useful to the Communists. He began scouting his options."

United Press International (UPI) reporter Ray Herndon, who lived in Vietnam from 1962 to 1967, also suspected that An had divided loyalties. When he accompanied An to the bird market on Nguyen Hue Street, An would inquire curiously about Herndon's visits to the field. He was particularly interested in descriptions of military units, their strengths and weaknesses. "I had a car and driver in Vietnam, which I leased to the Reuters bureau for two hundred and fifty dollars a month," says Herndon. "An would disappear with my car for several days at a time."

"'I have gone hunting,' he would say when he returned to Saigon. Then he would present my wife and me with a leg of venison or a piece of wild boar. Maybe it crossed my mind to wonder if he was a courier, running antibiotics and other supplies out to the Vietcong. My wife, who is Eurasian, was also suspicious of An. He seemed to show up in too many places at once and be too interested in observing what was happening. Of course, our side was spying on us too. The CIA put an agent named Don Larrimore on our staff. I caught him once inside my apartment riffling through my telephone book. So we were suspicious of everybody, An included."

I had long wondered why An was called to the countryside. Why make him cross enemy lines and report to Cu Chi, a hotly contested war zone northwest of Saigon? He was sometimes caught in crossfire, and once he had to spend the night hiding in a ditch. "An was summoned to Cu Chi in the same way we summoned our own assets to Saigon," says former CIA analyst and interrogator Frank Snepp, who now works as a TV producer in Los Angeles. "This is what you do in the business. You call people in for debriefing. It was a way to keep tabs on him. You want to make sure he hasn't been turned. You eye him. You see if he's still with you. It's very dangerous, but that's what you do."

An says he last went to the Cu Chi tunnels in 1966. After that, with the 25th Infantry Division stationed there, it was too dangerous. They had defoliated the jungle with herbicides and flattened the trees with Rome plows. "Before 1966, I went there all the time," he says. "After that, we relied on couriers."

I ask him why he needed to see his commanding officers in the jungle. "I believed I knew better than they did what was going on," he tells me. "They knew how to fight, but that was all. So their orders didn't mean that much to me. Sometimes they needed me to analyze with them. So I would help them."

With Reuters drying up as a source of news, An was not only disappearing from the office but was also freelancing for other journalists. Even when he was in the office he was often distracted by guests. "A string of visiting correspondents beat a path to our door to pick An's brain," Turner says. The parade included correspondents such as David Halberstam of the *New York Times,* which was permissible, since his paper was a Reuters client. But the situation got dicier when An spent time chatting with Reuters' competitors. "An was a huge reservoir of nuanced information, much of which Reuters had little use for, but it would have been great for thoughtful pieces in papers like the *Herald Tribune* and the *Christian Science Monitor.*" As Turner later learned, this was exactly where An's ideas were appearing.

Turner and An reached the breaking point in their relationship when Turner discovered that An, who had been absent from the office for several days, was helping a stringer for *Newsweek* named Beverly Ann Deepe write one of the background stories that she hoped would establish her as a serious journalist. Eventually An worked for Deepe as her legman before moving to his staff position at *Time.* Deepe was one of An's *déesses,* the female protective spirits who knowingly or unknowingly covered for him while he did his real work as a spy.

On learning what An had been doing, Turner exploded. "That's not on," he yelled. "I'm sorry. If you're working for other people, you can't be working for Reuters." Actually, it was all right to work for the Communists but not for *Newsweek.* One was the enemy. The other was the competition.

Compared to the paucity of news in the small Reuters operation, *Time* was a gold mine for An and the Communists.

"They had lots of inside dope," Turner says. "They wrote long reports, naming their sources. An would get an incredible depth of information just from reading these reports. They were full of news from journalists in the countryside, interviews with monks and other opposition figures, conversations with high government officials. They probably provided the finest overview you could get on the situation in Vietnam. These were the best files in the country. They were incredibly valuable."

"I always presumed that the CIA was reading *Time*'s cable traffic and appreciating the quality of their reporting," says Turner, who later worked for *Time* as a freelancer. "I sometimes wondered if the CIA wasn't the real audience for these reports. I mean no one back in New York seemed to be reading them. Correspondents would file fifteen thousand word stories from the field, which got homogenized into a seven hundred and fifty word article that said exactly the opposite of what had been reported from the field. It seemed to me that the CIA was the only reader who might appreciate the value of what *Time* was sending over their wires. I always assumed the CIA had a backdoor deal with *Time*. This is why people sweated their guts to get good information that was then ignored."

When I ask Turner if he ever ran a security check on An or discussed his suspicions with intelligence agents, he admits, "No one seemed to believe that An was a security risk, and I wasn't going to mention it to British or American intelligence. I was afraid they would clam up and not talk to me anymore." Turner himself was already a marginal figure in Saigon. "They regarded me as representing a British outfit, and I wasn't treated as well as if I had been in American news." In order to keep his own nose clean, Turner stifled his suspicions. The one person capable of blowing An's cover did his best to keep it in place.

"An has himself to blame," says Turner about An's departure from Reuters. "He schooled me in how to read the minds of Vietnamese. 'Don't believe what you're told. There is always another truth underlying the obvious.' As we used to say in Vietnam, if you think you know what's going on, you're not well informed. The more you learned, the more complicated it became. An gave me a good education in understanding the Vietnamese. I then applied it to him."

# Reliable
# Sources

When he left Reuters in 1964, An was out of a job but not out of work. The American presence in Vietnam was building. From seventeen thousand "advisers," the United States was preparing to introduce half a million combat troops. Included in the baggage to this buildup was a raft of journalists (more than five hundred would be accredited by 1966, all of whom needed translators and local reporters). As An's friend Frances "Frankie" FitzGerald remarked, "The news corps included senior editors from New York, cub reporters from hometown papers, Ivy League graduates, crime reporters with two-syllable vocabularies, spaced-out young photographers, combat veterans of Korea and the Second World War—everything, in fact, except a determined opponent of the war."

An freelanced for this flotsam of American journalists, his two major clients being Robert Shaplen, veteran correspondent in Asia for *The New Yorker,* and Beverly Ann Deepe, a twenty-seven-year-old, fresh-faced reporter with bangs and a beehive hairdo who was freelancing for *Newsweek,* the

*International Herald Tribune,* and the *Christian Science Monitor.* Deepe became his *déesse,* Shaplen one of his best sources.

"Brunette, gentle, and unprepossessing," Deepe was what former *Washington Post* correspondent William Prochnau calls a perfect example of "the girl-next-door world of the fading fifties." Deepe lent herself to this cause when she wrote that a woman journalist at war should be a "living symbol of mother, sweetheart, and the apple-pie world back home." Deepe grew up on a farm in Nebraska. She majored in journalism and political science at the University of Nebraska, graduating in 1957, and then got a master's degree from the Columbia School of Journalism. She traveled on a student exchange to Russia and Central Asia. Bitten with wanderlust, she saved her money while working as a political pollster during the U.S. presidential election in 1960 and then pitched up in Vietnam in 1962. Planning to stay for two weeks, she stayed for seven years— making her one of the longest-serving Western correspondents to cover the war.

An felt beholden to Beverly Deepe, Laura Palmer, and the other women correspondents who coached him in the etiquette of American journalism. They taught him how to punch up his leading sentences. They showed him how to be objective (the great god of American reporting). They helped him branch out from writing staccato wire service prose to penning longer opinion and editorial pieces. Unknowingly, Beverly Deepe served other purposes for An. She traveled widely through the country and was well received by soldiers who loved being gallant to a female reporter. She needed An to translate; he needed her to get access to his own investigative reporting from the field.

Deepe tended to report on America's activities in Vietnam with credulous enthusiasm. She reminded her colleagues of Alden Pyle, the "quiet" American who thought of Vietnam as a civics lesson on "the problems of freedom." The few critical remarks she ventured about the American enterprise in Vietnam were meant to improve U.S. strategy, in other words, to "win" the war. Deepe was brave and adventuresome, but she never got around to confronting the big questions that seven years in a war zone might have provoked in a more inquisitive mind. Her reporting on the battle at Khe Sanh brought her a nomination for a Pulitzer Prize. By the end of her lengthy tour of duty, she had acquired a military husband, Colonel Charles "Chuck" Keever, who ran the press center in Danang, and twenty-nine volumes of correspondence and articles, which are now stored in her office at the University of Hawaii–Manoa, where she teaches journalism.

Rather than remarking on her naïveté, An employed Deepe as the perfect foil for his own activities. Deepe lived in a fourth-floor apartment above a garage in the heart of Saigon. The apartment, consisting of one large room with a kitchen and a refrigerator cooled by a block of ice, faced the Rex Hotel, where civilian and military officials gave their daily press briefings. An explains the mutually beneficial arrangement he developed with Deepe: "I would stop by to see the colonel who commanded South Vietnam's office of central intelligence. He was a friend of mine. Every day, I picked up intelligence information, which I gave to Beverly Ann Deepe to write stories for the *New York Herald Tribune*. We were happy. We had all the information we needed. We just 'cooked' the story from the ingredients we were given. It was very simple."

On July 5, 1965, special correspondent Pham Xuan An published his own article in the *New York Herald Tribune*, entitled "Red Program for South Vietnam: One Bite at a Time." When I brought a copy of this article to An during one of our visits, he elaborated on its origins. "The article explains the Communist strategy, the program. Before the Americans sent in combat troops, they should know what the reaction of the Communists would be. That's why I wrote the story."

The article says that the Communists, at that point in the war, had sixty-five thousand troops in the south, supported by one hundred thousand regional and village militia. "These numbers are correct," An says. "The Americans and Vietnamese captured a lot of documents from the enemy. They gave them to the CID [Criminal Investigation Department] to be translated. I relied on the Vietnamese Central Intelligence Organization [CIO] and on Vietnamese military intelligence, Vietnamese military security, and the Saigon secret police to show me this material, which I read and analyzed every day." An covered his tracks by publishing only information that was already known in the south, and never anything that he got from his Communist bosses. "It was a one-way street," he says. "This was for security reasons."

"I couldn't say I was using these documents from the CIO. I had to say I was quoting 'reliable sources.' Communist documents are reliable enough," An says with a laugh, amused by the thought of "reliability" in this most unreliable of wars. An's editorials also served to alert the Communists to what was known about them in the south. "They should know that anything I wrote about the Communists relied on captured documents. They had to be careful. All the Communist resolutions, for example, I know better in English than in Vietnamese. This is the trouble with me," An says, smiling.

An had another source of information that was even more reliable than captured Communist documents. Every day, he saw the raw intelligence data on military interrogations, including interrogations of Communist defectors. These may not have been useful for his daily journalism, but they were invaluable for his spying. An kept North Vietnamese intelligence apprised of every breach in their operations. He was the bell on the American cat who, time and again, leaped into a Communist nest only to find it empty. Soon after the Têt Offensive in January 1968, a North Vietnamese agent named Tran Van Dac, also known as Tam Ha, defected to the south. It was a serious blow to the Communists. He was a high-ranking officer and political commissar who knew a great deal about their strategy, particularly their plans for the second stage of the Têt Offensive in May 1968, which would be a military failure if stripped of the element of surprise.

Tu Cang, who was then head of Communist intelligence in the south, rushed to Saigon to assess the damage. On his way into the city, he stopped to buy a newspaper. Splashed across the front page was a headline about Colonel Tam Ha's defection and a big photo showing him standing between a Vietnamese general and William Westmoreland, the commander of American forces in Vietnam. As soon as Tu Cang reached the city, An loaded him into his car. They drove to a military base on the outskirts of Saigon in neighboring Gia Dinh province. Within fifteen minutes, while Tu Cang waited in the car, An had walked into headquarters, borrowed the files, and walked out holding photocopies of Tam Ha's interrogation.

"Reading Tam Ha's testimony, I felt extremely angry with this traitor," Tu Cang is quoted as saying in *Pham Xuan An: A General of the Secret Service* (2003), one of An's three Vietnamese biographies. "He revealed everything: our campaign plan, tactics, weapons, the concealment of our troops, artillery, bullets, and even the location of the regional command headquarters. Faced with this situation, our senior leaders changed the whole campaign plan for launching the second stage of the offensive, losing minimum casualties. The outcome of this offensive eventually forced the enemy to deescalate the war and go to the negotiating table." This story is remarkable for a number of reasons, including the fact that Pham Xuan An is driving onto a military base with the head of Communist intelligence in the front seat of his car. "We were in a hurry," An explains.

Besides sharing some of his sources with her, An accompanied Beverly Deepe into the field. One day they drove out to visit John Paul Vann, who had resigned from the army but returned to Vietnam to run the United States Agency for International Development pacification program in Hau Nghia province, near the Cambodian border. Vann was a colorful figure who gave journalists good copy. A critic of America's strategy in Vietnam, he wanted a better, smarter war with closer engagement on the ground and less reliance on high-altitude bombing and long-range artillery. Vann was considered a world authority on counterterrorism until Neil Sheehan gave him a darker cast. As Sheehan revealed in *A Bright Shining Lie: John Paul Vann and America in Vietnam,* while Vann allowed people to assume that he was forced out of the army because of his outspoken criticism of U.S. policy, he was actually cashiered for statutory rape.

An and Deepe set off one morning in his little green Renault 4CV to drive fifty kilometers northwest of Saigon to Vann's Hau Nghia office. "I hadn't notified anyone first," An says about this trip in January 1966. "If they had known we were coming, they probably would have denied us permission. We drove to Tay Ninh and then turned left into Hau Nghia province. When we pulled into town, the Vietnamese general guarding Vann's headquarters was surprised to see us. 'Goddam it,' he yelled. 'I don't want you journalists coming here.' He gave me a real tongue-lashing. 'You're Vietnamese. If you die, I don't care. But you have an American lady with you, and if she's killed, I'll have lots of problems. The road you arrived on is attacked every day by the Communists. We have to sweep it for mines whenever we send out a convoy. People are ambushed and killed all the time.'"

Because Vann was away, An and Deepe met with Doug Ramsey, his second in command. They ate an early lunch in order to get back to Saigon before nightfall. The province chief sent a platoon to clear the road of mines and escort them back to Route 1. The next week, Ramsey was seized by the Communists, who would hold him captive for seven years.

"When they captured someone, they let me know about it," An says. "I told them, 'He's a nice man. You should release him.' 'But he speaks Vietnamese,' they said. 'We are suspicious of people who speak Vietnamese.'" It was not until the signing of the Paris Accords, after he survived B-52 strikes, starvation, scurvy, beriberi, and one hundred and thirty-six attacks of falciparum malaria, that Ramsey was released in 1973.

In the fall of 2007, I learned the rest of Ramsey's story from a former State Department official who wishes to remain anonymous. Not only did An save Ramsey's life, he also got the Communists to agree to exchange Ramsey for a Communist officer in Western hands. Unfortunately for Ramsey, the exchange was blocked by the CIA, which was busily interrogating its captive. A high-level confession could advance CIA careers. Ramsey could wait.

An had other good reasons to work for Beverly Deepe. "The American women journalists had one advantage over the men," he says. "The people they interviewed thought they could fool them. They thought they could get them to parrot their own ideas or prejudices. The women appeared to be agreeing with you during an interview, but later, when they wrote up their stories, it was completely different. They had their own ideas, and the men they interviewed, time and again, were proved wrong. These journalists looked sweet, but actually they were very tough."

"I consider her as my sister, my older sister," An says of Deepe. "I was protected by my personal goddesses. I hoped that one of them would have a chance to write about me, rather than a man. Unfortunately, my wish didn't come true."

An and Deepe found themselves in the middle of one big story she missed *because* she was a woman. In August 1965, they flew north to Danang and checked into the press center, a former brothel which had been turned into a hotel run by the marines. Here they encountered CBS newsman Morley Safer and his cameraman and soundman, who were also in town looking for local color. "I spent the day with Beverly Ann Deepe out in the field with a marine company," An says. "They were nice soldiers. They were doing public affairs, public relations, seeing the people, giving them gifts, providing them with medicine that tasted like candy. They were helping children whose bellies were distended with worms. They gave them colorful Band-Aids. The kids who looked hungry got extra C rations. We thought these were nice men. They said lots of nice things as they helped people."

"At three or four in the afternoon, we left the field and returned with the marines to their company base. They had rigged up a stainless steel water tank. They invited us to take a shower and served us a hot meal. We were good friends by the time we left that evening to return to the press center. Later that night, actually very early in the morning, the soldiers went out on the Cam Ne operation. We didn't follow them. It was nighttime. Beverly was a young lady. She didn't go out at night."

No one had mentioned to Deepe that the marines were going out on a military mission. Morley Safer and his film crew moved in to take their place. This allowed them to capture one of the defining moments in the war, when a village of three hundred thatch-roofed houses was burned to the ground by rampaging soldiers wielding Zippo lighters. "Cam Ne was the first time the marines burned an entire village. Safer got the scoop," An says, admiringly. He goes on to describe how the marines made a mistake. "They thought the village belonged to the Communist guerrillas. Actually it belonged to the government. The provincial chief wanted the villagers punished for not paying 'taxes,' which were bribes. The three soldiers wounded in the action were hit from the rear by friendly fire."

After witnessing a moment of deep national shame, Safer had the bravery to report it (for which President Johnson tried to get him fired). Safer had covered French counterterrorism in Algeria, which also involved immiseration of the civilian population, but what bothered him about Cam Ne, wrote David Halberstam in *The Powers That Be* (1979), "was the senselessness of it all, for even when the French had applied torture they had usually done it with a certain precision, they knew exactly what they were trying to find out. This seemed, in addition to

everything else, so haphazard and sloppy and careless, not as de-
liberate as the French cruelty and perhaps thus even worse."
When the footage from Cam Ne was shown to Americans on
the evening news it marked, said Halberstam, "the end of the
myth that we were different, that we were better."

In his assessment of Cam Ne, An is surprisingly forgiving.
"The Americans had never had colonies," he says. "For them,
Vietnam was part of a planetary strategy." He describes how
the marines were confused about Vietnam from the moment
they landed. "After being trained in North Carolina, an incredibly tough course where they stood in water for hours on
end, they charged off their landing craft to hit the beach at
Danang. And what did they find there? A bunch of pretty girls
with garlands draped around their necks. The enemy was
nowhere in sight. They were disconcerted. They didn't know
what to do. The marines were nice during the daytime, but
they behaved differently at night. Someone full of hate suddenly
gave an order to burn down a village."

Cam Ne was a "traumatic event" for An, a personal turning
point in the war. "It's like when the World Trade towers were
attacked by terrorists and many innocent people were killed.
Maybe these soldiers were nursing the poison of revenge. That's
unavoidable in war. It's like what happened later during the
My Lai massacre. Human beings have two parts, an animal
part and a human part. Sometimes the animal nature is so
strong that you lose your reason. The Vietnamese do this to the
Vietnamese. They don't know whether they are brothers or
enemies. Even God cannot explain it."

We return to this subject when I visit An's house on the
morning of May 20, 2004. Both of us have been up late watching CNN broadcast congressional hearings on the torture of
Iraqi prisoners at Abu Ghraib, another defining moment in
America's far-flung wars. Pictures captured on cell phones and
floated on the Internet show naked prisoners being led around
on leashes and hooded prisoners with their outstretched arms

and penises wired with electrodes. "One of the generals at the hearings said the situation in Iraq is something that America has not confronted for fifty years," An says. "He was referring to Vietnam. He was wrong about the date. He should have said thirty years."

An asks if I remember General Nguyen Ngoc Loan, the Saigon police chief who is shown in the famous Eddie Adams photo shooting a Vietcong prisoner at point-blank range, with the bullet flying out the back of the man's head. Taken during the Tết Offensive in 1968, the Pulitzer Prize–winning photo became another defining image of the war's corrosive cruelty.

"General Loan was actually a very sweet man," An says. "His father was a Communist in the Viet Minh during the French Indochina War. Loan was drafted when General de Lattre de Tassigny set up the Vietnamese armed forces. To avoid serving in the infantry, he took the exam to be trained as a French pilot. You buy time. You hope the war will be over before you commit the crime of killing your own people. Loan was sent to be trained in France. They made him the highest ranking officer in the Vietnamese air force.

"Loan was supposed to drop bombs on the Viet Minh revolutionaries. Instead, since the French had no system for recording the results, he bombed in the jungle and the swamps. He made sure he flew low enough to look down and see that no one was killed."

But after becoming chief of police in Saigon, "Loan was turned into a tiger, first a tiger cop and then a full-fledged tiger," An says. "He became very cruel. A commander has to know how to handle the animal part of human nature. If you don't control this aspect of your men, if you let them run wild, then you are finished. This is what happened at Cam Ne. These nice young marines were good people. They loved women, they loved children, and then suddenly when someone gave the order they burned down a village. The blame should be put on the person who gave the order. The same thing is true for the Communist Party, for the atrocities committed on our side."

If Deepe was a spunky welterweight, Robert Shaplen was a world-class writer, producing a steady stream of articles and books out of Asia for fifty years. Shaplen was the dean of the American press corps in Vietnam, a big, gruff, gravel-voiced, cigar-smoking man who was Far Eastern correspondent for *The New Yorker.* He lived in a hotel room overlooking Hong Kong Bay, except when he was in Saigon, where he stayed in Room forty-seven at the Continental Palace Hotel. Shaplen wrote four *New Yorker* articles a year, long, detailed, exquisitely nuanced examinations of government and military policy, informed by sources at the highest levels. "He was one of our favorite journalists," says former CIA officer Frank Snepp. "We had orders from the top to give him unbelievable access to the embassy and high-level intelligence."

Former *Newsweek* bureau chief Kevin Buckley, who also lived and worked at the Continental, describes how Shaplen, who occupied the central room over the front door of the hotel, opened his suite every afternoon for a cocktail party that drew the most influential journalists in town, including Pham Xuan An. "Following the daily military briefing at 4:45 P.M., we would stop off at café Givral or Shaplen's room or both," says Buckley. "He always had a bottle of Scotch, and there would be waiters bustling in and out with ice buckets, glasses, and soda. He was a great host."

"Shaplen presumed that his room was wired better than a recording studio," says Buckley. "Living next to him were the Canadian, Polish, and Indian diplomats who made up the International Control Commission. The ICC had been set up to monitor the 1956 elections, which were supposed to unify Vietnam. When the elections were canceled, these guys had nothing better to do for the next twenty years than eavesdrop on

Shaplen's telephone calls to the CIA. Whenever a question came up that needed to be answered, Shaplen would get on the phone and call down to the lobby. 'Hello, this is Bob Shaplen, get me extension 4—.'" Buckley lowers his voice and starts growling in the stentorian whisper that Shaplen adopted when speaking to his friends at the embassy.

Whether or not he worked for the CIA, Shaplen is known to have loaned his services to the U.S. government on at least one occasion, when he carried back-channel communications for the State Department between Washington and Hanoi. By mid-1966, the U.S. government had begun to fear for the welfare of American pilots and other prisoners held in Hanoi. Captured in the midst of an undeclared war, these men were labeled war criminals—what today would be called "enemy combatants." Anxious to make certain that they were covered by the Geneva Conventions and not tortured into making "confessions" or brought to trial and executed, U.S. Ambassador-at-large Averell Harriman asked Shaplen to contact North Vietnam.

Shaplen was dispatched from New York to Phnom Penh, where he was instructed to find his old acquaintance Wilfred Burchett. A Communist sympathizer and prolific reporter from Vietnam's "liberated" zones, Burchett was thought to be the quickest route to Hanoi. Shaplen penned a letter detailing America's concerns and offered a deal, either medical supplies or a reciprocal exchange of prisoners, following the release of U.S. pilots. Two days after Burchett delivered Shaplen's letter to the NLF representative in Phnom Penh, he got a reply. Referring to American prisoners as "criminal nationals," the letter declared, without naming a date, that the "prisoners [would] be returned to their families." (Another seven years would pass before this happened.) Shaplen asked Harriman for permission to write another letter thanking the Communists for "understanding the humanitarian aspects of the problem." He also wanted to clarify that his original letter, although coming from a "private person," had been authorized by the U.S. government.

"We gave him very good strategic briefings," says Frank Snepp, of the access Shaplen commanded at the U.S. embassy in Saigon. "Did some of this intelligence make its way to Pham Xuan An? You bet. An had access to strategic intelligence. That's obvious. This would have been vital information to get to the north. An was of paramount importance to the Communists for corroborating what they were receiving from other sources. He was also picking up information from the network of spies that operated in the interrogation centers. He knew the Communist cadre we had captured and what they were saying. The guy was worth his weight in gold."

Shaplen and An spent hours closeted together in Shaplen's hotel room discussing Vietnamese politics and the progress of the war, and Shaplen even wrote about An in a *New Yorker* article entitled "We Have Always Survived," published in 1972. An is "probably the hardest-working and most highly respected Vietnamese journalist in town," writes Shaplen, who begins his article with a lengthy description of café Givral. "Everyone who comes to Givral does so not only to exchange information but to play the subtle conversational games the Vietnamese play so much better than Americans can—testing each other, putting each other on, trying to humor somebody and to denigrate somebody else. Cabinet members drop by from time to time, as do other high civilian and military officials; President Thieu used to, when he was still an army officer." Shaplen describes how the exchange of information at Givral involved a formalized ritual. "There are three daily 'broadcast times' at Givral—one around ten in the morning, one in midafternoon, and one between five and seven, after the daily press briefings held at the National Press Center, across the way. The morning period is concerned mostly with business rumors and reports, and the two afternoon sessions with political and military matters."

Although An made a point of checking into "Radio Catinat," as the café was called, throughout the day, he also worked an extensive network of connections that stretched across other parts

of the city. "If Radio Catinat is the most central and most public place for the dissemination of information, true and false,
there are other places, not far off, which are also important, each
in its own way," Shaplen writes. An took Shaplen first to the
Ham Nghi animal and bird market near the old American embassy. "The market, which stretches for about half a block, sells
monkeys, civets, ocelots, rabbits, guinea pigs, and all sorts of
dogs, cats, fish, and birds—among the last being cuckoos from
Africa, pigeons from France and Mozambique, owls, myna
birds, parrots, skylarks, pheasants, and canaries. For those who
favor ancient folk remedies, bats are available; a well-regarded
cure for tuberculosis involves cutting the throat of a bat and
drinking its blood mixed with rice wine."

The military intelligence available in the bird market came
from studying the supply of crickets. As An explained to a reporter for *Le Monde*, "If there weren't any crickets in the market it was because the areas that supply them had been seized
by the Vietcong, and if crickets reappeared in the market, it was
because the government had recaptured those areas. The same
thing was true with rare birds and fowl."

Shaplen continues following An on his daily rounds. "Ad-
jacent to Ham Nghi is a street called Nguyen Cong Tru, where
each morning at about ten o'clock Chinese businessmen or
their Vietnamese agents meet in two or three cafés to determine
collectively what the day's black-market piaster rate will be and
also to set the prices of rice, pork, and other basic commodities.
Within half an hour after their decisions are made, the word goes
out to the two main commodity markets in Saigon and Cholon
and to the dollar black market. This Chinese-dominated strip
dates back to the days of the French, who operated out of the
same places through their Chinese compradors."

The daily price fixing is followed by a tour of Saigon's black
market. Here An records any shift in the mix of stolen goods or
uptick in commodity prices. "In the same block, and extending
along part of Ham Nghi, is the center of the sidewalk black-

market traffic in American goods," writes Shaplen. "Here, despite occasional crackdowns by the police, one can buy anything available at the American post exchanges and a wide range of other foreign products as well, including Japanese cameras and high-fi sets. Because police roundups have been more frequent in the past year or so, the more expensive items are no longer displayed, but they can be bought on a C.O.D. basis; that is, a Vietnamese woman running a stall will ask a customer whether he wants such-and-such a camera, and if he is interested he will give her his address and she will come around the next morning, camera in hand, and bargain. Almost all the goods are perfectly genuine—except the whiskey, which is usually diluted with rice wine. The markup on black-market goods ranges from forty to five hundred percent, but some things remain cheaper at the black-market dollar rate (now about four hundred and fifty piastres to the dollar) than they are at the post exchanges. It all depends on the subtle process of supply and demand, and on one's ability to bargain. Some of what is sold has been pilfered from the docks on its way to the post exchanges, and then the price is ordinarily kept low, but usually something like a case of beer, which sells for three dollars at the PX, will cost six or eight dollars on the black market. A carton of American cigarettes, which costs a dollar-seventy at the PX, will cost four dollars on the black market."

Having worked up an appetite by now, An and Shaplen stop for lunch. "In the same vicinity are a number of restaurants, each catering to a different clientele, and to these An took me in his search for tidbits of information. The Victory, a spacious place on Ham Nghi specializing in Chinese food, has much the same atmosphere in the morning that Givral has in the afternoon, but is not so crowded. Politicians, journalists, and important businessmen exchange information there every morning over tea or Chinese soup. The nearby Do Thanh is more of a middle-class place, for officials of sub-cabinet rank, field grade officers, and the second-rung diplomatic set. An, being a journalist who, though he works for the Americans, is also trusted by the Vietnamese, makes a point of visiting at least five such places each morning before he heads for Givral; then, after lunch, he goes to the official American and Vietnamese briefings and back to Givral. 'It takes a long time to build up your sources,' he says. 'You have to be frank and sincere, and you have to protect your sources. You must also do them favors—tell them things they want to know, buy them lunches and dinners, give them Tết gifts. Saigon operates in this pattern of social circles. If you're not qualified for one particular circle, you won't be accepted in its restaurant. The people will just ignore you. Journalists—the good ones—are the most useful informants, because they are in a position to hear things from so many different sources. The whole thing is like a school. You can graduate from one circle to another, just as you would from one class to another, once you've passed your tests.'"

In his book *Bitter Victory*, which he wrote after traveling through Vietnam and Cambodia in 1984, Shaplen refers to An as "surely one of the best-informed men in town. . . . In our conversations over the years, often lasting for hours, I discovered that the facts and opinions he furnished about the Communists, the government, and the many contending individuals and groups—including Buddhists and Catholics who opposed both sides in the conflict—were more on the mark than anything I could obtain from other sources, not excluding the American Embassy, which often knew surprisingly little about what was going on among the non-establishment Vietnamese."

"Pham Xuan An was one of the great double agents of the twentieth century, maybe of all time," says Peter Shaplen, Robert's son, who became a journalist and producer for ABC News. "He had entrée to all the high-level sources in Vietnam. The country consisted of a multitude of strange, shadow-like connections, and An was at the center of all of them."

Peter describes to me how his father, like An, was well connected. "When he went to Washington he would see friends at the CIA. Other friends in Hong Kong were Agency people. People said, 'Oh, he must be working for them,' but I don't think this was the case. He traded in information, he breathed it, he lived it. He would have been of incredible interest to the Agency, but was he a spy? I don't think so. For one thing, he was never rich. What money he had came from *The New Yorker.*"

Peter Shaplen has another reason for doubting that his father was a spy. "Bob couldn't keep a secret. 'Tell Western Union or tell Shaplen,' said one of his former wives. He lived big, he lived huge. He was a large man, six feet three inches tall, weighing two hundred pounds. He was a handsome guy with dark hair, who sat down at his typewriter at 7:00 A.M. and worked through lunch before heading off in the afternoon for a game of tennis. He had a booming, gravelly baritone, made raspy from smoking small cigars during the day and a big cigar at night. He liked his Scotch, his cigars, his women. He loved the life of a foreign correspondent. He relished the attention and being at the center of things. We're gossips," says Peter Shaplen. "That's what journalists are, gossips."

In the early 1970s, when Peter was beginning his own journalism career, he checked in to the Continental Hotel, where he was shown to his father's old room. Soon he was surprised by a steady stream of people knocking on his door—fixers, money launderers, journalists, ladies of the night, and other traffickers in the gossip that his father loved to retail. Word had got out that "Shap-ah-lain" was back in town, and people presumed it was Bob who had returned. Before he became ill during a visit to Saigon in 1988 and was flown back to New York, where he died of thyroid cancer, Robert Shaplen was writing one last story out of Vietnam: an article on Pham Xuan An.

According to his son, Shaplen felt "crushed" and rejected" when he visited Vietnam in the early 1980s and was told that An did not want to see him. (An told me that he too felt crushed when he learned that the government, without informing him, had blocked their meeting. He rushed to Phnom Penh to catch up with Shaplen before he left Southeast Asia but arrived too late.) In a letter to Edward Lansdale written in 1982, Shaplen mentioned that former *Time* reporter Stanley Karnow was claiming that An was a Communist spy. Lansdale replied, advising that whatever Karnow reported about Vietnam should be "taken with a grain of salt." Until his death in 1987, Lansdale refused to believe that An was anything more than a quick change artist who had flipped to the winning side at the last minute. Only when he was finally allowed to see An in 1988 did Shaplen get a firsthand report about An's long career as a spy. The reunion was not a happy one, at least for Shaplen, who felt heartbroken and betrayed. "Dad cried when he told me the story," Peter says.

The nature of Shaplen and An's early relationship was captured in a photo taken by Richard Avedon in 1971 and published in his book *The Sixties* (see pages x–xi). Better known as a fashion photographer than a war reporter, Avedon flew to Vietnam at his own expense in April 1971. The previous month, Lieutenant William Calley had been convicted of murdering twenty-two civilians in the village of My Lai and sentenced to life in prison. (Altogether, more than five hundred civilians were killed at My Lai. Calley was released and pardoned after three years of detention, mostly under house arrest.) When he arrived in Saigon, Avedon set up a studio in the Continental Hotel and started booking a ten-day photo shoot with napalm victims, U.S. generals, bar girls, and soldiers.

Shaplen arrived in Avedon's makeshift studio with four Vietnamese colleagues. In the photograph Avedon published, the journalists are dressed in their customary attire of white shirts and dark slacks. Pens and eyeglasses are tucked in their shirt pockets. At the center of the photo, a bemused Shaplen bends close, his right hand cupped to his head, a smile hovering around his lips, while An laughingly whispers something in his ear. Standing beside An is Cao Giao, looking professorial with his Chinese goatee and silver spectacles. Nguyen Dinh Tu, a journalist for Saigon's *Chinh Luan* newspaper, holds his pipe in his hand, and Nguyen Hung Vuong, Shaplen's assistant, smiles a toothy grin from the caved-in face of an opium addict.

On one of my trips to Vietnam I gave An a copy of Avedon's book. Together, we looked at the photograph of him with Shaplen, and then An got up to riffle through a drawer, where he retrieved a small black-and-white print, another shot from that day's session, given to him by Avedon. When I asked An to tell me about the published photo, he described the twenty-seven members of the Communist Party in Cao Giao's family and Vuong's work for the CIA, which resulted in his being arrested in 1978 and tortured for more than four years in Saigon's Chi Hoa prison. "Shaplen got all his information from the Three Musketeers," An says, referring to himself, Cao Giao, and Vuong. "He used all three of us because we covered every angle available. The information got funneled into Radio Catinat and then was given to Bob for his articles in *The New Yorker*."

The truth of An's statement is revealed when one consults Shaplen's notebooks. They show that page after page of Shaplen's minutely noted conversations with Pham Xuan An were redacted and published in *The New Yorker* as part of Shaplen's analysis of what was happening in Vietnam. There is nothing unusual about this. Shaplen had a good source, and he used it.

After the war, Frank Snepp broadcast an allegation that Shaplen's reporting was "shaped" or manipulated by the CIA. He claimed that Shaplen was one of the Agency's "favored" journalists. "We would leak to them on a selected basis, draw them into our trust and into our confidence, and then we could shape their reporting through further leaks because they trusted us."

In a statement released to the *New York Times* in Hong Kong, Shaplen called Snepp's accusation nonsense. "I, at no time, accepted at face value what anyone in the agency, Snepp included, told me about anything. When I did use agency information—and I discarded or discounted most of it—I always double-checked what I obtained with other American and other foreign sources." Avedon's photo captured Shaplen bending his ear to the best of these sources.

# The
# Perfect Crime

In 1963 Henry Luce, owner and publisher of *Time,* phoned Frank McCulloch, then managing editor of the *Los Angeles Times,* and asked him to go to Vietnam "to sort out the mess we're in over there." McCulloch thought Luce was talking about the war, but he was actually talking about the Time-Life bureau, where morale had plummeted after the bureau chief had quit in protest. McCulloch met Pham Xuan An, then a part-time stringer, on his first visit to *Time*'s Saigon office in February 1964. A year later he hired An for seventy-five dollars a week to work full-time as a local correspondent. "Two things impressed me about An," McCulloch told documentary film maker David Felsen during an interview in 2006. "He understood American journalism, and he was highly intelligent. Because he was so well connected, he knew Vietnamese politics intimately, and in 1964 when I first arrived in Vietnam politics, unfortunately, was a bigger story than the war itself. The coups d'état came and went so fast that if you were going to cover Vietnam you had to have Vietnamese know-how, and that's what An provided."

When McCulloch, a forty-three-year-old former Marine Corps sergeant, first arrived in Saigon, the Time-Life office had two demoralized employees who were still sore about Charley Mohr, the bureau chief, being forced to quit in a feud with the editors in New York. By the time McCulloch left Vietnam four years later, the Saigon office had twenty-five employees, including some of the war's best reporters. They filed fifty thousand words a month via a direct telex line to New York, and they collected massive amounts of information on every aspect of the conflict. "An spent a lot of time in the bureau, and all he had to do was listen," says McCulloch. "He had access to everything the bureau filed as a source, and I can think of lots of examples of hard, specific information that An would have made use of and reported to his superiors."

McCulloch cites as an example the fact that he was the first journalist to learn, three months before it occurred, that the United States would be sending ground forces to Vietnam. A friend in the military had tipped him the news and even supplied the precise numbers, revealing that the United States planned to station five hundred and forty five thousand troops in South Vietnam over the next year and a half. "I'm sure those were valuable figures for the Communists to have," McCulloch says.

"I'm never going to do that," President Lyndon Johnson lied to *Time*'s editor, when asked to confirm McCulloch's story; the magazine then killed the story. This would not be the only time that Pham Xuan An got a scoop from *Time* long before the magazine's readers back in the United States.

McCulloch was a hard-charging newsman who believed that a journalist's job is to "afflict the comforted and comfort the afflicted." The son of a Nevada cattle rancher, he had spent a couple of years trying to become a professional baseball pitcher before he began covering the police beat for the *Reno Evening Gazette*. When he broke important stories on how the mafia controlled gambling in Nevada, they threatened to kill him. McCulloch took this as a call to type faster. He broke other important stories on white racism in the South, corruption in the Teamster's Union, and Republican Party cronyism in Los Angeles. The cronyism story was a particularly brave piece, considering that McCulloch was managing editor of the *Los Angeles Times*. The paper was a house organ of the Republican Party, and its city hall reporter was a registered Republican lobbyist. McCulloch went on to edit other papers, including the Mc-Clatchy family's *Sacramento Bee*. At each paper the number of pages devoted to investigative reporting increased, and the stories got tougher.

The bald McCulloch was called "Buddha" by the Vietnamese as he traveled through the countryside. "He was a very scary guy, the journalistic equivalent of a Marine Corps drill sergeant," said Morley Safer, in an interview published in the *American Journalism Review*. "He could sometimes terrify the guys working for him with his bullet head. He demanded that they get it absolutely right, but at the same time he had a remarkable understanding of the problems his reporters faced. In his gruff way, he was very compassionate. He was a soft-hearted guy."

One day, when they were supposed to go out to lunch together, McCulloch found An sitting at his typewriter trying to file a story under deadline. "What's it about?" McCulloch asked. An told him. "Excuse me," said McCulloch, pulling up a chair to An's desk. "I'll take it from here."

"He started typing a mile a minute," An says. "He goes *ratatatatatat*, like a machine gun, and then he pulls the paper out of the typewriter and hands it to the telex operator. 'That's done,' he says, rising from my desk. 'Now, let's go to lunch.'"

During his four years in Vietnam, McCulloch turned a one-man operation run out of Room 6 in the Continental Hotel into a major bureau bustling with correspondents, photographers, contract employees, secretaries, telex operators, drivers, translators, and visiting editors from New York, who expected to see action in the field before being wined and dined in Saigon's best restaurants. McCulloch moved the operation into a villa at 7 Han Thuyen Street, facing the park in front of the Presidential Palace. The American embassy was a short walk down the street.

Under McCulloch, the bureau developed a particular rhythm. Reporters gathered early Monday morning to pitch story ideas and argue about what should be covered in the following week's magazine. Assignments came back from the editors in New York by Tuesday, and everyone scattered into the field. By late Thursday night or early Friday morning they gathered again in the office, swapping notes and writing up their stories for teletyping to New York, where the magazine closed and went to press on Sunday. "We all gathered for the writing Friday, Saturday, and into Sunday," says McCulloch. These weekend sessions were followed by "drinking a lot of beer and eating good French dinners."

"An wasn't part of the buddy system in the bureau," McCulloch told David Felsen. "He was more reserved, slightly aloof. But he was there all day long. When a correspondent was working on a political story, a coup or something like that, the first thing he would do is ask An what the background was, what had happened."

"An served more as a source for other reporters than he did as a reporter himself," says McCulloch. "But there was a period of time, in 1965 and early 1966, when the coups came—there were twelve coups altogether—when you'll find a lot of his reporting in the Time Inc. files." An did his best to keep his name out of these files. Once, when he was too prescient in predicting a forthcoming coup, the police called him in for an interrogation. After that, he tried to slip into the background. He was *Time*'s political analyst and cultural authority on Vietnam, but he rarely exposed himself as someone writing and filing his own stories. He talked. He consulted. He traveled throughout the country as a *Time* correspondent, but he allowed his colleagues to write the cables that would have got him in trouble if leaked to Vietnam's intelligence services.

"Another value An had as a reporter was his sure knowledge of the South Vietnamese government, particularly the corruption that was in it," says McCulloch. "He knew which generals were taking what kind of cuts. One general's wife ran a prostitution ring which covered five or six provinces. It must have been an enormous money maker." An had "intimate knowledge" of these scandals, which characterized South Vietnam's rulers until the last of them, General Nguyen Van Thieu, fled the country with several suitcases full of gold bars. *Time* never ran these stories either.

By this point in his career, An was well schooled in the rules of American journalism, how to keep himself out of the story and write the anodyne prose that passes for objectivity. "This made him an enormously valuable employee," says McCulloch. "In assessing who An was and what he did, people should know that he was a completely honest journalist. He didn't let Communist propaganda or positions intrude on what he reported. I'm sure as a spy that he took valuable information out of the bureau, but those are two very different things. Most people jump to the conclusion that if An hadn't worked there, *Time* would have gone on supporting the war until it ended. This isn't the case."

"He was enormously well read," says McCulloch. "He understood clearly what American journalism was about. He was a highly intelligent man, and a passionate Vietnamese citizen," qualities that made him "a delight to be with." McCulloch remembers a couple of visits he paid to An and his family in their house near Saigon's central market. "They were wonderful people, his wife and his sons." McCulloch remembers something else about these visits. "An kept two very large dogs. I've forgotten what breed they were, but they were big. They weren't aggressive, but they weren't afraid of anything either. An clearly loved both of them. When I was over there with the family, the dogs were very much present, and An wanted them that way, which is another reason why he seemed so American."

"An had come from a wealthy landholding family in the delta. We were told he had lost his land to the Vietcong, and this provided An with a perfect cover. He could and did sound anti-Communist."

"Did he tell you this story?" David Felsen asked McCulloch in their taped interview.

"I'm embarrassed to say I don't remember if he told us that story, or if it came from somewhere else," says McCulloch.

One reason An refrained from joining what McCulloch calls the "beery society" of American correspondents in Saigon was the fact that he had two jobs—a day job at *Time* and a night job that involved photographing documents and writing reports. After his children went to sleep, An transformed his two-room house and bathroom darkroom into a news bureau of his own. As his dogs guarded the door, he used a camera and lights bought for him by the Communist Party to work through the night photographing documents slipped to him by his friends in the Vietnamese intelligence agencies and the police. In the morning, he disguised his film canisters to look like *nem ninh hoa,* grilled pork wrapped in rice paper, or he hid them in the bellies of fish that had begun to rot. More fish and *nem* would be piled into baskets that looked like the offerings pre-sented at a Buddhist funeral. When An left his house and drove to the horseracing track where he walked his German shepherd every morning, he would deposit his *nem* canisters in an empty bird's nest high in a tree. For larger shipments, he hid his rolls of film under the stele of what he pretended was a family grave. An's wife sometimes followed him at a distance. If he were ar-rested, she would alert his couriers.

Throughout his career, An worked with Nguyen Thi Ba, a female courier who wore her hair pulled into a bun. From

1961 to 1975, she picked up his secret correspondence and film canisters. Eking out a living as an itinerant vendor of toys and knickknacks, she lived away from her children and was often sick with malarial fevers. "An, too, often suffered from diseases . . . I felt great compassion for him," Ba told Tan Tu, who coauthored one of the three Vietnamese biographies written about An. For years, Ba and An were the only people who fully understood the reality of each other's existence.

Using live drops, dead drops, couriers, and radio transmitters hidden in the jungle that linked him through the Central Office for South Vietnam (COSVN) to military headquarters in North Vietnam, An was supported by dozens of intelligence agents detailed to work on his behalf. Of the forty-five couriers devoted to picking up his messages from Ba and running them out of Saigon, twenty-seven were captured and killed. "There were times before my departure on a mission when my wife and I agreed, if I were arrested, it would be best if I were killed," An told the writer Nguyen Thi Ngoc Hai. "It would be more horrible if they tortured me for information that put other people's lives at risk. Sometimes it got so dangerous that, while my hands were steady, my legs were shaking uncontrollably. Despite my efforts to keep calm, the automatic reflexes of my body made me shiver with fear."

On a steamy day in January 2006 my translator and I ride our motorbikes out toward the airport to interview Nguyen Van Thuong, one of An's former couriers. In the scrub land surrounding the approach to the main runway, we find a new housing development full of three-story brick and stucco homes. With so much money to be made in Saigon's building boom, no one has bothered paving the streets. A jet roars overhead with its landing lights flashing. We stop at the big steel gate in front of Thuong's house and peer inside at a courtyard containing lotus flowers and a carp pond. After being admitted by Thuong's wife, who carefully locks the gate behind us, we walk up a flight of pink marble steps into a foyer filled with plastic orchids.

We enter a living room with shiny wood floors, big upholstered sofas, and a wide-screen TV, to find Thuong sitting in his
chair. He is a sturdy man with a large, square face and broad
chest. But he is only half a man—his lower half has been
chopped off. They began with his right foot and moved in successive amputations up from there. Thuong's left leg is completely gone. The right leg is cut to a knob that ends at the
knee. After each cut, he was given a chance to sell out, but he
maintained to the end that he was an illiterate farm boy who had
been roaming the countryside trying to dodge the draft. Thuong
sits ramrod straight as he describes how he became a Hero of
the People's Armed Forces.

He was born in 1938 in the Mekong delta near the Cambodian border. His mother was arrested by the French in 1947
and died on Poulo Condore. His father, a courier for the Viet
Minh, was arrested and died in prison under the Diem regime.
Continuing in his father's line of work, Thuong joined the intelligence services and started running messages for various
spy networks, including those of Vu Ngoc Nha and Ba Quoc—
two high-level spies in the South Vietnamese government—and
Pham Xuan An.

Thuong worked at the interface between the civilian couriers who ran messages from Saigon to the suburbs and the armed
couriers who ran them through the jungle and across the Cambodian border. It was a dangerous assignment, requiring alter-
nately that he melt into city crowds and crawl in darkness
through the Cu Chi tunnels. "I was the best person," says
Thuong matter-of-factly. "They counted on me to run all the important messages from the city to the countryside."

In November 1962, he was put in charge of transmitting
An's messages. For security reasons, he had limited knowledge
of who he was working for, and he still refers to Pham Xuan An
by his *nom de guerre,* Hai Trung. He had actually met An the
preceding year, when An was summoned into the jungle for one
of his debriefings. "In 1961, Mr. An was sent to the forest for

two weeks of study," says Thuong. "I cooked his food and took care of him while he was there."

"What was he studying?" I ask. "The policy of the Central Committee," says Thuong. "This was expected of everyone in the Party."

Thuong presided over a network of men and women who met three times a week in the park in front of the Catholic cathedral next to the statue of the Virgin Mary. After picking up messages concealed under a bench, he traveled north on National Route 13 into the forest. He carried an array of fake IDs. One said he was a captain in the Republican army. Another said he was a farmer. In special cases, as a last resort, he brought out an ID which identified him as a police intelligence agent. "Sometimes I carried An's messages directly from Saigon to Cu Chi. Other times, they passed through many hands," he tells me.

Thuong reaches into a tin box, an old Lipton tea container, and hands me a picture of himself. It shows a handsome young man wearing a sweater vest over a white shirt and black trousers. His eyes hidden behind lightly tinted sunglasses, he looks like a young professional on his way to work. In 1969, after fifteen years on the job, he was unmasked by a Communist agent who had gone over to the other side. "Many years later, after I was released from prison, someone told me that the documents I was carrying concerned plans to attack Cambodia. There was another document with the names of thirty-six spies who had been inserted into the Communist network."

One leg of Thuong's brown-checked pajamas dangles to the floor. The other is tucked under him, but the material is so thin that I can see the stumps of what used to be his legs moving under the fabric. I try to focus my gaze on Thuong's eyes as a fan blows hot air over us and he continues his story. Thuong was riding a motorbike down the road to Cu Chi when a helicopter swooped overhead. The "open arms" informer was onboard, pointing at him. A voice boomed out from a loudspeaker, calling him by his secret name, while soldiers used a rope ladder to drop to the ground. Thuong shot off the rotor with his pistol. The helicopter crashed into a field and exploded. Thuong hid his documents and a thousand dollars in cash in a ditch and began running across the rice paddies.

A battalion of paratroopers came for him. He was surrounded by four hundred American soldiers and three hundred South Vietnamese soldiers. With twenty-one bullets remaining, he killed twenty-one enemy soldiers. He jumped in a bunker to hide but was smoked out with gas and roughed up before being put on a helicopter and flown to an American military base. Here he confronted temptation. "A beautiful girl came to serve me. She invited me into the 'open arms' program. More beautiful girls came, singing songs, trying to persuade me to confess my identity. An American colonel began interrogating me in Vietnamese. I told him that I was a farmer, but they examined my feet to see if I had been wearing rubber sandals. They saw that I had been wearing shoes. They looked at my hands. I didn't have the calluses of someone who worked in the field."

The colonel promised Thuong a hundred thousand dollars and a sumptuous villa if he informed on his colleagues and came over to the American side. They would make him a lieutenant colonel. They would give him a Mercedes and lots of girls. As Thuong recounts what happened next, the house fills with the smell of lunch cooking in the kitchen. The already dripping air thickens with the odor of garlic and green onions. Thuong's wife opens and closes the front gate as family members stream through the living room. Thuong's son comes home from work and his son's two children and a granddaughter, who is wearing a blue school pinafore with a red scarf tied around her neck.

"I could have saved myself, but I chose to save my network," Thuong says. "Actually I knew the names of many people involved in several networks. This was against our general rules, where I was supposed to know only about one network, but I knew many of them. I could have led them up to the top, giving them the names of the most important spies who worked for us. They knew I was the key to cracking our intelligence network in the south."

Thuy Duong, the most beautiful of the temptresses, visited him one last time, pleading with him to join the American side. On refusing, he was whisked into another room, where the beating started. Eventually his captors crushed his feet and began amputating his limbs. Here the story gets a bit vague, for understandable reasons, but I suspect that it also takes on whatever coloration is required by the nature of Thuong's audience. In some versions, a Korean cuts off his legs. In others, a South Vietnamese and in others, an American. When I press for details, he tells me that Korean and American surgeons took turns.

"They cut off my right foot. I passed out. They cut off my left foot. Two months later they cut more. Every two months they cut off more of my body. Altogether, they put me on the table and cut my legs six times. The American colonel told them, 'You can cut away his entire body. Just be sure to leave his tongue in his mouth.'"

I feel lightheaded as the fan continues blowing hot air in my face and the house fills with the smell of rice and frying meat. Thuong was sent to a prison where Ba Quoc worked. This was the *nom de guerre* of Dang Tran Duc, a Communist intelligence agent who was employed by Dr. Tuyen and the secret police. The two men recognized each other but neither revealed the other's identity. Thuong was finally sent to Phu Quoc, an island prison camp like Poulo Condore. In 1973, following the signing of the Paris Peace Accords, after "four years and four days in enemy hands," he was released.

"Many years later I met Pham Xuan An, and he thanked me," Thuong says. "'Surely, you saved my life by hiding those documents,' he said." Thuong riffles through his tin box to pull out another photo of himself at an official government reception. He is sitting in a wheelchair holding a bouquet of flowers. Standing behind him, wearing a brown suit that swims around his skeletal frame, is a smiling Pham Xuan An.

An describes for me how he got his information "to the other side," as he calls it. "I wrote my reports and analyses in secret ink," he says. "You put a small bit of rice in a saucer, which you hold over a flame. After a while, the gluten and starch come out. You take a clean pen. I used what the French call a plume, a quill pen, made from a goose feather, which I trimmed with a pair of scissors. I dipped this sharpened pen in the rice starch and used it to write on what we call cement paper, because it is the same gray-brown color as the paper used to wrap bags of cement. I wrote my reports on this cement paper, which is hard to do, since you have to write very fast before the ink dries out. As soon as it dries you can no longer see where you were writing. You get lost in the middle of your report. This is why you have to write in the nighttime, under a bright light. You can't do this in the middle of the day, when people are walking around. So I would wait until midnight every night, after everyone had gone to bed, to begin writing my reports."

"You hold the light very close to the paper while you're writing. The rice starch ink, when it's wet, is shiny and reflects the light, but when it dries, you can't see anything. So you have to write very fast, which is why you should have your report memorized. You have to write it continuously, without pausing while you're writing. When you're finished and the ink has dried, you end up with what looks like a normal piece of paper. You wrap something with it, some egg rolls or rice, and give it to your courier to take into the jungle. Our base at Phu Hoa Dong wasn't very far away.

"When the report arrives, you mix up a solution of water, iodine, and one hundred percent alcohol. You use a piece of cotton to dab the solution over the document. The solution has to be weak with just a trace of iodine, not too strong. One small bottle of iodine and a small quantity of alcohol will last you a long time. You can buy them from any pharmacy for a few piastres. You dampen the piece of cotton and pass it over the paper. The iodine stains the rice starch, and suddenly the writing appears. You read the report and then burn the paper."

The rest of the Communist spying operation was equally primitive. When An visited the Cu Chi tunnels in the early 1960s, the only equipment for transmitting urgent messages to headquarters was a Morse code radio link to Cambodia. "These messages were then sent to the north, to the Politburo and to Pham Van Dong, who was in charge of strategic intelligence," says An. Dong was the third member of North Vietnam's ruling triumvirate, along with Ho Chi Minh and General Vo Nguyen Giap. He had earned his revolutionary credentials by spending six years in the tiger cages of Poulo Condore. A mandarin's son and former classmate of Ngo Dinh Diem, Dong, instead of going to work for the French, had helped found the Viet Minh. After managing the Communist takeover of South Vietnam in 1975, which involved sending four hundred thousand people to be "reeducated" in forced labor and prison camps, Dong served for a decade as Vietnam's hard-line premier.

With increasing frequency as Tết approaches, the bell on An's gate is pulled by visiting family members and friends. His dogs yap as guests drop by throughout the day to leave bouquets of apricot blossoms and other presents that are exchanged during the holidays. Thu Nhan accepts the gifts and chats briefly with the visitors on one side of the living room while An and I talk on the other. An never makes any claims about the importance of his intelligence. He minimizes his contribution to the war as nothing more than "long-range strategizing." Only after meeting his colleagues in Vietnamese intelligence and spending years piecing together his story did I begin to see a different picture. An provided strategic and tactical intelligence to the north, the kind of intelligence required to win battles and confound the enemy. In my *New Yorker* article, I wrote that An had been awarded four military exploit medals. He did not correct me, and it was only after An's death, when his medals were pinned onto a black field and framed under glass, that I learned he had been awarded sixteen medals, fourteen of which were associated with specific military operations. The medals credit An with winning or helping to win numerous battles that might otherwise have been lost.

An describes for me the trips that he used to make to the Cu Chi tunnels. "I would go stay for a few days to write reports and brief them," he says. "When using secret ink on rice paper, you can't write very much. Another way to do it was to go to Cu Chi and type up longer reports."

He also typed reports at home, using a portable Hermes typewriter bought for him by the Communists. "To keep my reports from being traced back to me, the typewriter had to be saved exclusively for writing these reports," An says. "Between thirty and a hundred pages, depending on the circumstances, these were long-range reports on how the war and political situation would evolve over the next few months. After the war was over, I threw this typewriter in the river."

The Communists also bought An a camera, a Canon Reflex, which he used to photograph his reports one page at a time. He left the film undeveloped, being careful to leave the leader hanging out of the roll by not rewinding the film completely. "This way, if the courier were captured, he could pull out the film and expose it. He would probably be killed, but no one would be able to read what I had written."

I ask An if he ever photographed secret documents. "Yes, sometimes I did this, but it was very dangerous," he says. "These documents were stamped secret, eyes only, top secret. You had to be very careful about how you handled this kind of material. They might be baiting you. Somebody hands you the document and you take it home and photograph it. Suddenly the police break into your house and arrest you. This is why I de-

veloped the habit of speed reading these documents and returning them immediately. This was sufficient for what I
needed. Remember, I worked in strategic intelligence. I wasn't
a spy. Spying is a different thing. You steal documents. You
take pictures of documents. The material you send into the
field is transmitted verbatim. I wasn't supposed to do this sort
of thing, unless they forced me to do it. This happened when
they didn't trust my way of analyzing things. They would demand proof, and I would give them some documents to support
my analysis. 'Without the documents, we can't understand what
you are telling us,' they would say to me."

As the war continued and An became increasingly important and his situation ever more perilous, he became less
deferential to his superiors. He had access to secret documents
and was privy to every aspect of the enemy's war plans and intelligence. His Communist bosses—like intelligence agents
everywhere—were hungry for this material. When they pressured An to steal it and film it, he refused. He was not going to
die for trafficking in pieces of paper marked top secret. Instead, he would narrate what he had read and recount the facts
in reports written to Ho and Giap. They had to believe him, because An's word was gold.

"If they didn't trust me I didn't care," he says. "For me it was
very simple. I worked for them. I worked for the right cause, for
the Vietnamese people. I didn't work for any individuals. If
they didn't trust me, I could just wash my hands and walk away.
Sometimes they said, 'We trust you, but we need more detail to
understand what you're saying.' In that case, I might send them
pictures of the documents. But this was a dangerous practice,
to photograph documents that were never supposed to be removed from someone's office."

According to An, "a spy faces three challenges. The first is
lies. He is in danger if the fictions and myths he is disseminat-
ing are recognized. The second is mistakes. If you are captured by chance, no one will save you. There is another kind of

mistake that comes from getting a story but not reporting it. For example, I was at dinner talking to someone who told me that Norodom Sihanouk was about to be overthrown in a coup. This was the start of the American invasion into Cambodia in April 1970, when they attacked the Sihanouk Trail. This was important information, but I didn't report it to the Communists. I should have, and if I had, I would have saved a lot of lives."

"Why didn't you report it?" I ask.

"I was too busy," he says. "I had hundreds of other things to report. My friends gave me the details of the coup, but I didn't pass them along. This was a big mistake. I deserve to be blamed. I should have told the Communists. Later I told them I had made a mistake." This rates as one of An's rare apologies to his handlers. His attitude toward them was generally dismissive. He was better informed and smarter than they were. They were poor northerners in tattered clothes and flip-flops, a dour, distrustful race, compared to the more jovial and privileged southerners. "Sometimes they challenged me," he says. "They doubted my information. Whenever they asked me for the names of my sources, I would say, 'I am the source. If you don't believe me, forget about it.'"

An shies away from the subject whenever I ask him for details about the secret documents he handled, but clearly they were pressed into his hands by everybody on every side. An had been a founding member of the Vietnamese Central Intelligence Organization (CIO) and trusted aide to Tran Kim Tuyen, its original director. He was presumed to work for the CIA, and he was free to peruse *Time*'s background files. Officers in the South Vietnamese military thought of An as the local weatherman. He was the forecaster you wanted to consult before planning a coup d'état or military campaign or other big change in the political climate. An could help figure out how to satisfy American patrons, while at the same time protecting the local constituency and making some money on the side. An was neither judgmental nor censorious. He indulged in none of the city's numerous sins, but he was always pleased to accompany friends whenever they dropped into dance halls or opium dens. The Americans were pumping huge sums of money into Vietnam. The South Vietnamese generals were stealing it as fast as they could but had to pretend they were representing America's interests. They wanted to lead their troops into "combat" while avoiding the enemy. An roamed the city's cafés and restaurants like a doctor on house calls. He advised people on how to distinguish the petty sins that could be winked away from the grave errors that would get you sacked or killed.

"I had hundreds of friends, everywhere," he says. "We would get together to discuss things. I would help them figure out these documents marked top secret or for eyes only. They would let me read them, and then we would discuss what they meant. Or they would ask me to help them edit the reports they were sending back to the Americans."

Where did these documents come from? "They came from the army, intelligence, secret police, from all kinds of sources," An says. "The commanders of the military branches, the officers of the special forces, the navy, the air force—they all helped me, and sometimes they needed my help. I had to return the favor. They had a problem. How were they going to deal with the Americans? For example, when the Americans landed their troops in Vietnam in 1965, the Vietnamese generals knew that they would be losing power to the American command. They used to be independent, making decisions on their own, except for having to deal with American advisers, but now the situation was changing." An describes a country full of anxious generals who had been instructed not to suffer casualties in the field, politicians who were mystified by the strange practice of stealing elections and calling it "democracy," and spies who were worried about competing intelligence agencies that were jeopardizing the drug traffic and other successful businesses. Masters of indirection and obfuscation, the Vietnamese had learned how to deal with a small American presence, but the new occupying force was another matter altogether. In the quid pro quo of people seeking An's advice and his seeking their information, documents changed hands, even if only briefly.

The political situation in Vietnam was altered dramatically as the first of what would eventually be a half million troops arrived in the country. "When the Americans sent in their troops in 1965, it presented problems for the Vietnamese who were running the south," An says. "I suggested people get together and discuss among themselves how they were going to deal with the Americans. 'Up to this point you have been independent. But now the question becomes, How are you going to maintain your command? If you aren't happy with the American advisers, you can kick them out.'"

This is useful advice for a Communist agent to give the generals who are commanding his enemy's army. As I listen to An tell this story, I relish its ironies. Many of An's apparently innocent remarks are loaded with these double and triple entendres. They are like pebbles careening down a mountainside. They ricochet through the scree of everyday assumptions and accumulate huge boulders of meaning before they hit bottom, with consequences large enough to flatten a country. An helps the South Vietnamese military shape its response to the arrival of American combat troops and at the same time provides this information to his North Vietnamese colleagues. He is a trusted adviser in the south and an invaluable informant to the north. "This is good advice," one imagines the South Vietnamese generals saying. "Let's throw out the Americans and face the Communists on our own!" On second thought, maybe this is not such a good idea, unless, of course, one is interested in losing this particular war.

Was An the honest broker or the master of a particular kind of disinformation, where truth was the destabilizing agent? The charge that An planted disinformation in the pages of *Time* is silly. This would have been a misguided assignment for a man so brilliant at planting information. An did not have to lie to anyone. His advice was the gold standard of accuracy. An could speak the same truth to everybody everywhere because he thought that eventually this truth would be self-evident. The logical end to the bloody war was a revolutionary victory for an independent Vietnam. This was the truth An ardently believed, even if it was not always the truth he revealed.

When An went to work for Time Inc. in 1964, one out of every five Americans was reading a Luce publication, either *Time,* the country's original weekly news magazine, or its sisters, *Life* and *Fortune.* Founded in 1923 by Henry Luce and his Hotchkiss prep school classmate, Briton Hadden (who died of a streptococcus infection in 1929), *Time* was part of a publishing juggernaut. With a combined weekly circulation of fifty million, Luce at the height of his power was America's unacknowledged minister of information. He wielded tremendous influence in shaping American opinion and defining public policy, and a job at one of Luce's magazines was reserved for journalists and photographers at the top of their game.

Nicknamed "Chink" because he had been born in China in 1898 to a Presbyterian minister, Luce developed a particular style for writing the news, which was at once omniscient, breezy, and splendidly self-assured. The world was divided with Manichean precision into "free" and "unfree" zones, mainly Communist, and it was America's duty to lead the struggle against this godless enterprise. Luce advanced his position most famously in an editorial written in 1941 for *Life* called "The American Century." According to Luce, America's political interests and its values and beliefs would define the twentieth century, and anyone opposing America would suffer the consequences. There was a bellicosity, a love of sport and war, in Luce's magazines and whenever America got into a fight, it was always by definition a good fight.

Until his death in 1967, Luce liked to wing around the world touring the outer reaches of his empire, dining with ambassadors and presidents. As he passed through Saigon, he would occasionally shake the hand of Pham Xuan An and his other employees. Six feet tall, a chain smoker with pale blue eyes and a beetle-browed intensity, Luce boomed out his opinions with utter authority. As Luce said of the Vietnam war on one of his visits to the Saigon bureau, "It's the right war in the right place at the right time. All we have to do is get this goddam situation cleared up and establish an American regency; then it will be over."

McCulloch tells a story about Henry Luce, or "Harry," as he liked to be called, visiting him "in country." As recounted in his interview with David Felsen, McCulloch arranged a dinner party in Saigon for Luce and the Australian ambassador, the CIA station chief, and other officials. Their negative evaluation of how the war was going upset Luce. "Luce got angrier and angrier until he hit the table and said, 'I know what the solution is. We put an American proconsul in here and clean it up and get out.'" There was silence around the table, Luce's outburst having ended the evening.

Practicing what he called "group journalism," Luce insisted that his publications speak with a unified, omniscient, corporate voice. To this end, he marshaled a huge, well-paid staff. His reporters made up one of the finest news-gathering organizations in the world, and his editors included some of America's most distinguished writers. Together, they produced a nameless, homogenized prose, published in unsigned articles that were utterly unreliable. This corporate product offered the perfect cover for a spy. An worked on everyone's stories, offering advice on large parts of the cable traffic going out of Saigon, while leaving hardly a trace of himself in the company's corporate paper trail.

Luce's correspondents were often dumbfounded when the magazine printed the exact opposite of what they had reported. It was as if New York were staffed by mad logicians. The correspondents wrote massive stories and compiled volumes of firsthand accounts. They interviewed all the top officials and gathered all the best documents. Their raw data were gold. The published magazine was lead. An was happy to keep himself removed from the editorial turf wars in New York and glad that his name rarely appeared in the magazine, except on the masthead. No one could trace stories back to him. No one could ferret out what he knew or when he knew it. The higher he rose in the company ranks the less he wrote. He was the background source, the adviser, leaker, tipster, legman, and translator—but not the author—of *Time*'s cable traffic from Vietnam. An was the confidence man in everyone's confidence. He was committing the perfect crime, with no evidence of breaking and entering, no fingerprints at the scene. There was just Pham Xuan An, smiling and joking as always, while peering out from behind the stack of papers piled on his desk.

Expecting that a famous journalist would have produced at least one noteworthy article, many people claim that An wrote *Time*'s obituary for Ho Chi Minh in 1969, but An denies authorship. "For a big story like this, correspondents from all over the world would contribute, along with freelancers and other people. Then the rewriters in New York would do a very heavy job on this material. They would sift through it and produce an article on deadline."

*Time*'s articles were anonymous, with no bylines, and it was not until 1970 that Murray Gart, chief of correspondents, put An's name on the masthead. The Saigon bureau chief at the time was Jonathan Larsen, son of one of the magazine's founding editors. An runs through the list of eight bureau chiefs under whom he served—Frank McCulloch, Simmons Fentress, William Rademaekers, Marsh Clark, Jonathan Larsen, Stanley Cloud, Gavin Scott, Peter Ross Range—uttering their names with such formulaic stiffness that he could be listing Vietnamese dynasties.

An developed the same kind of joking camaraderie with some of these men that he maintained with Edward Lansdale.

By translating the queer customs of the East into personal advice, he became the Dear Abby of sexual dysfunction, heightened pleasure, longevity, and other cures offered by Chinese medicine, providing various powders and potions to friends in need. "I gave Jonathan Larsen some good Chinese medicine for having children. 'This is very expensive medicine, rich in E vitamins,' I said. 'Take this every day,' and, while taking it, you should have sexual intercourse only with your wife. Don't go wild, spreading your sperm all over the place.' I don't know whether or not he listened to me, but he took my medicine."

In spite of accusations by *Time* editors in New York that the Saigon press corps was a weak-kneed bunch of whiners who covered the war from the rooftop bar of the Caravelle Hotel (this accusation, published in the "Press" section of the magazine, had resulted in Charley Mohr's resignation), a wartime assignment in Southeast Asia was grueling, dangerous, and sometimes deadly. Three Time-Life correspondents were killed in the war, and many were injured. The first casualty was *Life* photographer Robert Capa, who was killed on assignment in Indochina in 1954. The last casualty was photographer Larry Burrows, who for nine years did combat reporting, photo essays, and twenty-two covers for *Life* magazine before the South Vietnamese helicopter in which he was riding was shot down over Laos in 1971.

In a prolonged war with shifting boundaries and murky allegiances, being captured was a serious threat. An got reports from the Communists on who had been captured and where they were being held. On numerous occasions he vouched for his journalist colleagues and worked through back-channel contacts to get them released. In public, he feigned helplessness. While aiding his fellow *Time* journalist Robert Sam Anson, An came closest to getting discovered. Another attempt to free *Time* photojournalist Sean Flynn resulted in failure.

Flynn, son of French actress Lili Damita and Tasmanian-born actor Errol Flynn, who played the hero in *Captain Blood* and other sword-fighting movies, had dropped out of college and was drifting around the world, alternating between movie sets and war zones, when he reached Vietnam in 1965. Flynn idolized Audie Murphy, the war hero who played the quiet American in the first movie made from Greene's novel. Flynn rented what he thought was Murphy's apartment on the rue Catinat. Unfortunately he made a mistake. What he rented was actually the apartment of Michael Redgrave, who played the British journalist who was Audie Murphy's nemesis. It was from the balcony of this apartment that Redgrave had signaled for Murphy to be killed.

In April 1970, twenty-nine-year-old Flynn and fellow photographer Dana Stone left Phnom Penh on rented motorbikes to find the front lines of fighting in Cambodia. (Cambodia had become another Asian hot spot after Prince Norodom Sihanouk was deposed and U.S. troops invaded the country.) Captured by the Khmer Rouge in eastern Cambodia, Flynn and Stone were killed sometime the following year. "They were captured in Chi Pou, not far from Phnom Penh," An tells me. "They were killed immediately by the Khmer Rouge, but we didn't know it. All we knew at the time was that they had been captured."

As soon as news of the photographers' capture reached Saigon, *Time* mobilized a rescue effort. Supported by other bureaus with missing newsmen, they dispatched freelance journalist Zalin Grant, who had worked in army counterintelligence before writing for *Time*. "He needed two people to go with him to interview the refugees crossing the border from Cambodia," An says. "Vuong and I went with him to Trang Bang, where lots of refugees were pouring out of Cambodia. We asked them if they had seen these two photographers, Sean Flynn and Dana Stone." The rescue effort was carried on for another few years by British photographer Tim Page, who had been seriously wounded on the Cambodian border while working for *Time.* An was dispatched on another assignment involving Flynn. He was sent to clean out his apartment, which was "full of marijuana and a huge selection of guns picked up as war trophies. Fortunately, we got there before the police," An says.

An worked to save the lives of other captives, including a "dairy farmer" who was actually a colonel in the Australian air force. On other occasions he tried to keep the Communists from attacking strategic hamlets defended by conscripted peasants. "In 1967, Rufus Phillips and I learned about some fighting fifteen kilometers outside Saigon. He grabbed me and said, 'An, why don't we go out there and take a look?' We drove there in my small car. Rufe was a big man. He could barely fit in my car. Bob Shaplen could ride with me, but that was the limit. I couldn't fit in anybody bigger than that."

"We found that many poor peasants had been killed. They had been forced to work on the government side, as part of the self-defense forces. This is what you had to do if you didn't want to be drafted into the army. They had died in the attack on the village. These were farmers who lived in thatched-roof houses. Their children were wandering through the village in rags. Now that the soldiers were dead, their families couldn't even afford to buy them coffins."

"I complained to the policy makers," An says. He wanted the Vietcong to stop attacking Phillips's strategic hamlets, but I can tell from the way An shrugs his shoulders that his meddling failed. "I felt sorry to see people killed, Americans too," he says. "They were young and innocent. Human destiny is tough. We don't know if we are brothers or enemies. Only God can answer this question, but so far he has refused to answer. This is the problem."

On returning from the countryside, An found his four-year-old son whining and acting petulantly. "I slapped him in the face. I was thinking of the poor people who were dead and the children in that village who didn't have enough to eat. They didn't even own a porcelain bowl. They ate out of coconut shells, and here was my son in a comfortable house, with a good warm bed, and he was still crying. I wanted to take him into the field the next time I went, to see the fighting and the blood and the poor peasants dying. My wife thought this would be too much for him. 'Let him see the funerals,' she said, 'but not the blood.'"

Four months after Sean Flynn disappeared, An got involved in trying to rescue his colleague Robert Sam Anson, who was captured in Cambodia in August 1970. Anson was a twenty-five-year-old journalist who had arrived in Saigon the previous year. He had stashed his wife and two young children in Singapore to join *Time*'s five other Saigon correspondents in reporting what he called "the biggest, most exciting, interesting, dangerous story of all." Soon after his arrival, Anson concluded that "the war in Vietnam was murderous and immoral." It was "a neocolonialist criminal war of aggression." With no interest in publishing views such as these, *Time* banished Anson from the Saigon office and sent him to cover Cambodia—a hardship post, a dangerous little offshoot of the main conflict. Soon Anson was opposing another war that he found even more lethal and nonsensical than the one in Vietnam.

In a singular act of bravery, Anson tried to prevent a massacre in the Cambodian village of Takeo. Two hundred Vietnamese civilians had been rounded up by Cambodians and placed in an internment camp, where they would be killed. Anson drove out every day to check on the Vietnamese prisoners. He staved off the massacre for a few days, but one morning he arrived to find a great heap of bloody corpses, among them a few children who were still breathing. When Anson was later captured, It was An's description of his good deed at Takeo that convinced the Communists to release him.

After three weeks in captivity, Anson was given a pair of Ho Chi Minh rubber sandals as a going away present and released. He made his way back to Saigon and rushed into *Time*'s office to wrap Pham Xuan An in a bear hug of thanks. It would be another eighteen years before Anson learned for sure that An had saved his life, but Anson's wife had begged An for help, and he had promised to do what he could—a dangerous remark, implying that he really could do something. "I have a weakness for crying women and children," An admits. In 1988, when Anson visited An in Vietnam, he asked, "Why did you save me, if you were an enemy of my country?" An replied, "Yes, I was an enemy of your country, but you were my friend." To this day, Anson works with a photo of An on his desk.

Zalin Grant, the *Time* stringer with a background in military intelligence, claims that Pham Xuan An was "the first known case of a communist agent to appear on the masthead of a major American publication as a correspondent." This may be true, but *Time* has long been a genial home for spies, and Time Inc. has listed many intelligence agents on its mastheads. In one instance, the magazine sent a bureau chief spook to help the CIA lead a military coup. From its inception, *Time* took a pro-American stance that turned it into a cheerleader for military ventures around the world. This sometimes involved more concrete forms of aid, with the magazine providing cover for CIA operatives and lending itself to various covert operations. *Time* regularly published what it knew to be disinformation and propaganda, whenever these served what the magazine considered to be America's interests.

"World War III has begun," Henry Luce declared in March 1947. "It is in the opening skirmish stage already." He called for the creation of an American empire that would be "world-dominating in political power, set up in part through coercion (probably including war, but certainly the threat of war) and in which one group of people . . . would hold more than its equal share of power." Aiding Luce in this crusade was his right-hand man, Charles "C.D." Jackson. Luce praised him as "one of the most important experts in ideological warfare." Hired in 1931 as Luce's personal assistant, Jackson worked for the OSS in World War II. He was Eisenhower's psyops expert in Europe, and he helped shepherd the CIA into existence. On going back to work for Luce, Jackson was appointed managing director of Time-Life International, with a staff of nine hundred employees posted in sixteen countries around the world, and publisher of *Fortune* and *Life*.

Other intelligence agents who worked for Time Inc. included Dick Billings, a *Life* staff writer who spent time in Cuba trying to overthrow Fidel Castro, and William McHale, former *Time* bureau chief in Beirut and Rome who helped organize the Iraqi military coup in 1963 that eventually brought Saddam Hussein to power. McHale is said to have contributed a list of names, including Iraqi professors, doctors, and other members of the middle class, who were tortured and killed after the Ba'athist coup. *Time* provided cover for the CIA's first station chief in Paris, Philip Horton, and Paris bureau chief Enno Hobbing also worked for the CIA. The Agency moved Hobbing to Guatemala in 1954 to lead a coup against Jacobo Arbenz, Guatemala's elected president. Hobbing went on to serve another stint as a reporter in the Washington bureau of *Life*.

Henry Luce enthusiastically supported the CIA initiative launched in 1948 and known informally as Operation Mockingbird, which funneled government propaganda into domestic newspapers, magazines, books, and television. Described by founder Frank Wisner as a "mighty Wurlitzer"—a great pipe organ of propaganda—the operation had tentacles reaching around the world. Hugh Wilford, author of *The Mighty Wurlitzer: How the CIA Played America*, writes that the relationship between *Time* and the Agency was so close that "it was difficult to tell precisely where the Luce empire's overseas intelligence network ended and the CIA's began."

Wisner's activities first came to light in the 1975 congressional hearings chaired by Senator Frank Church, which also exposed Edward Lansdale's efforts to assassinate Fidel Castro and other CIA black operations. The Church Committee's findings, published in a multivolume report in 1976, revealed that one third of the CIA's budget for covert operations was spent on global propaganda. Some three thousand salaried and contract CIA employees worked on this enterprise, which at the time cost two hundred and sixty-five million dollars a year, making "the CIA propaganda budget as large as the combined budgets of Reuters, United Press International, and the Associated Press."

In the 1950s, the CIA ran a formal program for turning agents into journalists. Spies were "taught to make noises like reporters," one official explained, before being placed in a wide variety of media. Carl Bernstein, of Watergate fame, wrote in 1977 that "more than four hundred American journalists . . . in the past twenty-five years have secretly carried out assignments for the Central Intelligence Agency." The *New York Times* followed up Bernstein's article with an investigation of its own, which doubled the number of journalist-spies to eight hundred, including *Times* reporter James Reston and syndicated columnist Joseph Alsop, whose articles ran in three hundred newspapers. The Agency also financed the publication of as many as a thousand books a year.

The media outlets which harbored these covert agents-cum-journalists included most of the major newspapers and television networks in the United States. Support was provided by William Paley at CBS (whose news president had a direct telephone line to the CIA) and Arthur Hays Sulzberger at the *New York Times* (who signed a secrecy agreement with the Agency and provided cover to at least ten CIA officers). Bernstein wrote that CIA director Allen Dulles "often interceded with his good friend, the late Henry Luce, founder of *Time* and *Life* magazines, who readily allowed certain members of his staff to work for the Agency and agreed to provide jobs and credentials for other CIA operatives who lacked journalistic experience."

"Journalists provided a full range of clandestine services," said Bernstein, "from simple intelligence gathering to serving as go-betweens with spies in Communist countries. Reporters shared their notebooks with the CIA. Editors shared their staffs. Some of the journalists were Pulitzer Prize winners. . . . Most were less exalted: foreign correspondents who found that their association with the Agency helped their work; stringers and freelancers who were as interested in the derring-do of the spy business as in filing articles, and, the smallest category, full-time CIA employees masquerading as journalists abroad." At least twenty-two American news organizations employed CIA journalists, and a dozen American publishing houses printed the Agency's subsidized books. When asked in a 1976 interview if he had ever told journalists what to write, CIA chief William Colby responded, "Oh sure, all the time."

# New Year

Something odd happens when I phone An's journalist colleagues to talk about him. They remember him fondly and count him among their best Vietnamese friends, but they disagree on what he looked like. One person recalls that he was a bit shabby and down at the heels, with a hacking cough and lack of social graces. Others remember him as an elegant bon vivant who easily fooled them with his story about being the son of a rich landowner in the Mekong delta. He was tall. He was short. He was a sturdy, athletic man or a tubercular wraith. Like Woody Allen's *Zelig,* An slips into the picture at every key moment in Vietnamese history over the past fifty years. He is there at the battle of Ap Bac, the Buddhist crisis, the assassination of Diem, the fall of Saigon. He witnesses these historic events at a distance, displaced from the center. He lurks at the edge of the frame, commenting on the scene, with an ironic smile tugging at the corners of his mouth. But what exactly was An doing during the war?

After the overthrow of Diem, An comes into focus again during the Tết Offensive, the simultaneous attack on more than a hundred South Vietnamese cities and other targets during the New Year's cease-fire in January 1968. Planning for the offensive had begun two years earlier, when the head of An's intelligence network, a forty-year-old major known by his *nom de guerre*, Tu Cang, moved from the jungle into Saigon. Tu Cang was a famous cowboy, a hearty, affable man, who packed a pair of K-54 pistols and could plug a target at fifty meters with either his left or right hand. A former honor student at the French *lycée* in Saigon, Tu Cang had lived underground in the Cu Chi tunnels for so many years that by the time he reentered Saigon in 1966 he had forgotten how to open a car door. An replaced Tu Cang's jungle sandals with new shoes and bought him a suit of clothes. Soon the two men were driving around town in An's little Renault 4CV like old friends.

Pretending to be chatting about dogs and cockfights, they were actually sighting targets for the Tết Offensive. Tu Cang proposed attacking the Treasury to get some money. "They only hand out salaries there," An told him. A better target would be the courthouse, where lots of gold was stored as evidence in the trials of South Vietnam's legion of burglars and smugglers. He advised Tu Cang to bring an acetylene torch.

Tu Cang and An isolated twenty targets in Saigon, including the Presidential Palace and the U.S. embassy. Beginning at 2:48 A.M. on Wednesday, January 31, Tu Cang personally led the attack on the palace, where fifteen of the seventeen members on his team were killed outright. He himself barely escaped to the nearby apartment of Tam Thao, where he fired shots out the window and then hid with his two pistols held to his head, vowing to kill himself before being captured. When soldiers rushed into the apartment, Tam Thao convinced them that she was a South Vietnamese loyalist and perhaps even the mistress of the American officer—her boss—whose photo she prominently displayed. Later that morning, Tu Cang and An drove around the city, counting the bodies of the Vietcong soldiers who had died in the attack. (To commemorate the role these two men played in the battle, Tu Cang's pistols and Pham Xuan An's Renault are now displayed in the museum of military intelligence at army headquarters in Hanoi. The display includes the Canon Reflex camera An used to photograph his reports and secret documents. Also exhibited is one of the four suits of clothing that the Communist Party bought An for his travels in America.)

The Têt Offensive, engineered by General Tran Van Tra—the southern commander who had planned the ambush that killed An's French teacher—was a simultaneous assault by eighty thousand Communist troops on targets throughout South Vietnam. Apart from holding the Hué citadel for three weeks, the offensive was quickly suppressed, and it never sparked the popular uprising it was supposed to engender. The attack was a military disaster, with the Communists losing over half of their committed forces in the south and perhaps a quarter of their NVA regular forces from the north. "The offensive destroyed the Vietcong as a fighting force," An says. "Then the United States introduced the Phoenix Program, which was extremely effective in assassinating thousands of Vietnamese Communists and neutralizing the opposition in the south." As the war ground on for another seven years, the brunt of the battle would be increasingly borne by mainline forces from the north.

In spite of its failures, Têt was also a brilliant military success. The offensive shocked the American public and dealt a major psychological blow to the U.S. military. In March 1968, Lyndon Johnson quit the presidential race and partially halted the bombing of North Vietnam. In May, the Paris peace talks began, commencing the protracted negotiations that would end, seven years later, with America's disorderly retreat from Vietnam. Only when the cable traffic was released after the war did we learn that U.S. commanders had contemplated using nuclear weapons and chemical warfare to counter the attack. General Earle "Bus" Wheeler, former math teacher at West Point who was then chairman of the Joint Chiefs of Staff, cabled General William Westmoreland, former superintendent at West Point and commander of U.S. forces in Vietnam, asking 'whether tactical nuclear weapons should be used." He requested from Westmoreland a list of targets "which lend themselves to nuclear strikes." Westmoreland advised against using atomic bombs, at least for the moment, although he assured his boss that he would keep the idea in mind. "I visualize that either tactical nuclear weapons or chemical agents would be active candidates for employment," Westmoreland cabled Wheeler.

In spite of the bland assurances that Westmoreland publicly circulated at the time, he was seriously rattled by Tết. "From a realistic point of view we must accept the fact that the enemy has dealt the GVN [government of Vietnam] a severe blow," he cabled Wheeler. "He has brought the war to the towns and the cities and has inflicted damage and casualties on the population. Homes have been destroyed, distribution of the necessities of life has been interrupted. Damage has been inflicted to the LOCs [lines of communication] and the economy has been decimated. Martial law has been evoked with stringent curfews in the cities. The people have felt directly the impact of the war." In another cable to Wheeler, Westmoreland confessed that the Tết Offensive had allowed the Communists to inflict "a psychological blow, possibly greater in Washington than in South Vietnam."

"The plan was to liberate all of South Vietnam in one stroke," An says. "I doubted you could do it in one stroke, but I supported the Tết Offensive. After the United States began sending troops into Vietnam, I urged the Vietcong to organize a counteroffensive. By 1966 I was convinced they needed to do this to raise morale. This is why Tu Cang moved to Saigon two years before the offensive. He had to start planning. We had to do it."

Three months before the offensive, An was directed to stay in Saigon, where he would scout targets and develop the Communist strategy to take over the city. "The Communists wanted people to take a side," he says. "Either you side with the

Communists . . . I mean, the revolution, or with the puppets. They called the Saigon government the puppet government. The other side they called the revolutionary government."

To hide the fact that it was the real power directing the war in South Vietnam, the Communist Party pretended to defer to the National Liberation Front, which was revolutionary but not necessarily Communist. This is why An corrects himself, striking the c-word from his description. Only after 1975 was it publicly revealed that the NLF was indeed a Communist front. This revelation came as a surprise to some members of the NLF, who were shoved aside after the fall of Saigon. The Front was disbanded and many disillusioned partisans joined the boat people fleeing Vietnam.

As organized by Tran Van Tra, the Tết Offensive was to be followed by a second wave of attacks in May 1968. At the onset of what was called the mini-Tết offensive, the Communists began shelling Saigon indiscriminately with 122 mm Russian rockets, blowing up buildings and killing scores of civilians. "I sent a message to the commanders in the field asking them to stop firing on the city," An says. "I told them to stop the shelling. It had no military objective and was alienating people."

"What happened next?" I ask.

"The shelling stopped. Maybe thanks to my request. Maybe on their own. They were my superiors. They never told me why they did what they did.

"A Catholic priest later explained to me why sending rockets into Saigon and killing innocent people was an effective strategy. 'It's very simple,' he said. 'The people in Saigon were spending their lives loafing around making money out of the Americans. They didn't care which side won, just so long as they could sell things and rent their houses at a high price. The Communists wanted them to take sides.' Either you are with the Communists . . . I mean, the revolution, or you are with the puppets." I notice that An is again correcting himself by reflex, omitting mention of the Communists.

He admits that the priest has a point and his logic is compelling, "but I'm too sentimental for this sort of thing," An
says. "That's my problem. I don't like to see innocent people
get killed."

When I ask him if he ever regrets the role his intelligence
played in the deaths of innocent people, An doesn't waiver.

"No," he replies. "I was fulfilling my obligations. I had to do
it. I was forced to do it. I was a disciplined person."

"So you have no regrets?"

"No."

The author of seven books published on the Vietnam war, Tu
Cang is a sturdy, handsome man with the self-assurance of
someone who has cheated death many times. "I used to be
very strong," he says, before enumerating a list of war wounds
that have left him "sixty-one percent incapacitated." He rolls
down his sock to show me where a bullet passed through his
ankle. A meter of his intestine was lost to a stomach wound. He
has scars on his head from B-52 bombing raids and psychological scars, as well. "I have a recurring nightmare about being
strangled by an enemy intelligence agent," he says. "One night,
thinking I was striking my attacker, I accidentally hit my wife
and knocked out her two front teeth. Since then, we have slept
in separate beds."

Nguyen Van Tau, as he was called by his parents, was a
seventeen-year-old scholarship student at Lycée Pétrus Ky
when he left school in 1945 to join the revolution. He slipped
back into the city a year later to marry his high school sweetheart.
When he left again for the jungle, she was pregnant. Twenty-
seven years later he returned to Saigon to meet his daughter for
the first time. Tu Cang spent his entire adult life fighting the
First and Second Indochina Wars before heading to Cambodia
in 1978 to fight against China and its Khmer Rouge proxies. Tu
Cang boxed Vietnamese style, while An boxed English style, but
both men were natural athletes, animal lovers, and raconteurs.

While shuttling between life underground in the Cu Chi tunnels and intelligence work in Saigon, Tu Cang was An's direct leader in the Communist intelligence services from 1962 to 1970.

"The U.S. soldiers pumped gas down the tunnels and cleared off all the trees and animals with Agent Orange," Tu Cang says. "We thought it was raining when they dropped chemicals on us from their airplanes. We came close to death many times." He circles his arms overhead to show me how American paratroopers dropped down from the sky like airborne ferrets to chase him underground. In addition to commanding the intelligence network in Saigon, Tu Cang directed the city's guerrilla terror campaigns. "We were divided into frontline soldiers and inner-city soldiers," he tells me. "The second of these exploited the enemy's weaknesses, attacking restaurants and bars. We worked in teams of six or seven *sapeurs dans les villes*, inner-city terrorists."

In 2004, on my first visit to Tu Cang's house, I drive down a dirt alley to a walled compound that used to be a farm before the city grew up around it. After touring a garden filled with prized orchids, my translator and I kick off our shoes and enter the salon, an airy room with a red tile floor. At the back of the room hangs the rope hammock in which Tu Cang takes his afternoon naps. A large man with a winning grin, he has a high-domed forehead crowned with thinning black hair. Barefoot, he sits with his knees pulled up to his chest. A brown and white dog sleeps at his feet. His wife, a sharp-eyed woman with her gray hair pulled into a bun, bustles around us, pouring tea and straightening the house. At one point, she stops dusting and picks up a book I am carrying, one of the three Vietnamese biographies on Pham Xuan An. She leafs through it, carefully noting every underlined passage and marginal note. Tu Cang tells us that his wife was a sergeant in the army, a liaison officer with four military exploit medals. He himself has thirteen medals and was recently named a Hero of the People's Armed Forces.

Speaking to me in the schoolboy French he learned sixty years ago, before lapsing into Vietnamese, Tu Cang explains how he worked for the North Vietnamese Army, rather than the southern forces supposedly directed by the National Liberation Front. "The NLF was created for diplomatic purposes," he says. "It gathered together people in the south who weren't Communists. But it was under the control of the Party."

"Did the southerners know this?"

"No," he says. "Not everyone knew the NLF was directed by the Communist Party."

When I ask if I can see his famous K-54 Chinese semiautomatic pistols, Tu Cang tells me that his guns, along with An's Renault 4CV, have been sent to Hanoi for display in the museum of military intelligence on Le Trong Tan street. Unfortunately, entrance to the museum is reserved for employees of Vietnam's intelligence services. Other than An's car, which is now up on blocks, the museum is filled with telescopes, radio transmitters, decoders, and the camera An used to photograph secret documents.

"Are there any poison-tipped umbrellas?"

"We are not like the Russians," he says.

I ask about An's two instructors in military intelligence, one schooled by the Chinese, one by the Russians. "I don't know anything about Russians or Chinese," he says. "Only the Americans trained An. He was like me. I never studied intelligence. I just did it. People knew how to keep secrets. That was the key to our success. Our organization was simple. There was nothing fancy about it."

When I ask Tu Cang if he ever made any mistakes, like jeopardizing his network by firing at American soldiers, he reaches down to scratch his foot. Then he waves toward the horizon outside the open door. "Mistakes were unavoidable," he says.

I ask him if it was a good idea, when they were planning the Tết Offensive, for Tu Cang and An to drive around Saigon together. He laughs heartily. "This seemed to be a weak point in our plan, but I thought we could pull it off. I believed in my cover. I thought it was solid. I even went to the office of *Time* magazine with An."

Tu Cang pretended to be an old schoolmate of An's who shared his interest in birds and dogs. "We spoke French to each other because An's dog was trained in French. He was a German shepherd who once belonged to Nguyen Cao Ky. Nobody thought Communist spies would walk around the city with such a high-class dog. I wore what An wore, casual shirts and slacks. When I first arrived in the city in 1966, he looked at me and said, 'This guy has just come from the forest. Your sandals make you look like a pickpocket. I have to take you to a shoe store and get you some shoes.' He also bought me new clothes that he rumpled up so they wouldn't look too new."

Following his makeover, Tu Cang and An "looked like friends in the city," he says. "We held Party meetings and discussed work in luxurious restaurants where the tables were placed far from each other, and no one could overhear what we were saying. An always brought his dog with him. It was a very intelligent dog that understood foreign languages, and people were afraid of it."

Tu Cang pretended to be the owner of a rubber plantation in Dau Tieng, next to the famous Michelin holdings. He knew the area well because the drivers of the rubber trucks were part of his network, and he used to ride with them in and out of the city. In Saigon, Tu Cang played the role of a bon vivant who had all the time in the world to spend chatting with his friend An when they met on the Continental terrace or strolled next door for a cup of coffee at café Givral.

As we discuss his planning for the Têt Offensive, Tu Cang occasionally grabs my notebook and sketches battlefield maps and other plans for the campaign. "Our attacks on the U.S. embassy and Presidential Palace were feints," he says. "The

United States had troops ringing Saigon. We wanted to draw them into the city. We ourselves had divisions on the outskirts, waiting to break through."

"The information he gave us was very important," Tu Cang says of Pham Xuan An, the preeminent spy in his Saigon network. "He knew in advance where the Americans would send their forces. He alerted us to upcoming attacks and air raids. In 1967, for example, he told us when B-52s would be bombing our headquarters. This allowed us to get away. He saved the lives of lots of people. We also found out from An what the Americans knew about us. This too was very important." Then Tu Cang tells me about the twenty-five agents in his unit who were killed running Pham Xuan An's intelligence out of the city.

An's role in the Têt Offensive marks what the Vietnamese consider the high point of his career as a spy. "After the first stage of the general offensive, I sent back a report from the city to senior leaders, saying that the situation was rather unfavorable," Tu Cang is quoted as saying in *A General of the Secret Service*. On the morning after the offensive was launched, while driving through the city with An, he was shocked and depressed to find the streets littered with the bodies of his fallen comrades.

But after listening to An interview Vietnamese and American officials, Tu Cang reached a different conclusion. "I changed my opinion," he says. "A colonel told us that the offensive had dealt a heavy blow to the South Vietnamese army, and American officials told us that the antiwar movement was on the rise in the United States and American prestige had gone downhill. After that, I changed my mind and reported that the offensive would not bring about satisfactory results militarily, but its political and psychological impact on the enemy would be great. Senior leaders held that this report had correct assessments. The previous one was criticized."

It was Pham Xuan An who convinced Tu Cang and his Communist leaders that the Têt Offensive was a political victory. An understood the psychological value of the operation. It was a propaganda coup, a master stroke of Lansdalian PR, with resounding consequences in Vietnam and the United States. "All the Vietnamese supported it," An says of the Têt Offensive. "They knew it would force the Americans to negotiate and it succeeded. It *did* force them to negotiate."

Not all of An's colleagues had supported the offensive. It was not like General Giap's heroic battle at Dien Bien Phu. Têt was a modern move, a kind of psyops ballet, which could only succeed if given the right spin. Many of the targets under attack had been held only briefly, sometimes no longer than was required to snap a picture of the U.S. embassy or an American airbase under attack. Even Tu Cang, in his first report back to COSVN, had missed the point. He was depressed about the dead bodies of his colleagues, with the Communists having lost forty-five thousand soldiers, ten times more than the other side. Then An, with his eye on the *Time* wire and the news pouring in from around the world, explained the larger picture. Americans were shocked and dismayed that nothing in Vietnam, not even the American embassy, was safe from attack. The South Vietnamese government was not defendable, and the American government had been shaken to its foundations. The offensive would drive President Lyndon Johnson from office and General William Westmoreland from command. It opened the credibility gap—the disparity between official propaganda and firsthand reports from the front—and it engendered in the United States a fundamental distrust of government that persists to this day.

An was the one person uniquely positioned to explain to General Giap and the Politburo how Têt was playing around the world. He interpreted its psychological impact for his colleagues and convinced them of its importance. Once he had converted Tu Cang to his view, the two of them worked assiduously to get the rest of the Communist command to accept their interpretation of events, and they obviously succeeded, as evidenced by

An's official biography, which says that he would have been made a Hero of the People's Armed Forces—Vietnam's highest military honor—for what he did during Tết alone. "However, because he was working inside the enemy ranks, the conferment was delayed in order to ensure absolute secrecy."

Arriving at 7:00 A.M. to pick up Tu Cang for a day's journey out to the Cu Chi tunnels, we find the old warrior standing outside his gate wearing green army fatigues and a short-sleeved white shirt. He is holding copies of his books, which he intends to present as gifts to the soldiers who are still stationed at Cu Chi. Accompanying us for the day is Thuy Nach, the Vietnamese wife of a retired U.S. foreign service officer. Thuy, a small, dark-eyed woman of encyclopedic intelligence, has been helping me as a translator. She and Tu Cang compare notes on how they used to rank among the brightest students in their colonial high schools. Forgetting for the moment that they chose opposite sides in the war, they soon discover that they can recite Vietnamese poetry and sing the old patriotic songs together.

Driving into the countryside northwest of Ho Chi Minh City, we pass through miles of truck traffic and commercial sprawl. Welders torch rebar on the edge of the road next to vendors selling cassette tapes, orchids, and cigarettes. Around us flows a stream of motorcycles as we pass a parade of diesel-belching trucks and bicycle carts loaded with pigs and chickens in bamboo cages. A nation of tight-knit family clans centered around ancestor worship and commercial trading, the Vietnamese are the world's least likely Communists. Their primary allegiance is not to the state but to the family. The unnatural implantation of Communism into Vietnam was a historical accident. The Party's anticolonialism briefly lined up with Vietnam's nationalist aspirations, but today the people doing business around us look more like students of Adam Smith than Karl Marx.

Tu Cang takes my notebook and draws in it a map of the rubber plantation he supposedly owned sixty kilometers north of the city and all the landmarks he passed on Route 13 as he traveled into town to meet Pham Xuan An. With couriers and safe houses along its length, Tu Cang knows every inch of the route we are traveling.

For ten slow miles we honk our way through swirling eddies of Hondas, Vespas, oxcarts, and rickshaws, until we cross a canal that feeds the Saigon River. Here the countryside opens into emerald green rice paddies and fish ponds edged with palm trees and coconuts. White cranes flit over the fields, which are dotted with black water buffalos and women in conical hats. Schoolchildren walk along the highway, wearing neatly pressed white shirts and red kerchiefs tied at the neck. Tu Cang draws another map showing me the battle plan for the 1968 Tết Offensive, including the feints on the U.S. embassy and the Presidential Palace which were supposed to draw American troops into the city and leave Saigon's perimeter momentarily undefended. "We had two divisions here, hiding in the rice paddies," he says, pointing out the window. "There were ten thousand soldiers on this road, but they never made it to the city. Our cover was blown. The 25th Infantry Division attacked and killed many soldiers in these fields."

Tu Cang taps me on the shoulder and points over a weedy parade ground toward a mass of low-lying buildings. "This was the American base, the 25th Infantry Division, Tropic Lightning," he tells me. All the gas and tunnel rats, Rome plows and pesticides which for years were directed at killing him came from here. We drive on through countryside covered with dwarf trees. "We were not successful," Tu Cang says of the Tết Offensive. "We caused panic. It was a psychological success, but it was not a military success." He tells me that the strategy was borrowed from the Tay Son warrior Nguyen Hue, who in 1785 defeated the Chinese by catching them off guard during the Tết festivities. "The Tết Offensive had three goals: to take over Saigon, to kill the puppet forces, and to make a big noise. For the first goal, we failed. For the second goal, we failed. Only for the third goal did we succeed."

After passing a former police checkpoint, Tu Cang tells the driver to pull over. We stop at a little white house with a brick patio. The front yard is filled with bamboo frames that are covered with drying rice paper used for wrapping spring rolls. A silver-haired woman dressed in flower-print trousers and blouse greets us. She smiles up at him as Tu Cang wraps his arm around her. It is the embrace of old soldiers, bonded through their memory of death and surprised to find themselves still alive. Nguyen Thi Se was one of Pham Xuan An's couriers. She hid Tu Cang in her house and fed him. After she was caught bringing him a radio, she was sent to prison and tortured for three years.

As we walk behind her house into the garden, the air is sweet with the smell of frangipani. We stroll among palm trees and jackfruit trees, with their pendulous green fruit hanging low to the ground. The garden is nicely irrigated and tended. It includes a banana grove, a sty full of happily grunting pigs, and several conical, hat-shaped haystacks that are used to fuel Se's stove and feed her buffalo. At the foot of the garden floats a sampan tied to a tree on the banks of the Saigon River. Jumping into the small, flat-bottomed boat, Tu Cang shows how he used to escape from the Americans when they came to search the house. The river here is wide and brown with topsoil washing down from the mountains. "The water used to be clear and drinkable," he says, "but now it is polluted and all the fish are dead."

Crossing a canal and walking into a forest of thick-trunked bamboo, Tu Cang points to where he hid a radio transmitter and a communications team along the river. "This was a good place to operate," he says. "From here we could easily melt into the forest. We used Morse code and a radio, a PRC-25 captured from the Americans, to communicate with our headquarters over the Cambodian border. One time the Americans picked up our signal. They fired on the house with two hundred rounds. They used to bomb the garden regularly. We would jump in the canal and hide until the bombing stopped."

Tu Cang takes my notebook and draws another map. It shows how this house, lying only a few hundred meters up the road from the headquarters of the 25th Infantry Division, marked the southern end of the Cu Chi tunnels. The network stretched north from here along the river, which allowed for quick escape and provided a natural barrier against American tanks.

Standing in the garden where he lived for a decade like a mole popping in and out of tunnels to avoid bombs and artillery shells, Tu Cang pauses, brushing his hand over his face and looking up at some birds flitting through the trees. "All my old comrades are dead," he says, speaking in the French he learned as a schoolboy in the 1940s. "I miss them when I stand here and look at this garden where I used to live."

Tu Cang starts to sing an old revolutionary song about Vietnamese children fighting the French with bamboo poles sharpened into pungi sticks. Thuy Nach joins his high, sweet tenor. She too knows the words to all these songs, which she learned as a child living in a Viet Minh zone in the north. Together they stand in the garden singing "Autumn Victory of 1945."

*Small as you are, you can still kill the French.*
*Even with wooden guns, you can load, aim, and fire.*
*You will dye the whole forest red with the blood of the enemy.*

"Most of my soldiers were women like her," Tu Cang says, beaming down on the diminutive Thuy. He is pleased that she knows the old songs. This means she is still Vietnamese at heart, even after moving to the United States and marrying an American diplomat.

A mile down the road from Nguyen Thi Se's house we stop at the Cu Chi theme park, where a stretch of tunnel has been opened to visitors. After an introductory film, a guide outfitted with a pointer made from an old auto antenna begins lighting up a diorama that resembles an ant farm illuminated by Christmas lights. Two hundred and fifty kilometers of tunnels were built with man traps made from pungi sticks, air locks against gas attacks, and choke points designed to catch big-boned Americans. Thousands of men and women died in these dark burrows stretching twenty miles west into Cambodia, but for all the military force expended on destroying them, the tunnels managed for thirty years to hide as many as ten thousand soldiers within striking distance of Saigon.

We spend the morning touring displays filled with life-size mannequins demonstrating how Vietcong soldiers manufactured land mines and hand grenades. There is a shooting range where for a dollar a bullet I can fire an AK-47 on full automatic at targets shaped like elephants, tigers, and camels. All morning we have heard the sound of shots ringing through the small, second-growth forest which has grown up at Cu Chi. Occasionally I look over at Tu Cang to watch him hunch his shoulders and glance around for cover. "I hear the sound of firing, and I become alert," he explains.

Our final stop is a collection of long wooden tables set up in the forest where girls dressed in the black pajamas of Vietcong soldiers serve hot tea and manioc dipped in a mixture of peanuts, sugar, and salt. "When I lived here, this is all we had to eat," says Tu Cang, sitting at one of the tables. "I lived on it for years. It made me sick." He recalls B-52 bombing raids that made him bleed from his ears and malnutrition that left him covered with red spots. Before long, the guides have gathered around to hear Tu Cang tell his stories. When he asks if they know the songs that the soldiers used to sing when they sat here eating manioc, the girls shake their heads. Tu Cang starts singing. He is joined by Thuy and then the guides chime in. The *rattattat* of AK-47s resounds through the forest as Cu Chi is filled again with voices calling for Vietnam to dye its land red with the blood of the enemy.

A part from the Tết Offensive, the other big story of 1968—although it would not be revealed until the following year—was the My Lai massacre. On March 16, 1968, a company of soldiers who had been in Vietnam for three months and had lost ten percent of their men to snipers and bombings walked into a village seeking revenge. Finding no enemy soldiers in the hamlet known as My Lai 4, they began raping and shooting more than five hundred women, children, and old men. It took them a day to kill everyone, and they stopped in the middle to eat lunch. Of the thirteen soldiers later charged with war crimes, only one, Lieutenant William Calley, was convicted by court-martial of murder and sentenced to life in prison at hard labor. The sentence was reduced to ten years, and then Calley, because of time already spent under house arrest, was released after spending six months in federal prison. As the mother of one of the soldiers at My Lai told Seymour Hersh before he broke the story, "I gave them a good boy, and they sent me back a murderer."

After the Tết Offensive in January and mini-Tết in May, which provoked America's disengagement from the war, *Time* moved its offices back to the Continental Hotel, where it rented two rooms overlooking café Givral on the old rue Catinat (then known as Tu Do Street). An was in his element, never having to walk more than two steps from Givral to the Continental terrace and La Dolce Vita, as the hotel's restaurant was ironically named. An presided over Radio Catinat, the rumor mill. He attended the military briefings known as the Five O'Clock Follies, and when Bob Shaplen was in town, he regrouped for cocktails in Shaplen's room at the Continental, which included a heavy teak desk and a cork board for Shaplen to pin his maps. When An and Shaplen wanted to talk privately, they would step outside onto the balcony and peer through the tamarind trees which lined the street in front of the hotel. Cocktail hour lasted until everyone went off to dinner at Augustin's or Brodard's or another of Saigon's pleasant French restaurants. The evening ended with a late-night coffee at Givral's or a round of drinks on the roof of the Caravelle Hotel.

While he lived the public life of a *boulevardier,* An's private life was more abstemious. Tu Cang recalls that An's house was tiny, a mere ten meters by twenty. Living as simply as possible, An says he was saving his money for the moment that he would be unmasked, leaving his wife and four children to fend for themselves. "I accepted that sooner or later I would be caught, like a fish in a pond. Maybe a small fish can escape through the net, but not a big fish. I was prepared to be tortured and killed. This was my fate."

Chin Chi and Tam Thao, An's fellow spies, have drawn me a map of where he used to live in the dense warren of houses that lies between Saigon's central market and Cholon, the city's Chinese district. An has added his address, 121/55 Le Thi Rieng. A double-barreled address like this means that he lived not on the main street but in an alleyway behind it. "Look out for the water tower," Tam Thao says. "When you see it, you'll know you're close to An's house."

The day I set out to see where An lived while writing reports in invisible ink and photographing secret documents, I begin with a tour of his old haunts in central Saigon. From my balcony at the Continental Hotel, I look down the old rue Catinat toward the Saigon River. In French provincial fashion, the trees have been gussied up with whitewashed trunks, and below lies another colonial legacy, the municipal theater which served for two decades as South Vietnam's national assembly.

Across the square in front of the theater is the old Caravelle Hotel, which is dwarfed by the new addition that towers over it. Correspondents once gathered in the Caravelle's rooftop bar to watch the tracer bullets and rockets that lit the night sky on the outskirts of Saigon.

To my right I look across Catinat, now named Dong Khoi, onto the Eden Building, an enormous, dun-colored edifice that fills the entire block between the Continental and Rex hotels. Once home to the Associated Press and other news agencies, the Eden is now a mildewed wreck inhabited by families that live in unplumbed rooms. The balconies are littered with outdoor showers and chicken coops. Flowers and vines grow wild up the crumbling facade, and as soon as its residents can be evicted, the Eden is destined to become another molar extracted from Saigon's gap-toothed mouth.

Two blocks up the street, toward Saigon's red-brick cathedral, I spot the apartment building at 22 Gia Long Street that once served as a CIA safe house. On top of the building sits the flat-roofed elevator hoist house that was used on April 30, 1975, as an emergency helicopter landing pad. This is where a queue of refugees climbed a rickety wooden ladder up to the helicopter that had come to rescue them—an image captured by Hubert Van Es in his iconic photo of the last flight out of Saigon, taking off from the roof of the U.S. embassy. It was neither the last flight nor the embassy rooftop, but the photo was so poignant in capturing the ignominy of America's pell-mell retreat from Vietnam that this is what it was called.

Directly below the Continental, at the base of the Eden Building, sits café Givral. Built with curved windows looking onto the two busiest streets in town, this fishbowl of a restaurant was the perfect lookout for surveying wartime Saigon. Across the street lay the open-air terrace and bar of the Continental Hotel. On either side of the café stretched the fancy shops that filled the ground floor of the Eden Building. Americans sat in the booths next to Givral's windows, while the Vietnamese sat inside toward the bar, talking discreetly as they sipped iced coffees sweetened with condensed milk.

The inner courtyard of the Continental, with its famous garden, remains unchanged from the days when An and Tu Cang sat here planning the Tết Offensive. In this cloistered space with tables set under flowering frangipanis, I sit next to espaliered trees in Chinese vases, a palm tree whose trunk is decorated with red foil, a fishpond filled with carp, and a belle epoque lamppost that could have been designed by Gustave Eiffel himself. Over my table rises a frangipani with wildly waving arms that stretch thirty feet into the air, before arriving at a fringe of spatulate leaves and white flowers that scent the air with a heady tropical aroma.

The day has already turned vaporous, with the sun beating down through a layer of diesel fumes and dust, when Viet, my Honda man, and I head to the Ben Thanh market. Sighting the telltale water tower that Tam Thao has given as a landmark, we turn down an alley no wider than my outstretched arms, before the track appears to end at a pagoda with fish and fruit vendors squatting in front of it. Asking for directions to An's house, we are told to knock on the door of an old woman who has lived here for many years. We find her at home chewing betel nut, and, yes, she remembers the journalist who parked his car out on the boulevard and who, because of his press pass, was the only person in the neighborhood allowed to come and go at all hours of the day and night.

The old woman directs her niece to lead us through the maze of streets behind the pagoda. We follow her down a crevasse beside the temple, which I hadn't noticed before. We jog right, left, right. With the alleyway narrowing at every turn, my elbows graze the walls if I hold my arms akimbo. A crowd of onlookers gathers as people come out of their houses to stare at the commotion, and soon the entire neighborhood is involved in deciding exactly which house was Pham Xuan An's and which his parents'. Finally we agree that my map is right. I ring the bell at 121/55. A young man opens the gate in front of a new three-story structure and confirms that this is where the famous journalist lived, although his house has been knocked down to make way for a modern replacement.

# A Country
# Created by
# Salvador Dali

An scored more coups in the years following the Têt Offensive, some as a spy, some as a journalist. Occasionally, during our conversations, I find my head spinning as I imagine him shifting through the multiple roles he played during the war. When the South Vietnamese army invaded Laos in 1971, An tipped off the North Vietnamese. His advance warning, including the battle plans for what was called Lam Son 719, allowed the Communists to inflict eight thousand casualties. Abandoned in the Laotian jungle at the end of this disastrous invasion were one hundred helicopters, one hundred and fifty tanks, and any hope that the South Vietnamese army could defend itself against the north.

"When we lost the battle in southern Laos in 1971, we were hoping to cut off the Ho Chi Minh Trail, after an earlier raid into Cambodia to cut off the Sihanouk Trail," An says.

"What do you mean when you say *we* lost the battle?" I ask.

"I am referring to the nationalist side. I am sorry. I am confused," An says, laughing.

It is my turn to be confused when he continues talking about the battle from the southern perspective, perhaps to deflect attention from the lethal consequences of his spying. With the battle of Ap Bac and the Ho Chi Minh campaign, Lam Son 719 is one of the major Communist victories that can be attributed, at least in part, to Pham Xuan An's intelligence. The South Vietnamese forces had presumed that their firepower and American air cover would prevail, but these supposed advantages proved useless against an enemy that knew their every move in advance. An's tactical intelligence allowed the People's Army of Vietnam (PAVN) to target South Vietnamese troops with a devastating array of mortars, rocket batteries, and artillery, including 130 mm guns that were capable of firing eight rounds a minute at targets as far as eighteen miles away.

By January 1973, the Paris Peace Accords had been signed, ushering in the "Vietnamization" of the war, and by March most of America's ground forces had left Vietnam. Throughout the Paris negotiations, relying on leaks from the head of South Vietnam's Central Intelligence Office (CIO), An had kept both *Time* and the Communists informed about Henry Kissinger's negotiating feints and South Vietnam's opposition to the accords, which President Thieu saw as a sellout leading to the south's eventual demise. Thanks to An's information, the Communists trumped Kissinger in Paris and *Time* trumped *Newsweek* in New York. "We scooped them with a better story. It was a good day for us," he says.

An once again deftly interpreted the political situation when he witnessed the Watergate scandal and Richard Nixon's resignation in August 1974. He knew that Congress would never allow the president to reintroduce U.S. ground forces into the war. With American military power constrained, An urged the Communists to mount their final assault. They were timid militarily, until An convinced them that the moment had finally come to seize Saigon. The last of An's military exploit medals was awarded for the role he played in the Ho Chi Minh campaign—

the final battles in the war which ended with the fall of Saigon on April 30, 1975. An's last deed in the war was an act of friendship. Hours before the city fell, he arranged the escape of his old patron, South Vietnamese spymaster Tran Kim Tuyen. In Hubert Van Es's famous photo of the last flight out of Saigon, the final person climbing the rickety ladder up to the waiting helicopter is Tran Kim Tuyen. Out of the frame, down below on the street waving good-bye with tears in his eyes, stands Pham Xuan An.

"Tuyen had suddenly appeared in my office," An says. "He had waited too long to get out, and now he was trapped. Maybe God had decided that I had to help the man. I think he deserved that I return the help he had given to me. So he was the last man who stepped on the last CIA helicopter to get out. I was not wrong," he concludes.

In the summer of 2007, I met Vietnamese refugee Tran Tu Thanh for dinner at a restaurant outside of Washington, D.C. Thanh had worked for General Nguyen Ngoc Loan in police intelligence. He interrogated captured soldiers, and, as a friend of An's, he had inadvertently provided him with some of the information he sent to the north. The son of a math professor who had once served as South Vietnam's deputy prime minister, Thanh was captured at the end of the war. He was imprisoned and tortured for fifteen years. For four and a half of these years, he was shackled at the ankle and held in a box the size of a coffin.

"Why would An spend the last day of the war working so hard to get Tuyen out of the country?" Thanh asks, as we begin our dinner. He speculates that An must have had a good reason for getting Tuyen removed from the scene. If Tuyen had been captured and tortured, as he surely would have been, what name might have come to his lips? This would have been embarrassing for his former colleague and loyal assistant An. If all that talk about An being a double agent were true, then Tuyen was the best source for confirming these rumors.

On May 12, 1975, *Time*'s corporate newsletter, *F.Y.I.*, featured a photo of Pham Xuan An on the first page. Moments before the Communists rolled into Saigon, he is shown defiantly smoking a cigar in front of Saigon's city hall. His black hair is slicked back from his forehead and he squints toward the horizon, as if scouting out the rumble of tanks. "Reporter Pham Xuan An put his wife and four children on the plane but decided to remain in his homeland," the article reports. The reason he offers for remaining is deliciously cryptic. "I am a Vietnamese and a journalist and evacuation is only one chapter of the story."

In the days before the nationalist government collapsed, *Time*'s editors launched one abortive escape attempt after another. Twice they flew chartered airplanes into Saigon that were turned back at the airport. None of the usual bribes worked for securing exit visas, and the U.S. government was frozen in denial that the war's end had arrived. Murray Gart, *Time*'s chief of correspondents, flew to Hong Kong and rented a hundred-passenger ferry boat to sail to Vietnam, but the boat was captured by the South Vietnamese navy who used it for their own escape. Gart flew to Washington and camped outside the office of Henry Kissinger. At the end of the day, the secretary of state finally appeared and promised to telex the ambassador in Saigon for help. Within a week, every member of *Time*'s staff, other than An, had been airlifted out of Vietnam.

"Five rolls by Mrs. An shipped this afternoon. Film will be processed either at Clark or Guam laboratory," read the coded cable to *Time* headquarters, announcing that An's wife and four children had been airlifted to a U.S. base in the Pacific. After passing through the Guam "laboratory" and Camp Pendleton in California, An's family was resettled in Washington, where they stayed with An's *déesse* Beverly Deepe. On April 30, 1975, the day Saigon fell to the Communists, An cabled headquarters in New York that "the office of *Time* is now manned by

Pham Xuan An." After giving a rundown of the day's events in the south, An filed three more reports before the line went dead.

When his former colleagues first learned An's story from rumors that began circulating in the 1980s, each invariably recalled a questionable incident that was suddenly explained by the news. Nick Turner, An's former boss at Reuters, confirmed his suspicions about An's unannounced absences from the office. H. D. S. Greenway, known to his friends as David, suddenly understood why his former colleague at *Time* knew more than he did about the battle of Lam Son 719.

"I had been up on the border near Khe Sanh, watching badly mauled soldiers retreating from Laos," Greenway told me. "I described them as survivors from the original column leading the attack. 'No,' An said, without the slightest hesitation. 'The original column was wiped out. What you saw were survivors from the attempt to rescue the column, which also failed.' Later, when I thought back on it, he seemed remarkably well informed. This is the kind of insight you'd have only from knowing what both sides in the battle were doing."

Nayan Chanda, who was working for Reuters and the *Far East Economic Review,* remembered seeing An standing in front of the Presidential Palace on the last day of the war as Communist tank 843 smashed through the iron gate. "There was a strange, quizzical smile on his face. He seemed content and at peace with himself. I found it odd," Chanda says. "His wife and children had just been airlifted out of the country, and he didn't seem to have a care in the world." Chanda later realized that An was celebrating the Communist victory he had supported for thirty years.

Aside from Chanda's fleeting glimpse, An kept his cover in place after 1975. "It was a dangerous moment for me," he says. "It would have been easy for someone to put a bullet through my skull. I was afraid they would kill me and barbecue my dogs alive. All I could do was wait for someone from the jungle to come out and recognize me."

An and his mother moved into the Continental Palace Hotel, where they occupied Robert Shaplen's old room. (Shaplen had pressed the key into An's hand as he left the country.) Eventually An moved into *Time*'s two-room office. He was summoned for repeated interrogations by the police until intelligence officials intervened. People began to suspect that he was "a man of the revolution" when they saw him ride his bicycle to the military supply depot and leave with bags of rice and meat tied to his handlebars. They assumed, though, that he was an "April 30 revolutionary," someone who had jumped to the Communist side only after the fall of Saigon.

Not even military officials as highly placed as Bui Tin, a North Vietnamese colonel and intelligence agent, knew An's story. Working as deputy editor of the North Vietnamese army newspaper, Tin rode a tank up to the Presidential Palace on April 30. Accidentally finding himself the highest ranking officer on the scene, he accepted the surrender of the South Vietnamese government and then sat down at the president's desk to file a dispatch for his newspaper. Like most journalists newly arrived in Saigon, the next thing he did was go looking for Pham Xuan An. As Tin recalled, "On the morning of May 1, I went to meet An at his office in the Continental Palace Hotel. I had no idea at the time that he was a spy. All he told me was that he was a correspondent working for Time-Life. He introduced me to all the journalists in town, and I helped them send their articles abroad. Three months after the end of the war, I still didn't know An was a spy."

An was supposed to follow his family to Washington and carry on his work as a Vietnamese intelligence agent, but this assignment was blocked at the last minute. Hints of the power struggle over An—between the military intelligence agents who wanted to send him to the United States and reticent officials in the Politburo—were revealed to Bui Tin only when the government moved to get An's wife and children repatriated to Vietnam. Bucking the tide of refugees flooding out of the country, An's family would spend a year trying to get back into Vietnam by means of a circuitous route that passed through Paris, Moscow, and Hanoi. Nguyen Thi Binh, An's childhood friend, finally got them home. An's family had been camped for four months in the corridors of the Vietnamese embassy in Paris, buffeted between Vietnam's competing intelligence and security departments, when one day Binh found them sitting there. Vietnam at the time had *two* embassies, one run by the Communists and the other by Ambassador Binh, who was representing the National Liberation Front. Following her work as NLF negotiator at the Paris Accords, Binh's last act of diplomacy was to arrange safe passage home for An's family.

As the last man remaining in *Time*'s Saigon office, An became, by definition, bureau chief. His name remained on *Time*'s masthead until May 3, 1976. He answered queries and filed reports for a year after the fall of Saigon, but he wrote less and less as the gray net of state security closed in on the city. "After 1975, Saigon turned into Ho Chi Minhgrad," he says. "They cut off the teletype machine and made every story go through the PTT. They crossed out this, crossed out that. The censorship was so tight it was like back in the days of Graham Greene. I didn't file many stories because I didn't know how to dodge the censors. All they wanted was propaganda for the new regime, so I spent my days going to cockfights and fish fights."

The first official announcement of An's wartime allegiance came in December 1976, when he flew to Hanoi as an army delegate at the Fourth Party Congress. Friends who saw him walking around Hanoi in a dark green military uniform, which he was wearing for the first time in his life, were astounded by An's transformation from journalist into beribboned hero. "So many VC from the south were surprised when they saw me," An says. "They thought the CIA had left me behind."

Nguyen Khai, the well-known Vietnamese author who would later write a novel about An, was one of these people. "You belong to the revolution!" he exclaimed. "I belong to everything," An answered. "The French, the Americans, and now the revolution too."

As hundreds of thousands of Vietnamese disappeared into prisons and labor camps, An was also sent to what he jokingly called "reeducation." In August 1978, he was enrolled for ten months' instruction at the Nguyen Ai Quoc Political Institute in Hanoi. This was a training course in Marxist-Maoist thought for high-level cadres. "I had lived too long among the enemy," he says. "They sent me to be recycled."

Always a bad student, An finished near the bottom of his class. "They didn't like my jokes," he says of the dour northern-ers who were trying to teach him to speak the "new" Vietnamese full of political terms borrowed from China. An suffered through the bone-chilling rains of a Hanoi winter, sleeping on a wooden bed with a cotton mattress. "I wore a Chinese cotton jacket that made me look like a mummy. I asked for a Russian jacket but I was still cold, so I went back and asked for a one hundred and eleven degrees centigrade jacket. 'What's that?' asked the head of the institute.' 'Three girls,' I said, 'one sleeping on my right, one on my left, and one on top of me.'"

"They didn't like me at all," An says of his political reedu-cators. "But I haven't made a big enough mistake to be shot yet."

An was put in the political deep freeze for a decade. He was forbidden to meet with former American colleagues visit-ing Vietnam, and speculation abounds about why he was shuf-fled into seclusion. He was too close to the Americans, too fluent, and too well versed in Western politics. He had allowed spy-master Tuyen to escape. He refused to finger Vietnamese col-leagues who had worked for the CIA. Perhaps, as An himself was heard to complain, the Communists considered him a *rentier* who had collected money from the peasants living on his land.

In the meantime, he was biding his time, waiting for the anti-American climate to change as Vietnam went on to fight other wars against the Cambodian Khmer Rouge and their Chinese allies. On January 15, 1976, he was named a Hero of the People's Armed Forces—the country's highest military honor. By 1978 he was a lieutenant colonel, by 1981 a senior lieutenant colonel, and by 1984 a full colonel. By 1990, still serving as an active duty officer, he had risen to the rank of general.

As he looked out on Saigon through the gates of the villa into which he had retreated, An saw no signs of a Communist idyll. The city was overrun with humorless apparatchiks and carpetbaggers from the north. Prison camps sprouted in the countryside, and social ostracism and revenge were the order of the day. Like Voltaire, An devoted himself to cultivating his garden. Actually, his wife, Thu Nhan, cultivated the garden, but part of it was always reserved for the cages holding An's fighting cocks and exotic birds.

On those occasions when An left his house and tried to contribute to rebuilding postwar Vietnam, he was rebuffed. He proposed renaming the little park in front of the Catholic cathedral Morrison Square, after American Quaker Norman Morrison, who had doused himself with gasoline and burned himself to death outside Robert McNamara's office at the Pentagon. McNamara had stood at his office window and watched Morrison burn, and as he later wrote in his 1995 memoir, *In Retrospect,* "Morrison's death was a tragedy not only for his family but also for me and the country. . . . I reacted to the horror of his action by bottling up my emotions and avoided talking about them with anyone—even my family. Marg [McNamara's wife] and our three children shared many of Morrison's feelings about the war . . . and I believed I understood and shared some of his thoughts." Known in colonial times as the Place Pigneau de Béhaine, after the eighteenth-century French missionary who opened Vietnam to European colonial influence, and during the Vietnam war as John F. Kennedy Square, the little park in front of the cathedral is currently named after the Paris Commune.

In 1981 former *Newsweek* correspondent Arnaud de Borchgrave, in congressional testimony before the U.S. Senate subcommittee on security and terrorism, denounced Pham Xuan An as a "disinformation agent." The charge was overblown but An's old competitor was getting his revenge for having been scooped by An during the Paris peace talks. The same year, Stanley Karnow, writing in the *Wall Street Journal,* characterized An—whom he was forbidden to meet during a visit to Saigon—as "a senior official in the Vietnam government." These reports confirmed what others had known since An first donned a military uniform and started riding his bicycle to monthly Party meetings in 1976.

"We thought this was a joke," David Greenway says when I ask him about the charge that An was an "agent of influence" whose job was to manipulate the news and plant stories in *Time.* Greenway, who was injured covering the Têt Offensive in Hué, left *Time* in 1972 and later became editorial page editor of the *Boston Globe.* "The editors at *Time* weren't listening to us. None of *Time*'s reporters was manipulating the news. He wouldn't have had any better luck than the rest of us."

Far from planting stories, says Richard Pyle, former bureau chief in Saigon for the Associated Press, "An saved *Time* from embarrassing itself by publishing stories that weren't true. It was sleight of hand on his part. Without revealing how he knew what he knew, he'd let you know whether you were on the right track."

After learning the news about his former Saigon political correspondent, Murray Gart, chief of correspondents at *Time* during the war, is reported to have said, "An, that son of a bitch. I'd like to kill him." Peter Arnett was similarly critical of An. The two journalists had often met at Givral's to swap stories. "It's still a raw point for me," Arnett says. "Even though I understand him as a Vietnamese patriot, I still feel journalistically betrayed.

There were accusations all throughout the war that we had been infiltrated by the Communists. What he did allowed the right-wingers to come up and slug us in the eye. For a year or so, I took it personally. Then I decided it was his business."

With rare exceptions—and even Arnett praises An as a "bold guy"—An's colleagues are united in their support of him. "Was I angry when I learned about An?" says Frank McCulloch, who first hired An to work for *Time*. "Absolutely not. It's his land, I thought. If the situation were reversed, I would have done the same thing."

McCulloch, who now lives in a retirement community in California after a distinguished career as the managing editor of the *Los Angeles Times*, the *Sacramento Bee*, and other news-papers, recalls An as his "colleague and star reporter. . . . An had a very sophisticated understanding of Vietnamese politics, and he was remarkably accurate." McCulloch bursts into laughter, "Of course he was accurate, considering his sources!"

Remembering An with fondness and respect, McCulloch says it gave him "great pleasure" to organize a subscription fund in 1990, which raised thirty-two thousand dollars to send An's eldest son, Pham Xuan Hoang An, to journalism school at the University of North Carolina. The list of subscribers to the fund reads like a *Who's Who* of Vietnam war reporters. (Hoang An, known to his friends and family as "Little An," earned a law degree from Duke University in 2002. Working for the Viet-namese Ministry of Foreign Affairs, he accompanied Vietnam's president to the White House when he made his first official visit to Washington in 2007.)

"Let's say that the United States in 1966 had been occupied by a million Vietnamese troops who were here to tell us how to run our country," McCulloch told David Felsen. "What if I had a chance to defeat them and send them away? I would have done exactly what An did."

"How did An show you that he loved his country?" Felsen asks.

"By not trying to show me how much he loved his country," McCulloch answers. "An didn't demonstrate his deep love for his land and people. He practiced it. He believed in it, and he did it. I still have vast respect for him, as a human being and as a Vietnamese citizen and patriot."

McCulloch remembers the day he learned from Stanley Karnow's article that An was a spy. "It dismayed me, it distressed me, and it certainly surprised me. But there are a lot of hard-nosed journalists and U.S. government people who still think a lot of An. People ask me if I personally feel betrayed, and the answer is no, because as a journalist he functioned with total honesty. He was guided by and stuck by the rules of journalism. As for his other role, he did what he thought he had to do as a citizen and patriot of Vietnam."

The interviewer presses McCulloch. "So you weren't betrayed as a journalist, but you were betrayed as an American? Are you a journalist first and an American second?"

"No, I don't feel that," says McCulloch. "I assume that some of the intelligence An gathered in the bureau resulted in American losses and American deaths, and I deeply regret that and feel some personal responsibility for it. But I cannot criticize or condemn An's role as a Vietnamese citizen. That's his right."

As his story surfaced, An was hurt by the charge that he killed American troops and was responsible, even if only inadvertently, for the deaths of journalistic colleagues. "I saved their lives," he says emphatically, and it was true. He saved the life of Mills Brandes when the CIA agent and his family were touring the countryside and took a wrong turn, which resulted in their being captured briefly by the Communists. He saved the lives of Doug Ramsey, Bob Anson, and Tran Kim Tuyen. He often intervened to keep peasants from being tortured or shot by South Vietnamese troops. He helped South Vietnamese officials flee the country in 1975 as defeated warriors and, later, as refugees sailing across the South China Sea. An played the game fairly, as a gentleman, but none of this counters the un-

fortunate reality that he lived and worked in the midst of a
bloody war that killed several million people.

When I went to see him, An often reiterated that Vietnam
fought *three* Indochinese wars, the first against the French, the
second against the Americans, and the third against the Chinese.
Following a series of provocations, with Cambodian forces crossing the border to kill Vietnamese villagers in the Mekong delta,
Vietnam invaded Cambodia on December 25, 1978. Phnom
Penh was captured a few days later, and for the next decade Vietnam would be mired in a guerrilla war against Pol Pot and the
Khmer Rouge, who were armed by the Chinese. Knowing more
about how to wage guerrilla wars than fight them, Vietnam lost
more than fifty thousand soldiers in this third Indochinese conflict, before the last shot was fired in March 1990.

In February 1979, China invaded Vietnam across its northern border. They captured the cities of Cao Bang and Lang Son,
before withdrawing at the end of a bloody, twenty-nine-day
war, which resulted in thousands of casualties on both sides.
Today the border bristles with troops—Vietnam has more than
thirty divisions facing China—and the war continues with cross-
border raids and diplomatic disputes involving the Paracel and
Spratly islands, two rocky archipelagos in the South China Sea
rich in fish and subterranean oil.

In 1990 Colonel An was elevated to the rank of general. At
the time, Vietnam was beginning to adopt *doi moi*, the "renova-
tion policy" that opened the country to the West. An explains his
promotion with a joke. As Western journalists began returning to
Vietnam, people would ask to see "General Givral," and to
avoid embarrassment, the government decided to raise his rank
to match his title.

When I first met him in 1992, An was a pleasant host to anyone who troubled to pull the bell on his gate. He had resumed
his old role as cultural informant and commentator on all
things Vietnamese. An was a genius at the art of conversation,
a brilliant raconteur and jokester, as well as an astute analyst.

While we talked so amiably, I also had the feeling that he was monitoring our conversation, recording it in his head so faithfully that he could play it back later word for word. Sometimes, the following day, or even two or three days later, he would return to something he had said and clarify or correct it. Sometimes he asked me not to repeat something he had said, which made me wonder why he said it in the first place. As An wrote to his old college girlfriend Lee Meyer, after she got in touch with him and they began corresponding in 2000, "I have not written anything worthwhile for the last twenty five years but [have spent my time] yakking and yakking with former foreign colleagues who have happened to come here to visit with me."

In 1997 the Vietnamese government apparently denied An permission to visit the United States for a conference at the Asia Society in New York, to which he had been invited as a special guest, and it was not until March 2002 that the seventy-four-year-old, emphysema-stricken general was supposedly allowed to retire. (He "retired" again in July 2005, but he was actually working up to the day he died.) "They wanted to control me," he says. "That's why they kept me in the military so long. I talk very wildly. They wanted to keep my mouth shut." All we can say for sure is that for at least thirty years after the end of the war An was still an active member of Vietnam's intelligence service.

There was often a touch of bitterness in An's voice when he talked about life in postwar Vietnam. The government could be stupid or corrupt. The opportunity to build a united, prosperous Vietnam had been squandered on ideological blunders, like the decision in 1978 to nationalize the rice markets and seize the property of urban merchants, which resulted in a flood of ethnic Chinese boat people fleeing the country. If An occasionally criticized Vietnam's party cadre, he reserved his fiercest comments for China, which he considered an ever-present danger and the worst colonial meddler in Vietnam's history. It was China in the 1950s that had forbidden North Vietnam from launching the war against Diem and the Americans.

While An watched his fellow revolutionaries in the south get wiped out, the Vietnamese Communist Party had held back, at China's insistence. It was only when the southerners began attacking Diem on their own without Hanoi's approval that the north belatedly jumped into the battle. "The Chinese were afraid of getting their nose bloodied, as in Korea," An says. "Only when the Americans escalated were they forced to support us. But we Vietnamese keep our mouths shut. We are so damn afraid of big brother," An says, using Vietnam's familial term for its huge neighbor to the north.

By 2002, the year of An's first official retirement, the Vietnamese Communist Party considered him sufficiently accessible to commission a biography, *Pham Xuan An: Ten Nguoi Nhu Cuoc Doi* (Pham Xuan An: A Life Like His Name). The title of the book plays on the word *an*, which in Vietnamese means "hidden." An dodged most of the questions put to him by the book's author, Nguyen Thi Ngoc Hai, about what he had actually done during the war, but Hai was an energetic reporter who tracked down An's colleagues and collected information that An himself would not divulge. Her book appeared at the same time as a fifty-three-part series of newspaper articles published in *Thanh Nien*, official newspaper of the Ho Chi Minh Communist Youth League. An English translation of some of this material was published in 2003 as *Pham Xuan An: A General of the Secret Service*. A third biography, *Nguoi im Lang* (The Silent One), was written by author Chu Lai for Tong Cuc II (TC2), the Vietnamese intelligence service. Another book-length series of articles was published in *Vietnam News* in 2007, and *Thanh Ninh* in May 2008 began producing a second series of articles on Pham Xuan An. In the meantime, two biographies have been published in the West: *Un Vietnamien Bien Tranquille* (The Quiet Vietnamese), by former *Le Monde* reporter Jean-Claude Pomonti, and *Perfect Spy*, by American professor of government Larry Berman.

After he retired, An also began to appear on television and in movies. An hour-long appearance on a Vietnamese talk show was followed by a four-hour TV documentary aired in December 2007. French television producer Alain Taieb filmed a documentary about a reunion at the Continental Hotel between Pham Xuan An and Philippe Franchini, the hotel's former owner. One of An's more intriguing roles was the part he played in Australian director Philip Noyce's remake of *The Quiet American*. Instead of British journalist Thomas Fowler having two men working for him, an Indian assistant and a Communist agent, Noyce combined them into one man, Mr. Hinh. "He told the Chinese American actor who was playing the role to come see me," An says. "He knew I was a guerrilla at the time who worked in the city. I would brief him about Communist activities, how we acted and what we did."

Noyce, in the press kit released with the film, describes how he decided to alter Greene's novel. "The change was inspired by an intriguing story that I heard of a very famous Vietnamese patriot, General An. As a special agent he spent thirty-five years working for the French as a censor, for the Americans in intelligence, and finally working for Reuters and *Time* magazine, while at the same time he was working for the Vietnamese people as a spy. I thought this was a wonderful character, this triple agent, so we developed the character of Mr. Hinh around General An." The press release goes on to describe how Noyce and Tzi Ma, the actor who plays Hinh, "spent days with General An during filming absorbing his history and developing an analysis of the character." One of the consequences of writing An into the script of *The Quiet American*—of making him both Fowler's assistant and the Communist agent—is that An becomes the assassin who kills CIA officer Alden Pyle. Maybe this is an accident occasioned by altering the plot. Maybe this is not an accident.

Whenever I am in Paris, I try to meet Philippe Franchini for an afternoon drink at the Bistro des Amis near his apartment on the Left Bank. The Vietnamese owner greets

Philippe as *patron,* and there is something about this unas-
suming man, short and stout, but almost feline in the way he
glides down the street, that makes it appropriate to call him
"boss." Franchini is a painter with glancing brown eyes and a
quick gaze that seems to take in the world around him with immediate precision.

A great storyteller, Franchini can settle into a *banquette* and
nurse a glass of wine through an afternoon of conversation.
Pham Xuan An had the same talent and so too, apparently, did
Ho Chi Minh. Truong Nhu Tang, a founder of the National
Liberation Front, describes an afternoon he spent with Ho
when he was a student in Paris. "That afternoon was a short
course in the history of Vietnam, taught to us over tea by
Uncle Ho. He had done it all in the traditional Vietnamese
manner with which we felt so comfortable, with touches of light
humor, legends, anecdotes, and moral tales to amuse and instruct at the same time."

It was no accident that Pham Xuan An and Philippe Franchini were friends. They loved telling jokes and laughing at
human foibles, their own included. Their judgments were keen,
their instincts finely honed. Other people sought them out as
wise men, but there was not an ounce of pretension in their wisdom. They were humble, noble characters, who ruled over the
*banquettes* in whatever cafés they found themselves.

Alain Taieb in his movie about Franchini and An put them
together in the garden of the Continental Hotel, supposedly to
watch them reminisce about the old days, when Franchini
owned the place and An worked upstairs on the second floor in
*Time*'s two-room office overlooking café Givral. An and Franchini skip the reminiscing and cut right to the chase. An wants
the world to know that Franchini is an honorable man. He inherited from his father a grand hotel that was a sinkhole of
bad debts, and instead of walking away from these debts he paid
them off one by one over the course of a decade. Franchini lost
everything at the end of the war when the hotel was seized by

the Communists, but his family honor was saved. An's words bring tears to Franchini's eyes.

Franchini is a *métis*, a mixed-race Eurasian with a Corsican father and Vietnamese mother. "In Vietnam, no one trusts *métis*," he says. "They know too much. They pass for Europeans while staring at the world through Asian eyes. They are spies in the houses of their fathers and mothers. They are useful but treacherous."

Pham Xuan An is also a *métis*, a cross between Vietnam and America. He too is a spy in the houses of his mother and father, a fish swimming in all the waters of the world. If the history of Vietnam is one long story of treachery and ambivalence, the *métis* incarnates this history in his skin, with Franchini and An being exhibits A and B.

Today Franchini works as one of France's busiest *nègres*, a ghostwriter who pens the books of politicians and TV personalities. When Franchini launches into a story, it is so richly embroidered that I imagine him working it up later that evening into a book chapter or screenplay. "I would never dare to write about Pham Xuan An," he tells me. "He lived in a world where nothing was the way it appeared. You can't just write the facts of his life. The interest is psychological, and with the Vietnamese there is always something ambiguous, something mysterious. It's a country that could have been created by Salvador Dali. You know his surreal painting of *les montres molles*, the soft watches? Everything in this painting, called *La persistencia de la memoria*, is twisted, deformed, pliable. Time and space melt into each other, and everything is surrounded with an air of mystery. This is Vietnam. It is an ambiguous world, just like the one imagined by Salvador Dali."

Four-star general Mai Chi Tho, An's former boss, emerged after the war as one of Vietnam's most powerful figures, serving as head of the Party committee governing South Vietnam and as minister of the interior. At Tho's villa in central Saigon—

the former Swiss embassy—I am ushered into a sumptuous reception room on the ground floor, which is filled with mahogany furniture and sculptures carved from rocks gathered at Vietnam's famous revolutionary sites. Dominating the far end of the room is an altar covered with flowers and bowls of fruit. Above the altar are four hand-tinted photographs of Tho's mother and father and his two famous brothers: Dinh Duc Thien, the two-star general who helped build the Ho Chi Minh Trail, and Le Duc Tho, the four-star general and Nobel Peace Prize winner who snookered Henry Kissinger at the Paris Peace Accords.

Standing at the altar, Mai Chi Thao holds a lighted bundle of incense in his hand and bows before his father's picture. Today is his father's death day, not customarily a time for receiving strangers, but Tho knows my stay in the country is short. He places the incense on the altar and comes to shake my hand. Dressed in gray slacks and a purple shirt, he is an imposing, white-haired man with a direct gaze. Bigger than most Vietnamese, Tho had an extra-large tunnel dug for him during the ten years he lived underground at Cu Chi.

Schooled in all the best prisons in Vietnam, including what was later known as the Hanoi Hilton, where John McCain spent five years, and Poulo Condore, the Devil's Island where two-thirds of his fellow inmates died before he was released in 1945, General Tho is a war-hardened opponent who today is an affable host, offering his American visitor tea and fruit. "It was really hard work, but we had to do it," he says of his effort to raise the funds that sent An to America in 1957. "The Party had very little money, but we thought the effort was worth it—An was the first person we sent to America—to learn the culture of the people who were taking over from the French to become our enemy."

"An was the perfect man for the job," he says. "It was a major coup for us."

When I press Tho about the missed opportunity to send An to the United States again in 1975, he stares at me through his steel-frame spectacles. "I don't know how this story got out in the open," he says, obviously regretting that I know enough to ask the question. "He would have been great if we had sent him to the United States," Tho says, indicating that it was not his decision to hold him back.

I know before I ask that my next question will go unanswered. "What exactly did An do for you?"

Minister Tho smiles and offers me another cup of tea. "An had the best sources and access to secret information. He had his ear to the ground like no one else in Saigon. If you wanted to know what was happening, An was the man to ask. After the war, we made him a general and a Hero of the People's Armed Forces. Without giving you any details, that alone should tell you the importance of what he did for his country."

At another meeting with Tho the following year, I ask him to list Vietnam's top spies. (At one point, the CIA estimated there were fifteen thousand of them.) Heading Tho's list is Pham Xuan An, followed by Dang Tran Duc, also known as Ba Quoc, who succeeded An in working for South Vietnamese intelligence. Two entrepreneurial spies, Vu Ngoc Nha and Pham Ngoc Thao, are listed in third and fourth place.

Vu Dinh Long, better known by his *nom de guerre* Vu Ngoc Nha, was born into a landowning Catholic family in Phat Diem, the North Vietnamese village that figures prominently in *The Quiet American.* It was here in the midst of a pitched battle between the Viet Minh and their Catholic opponents that Alden Pyle and Thomas Fowler began their own fight to the death over Phuong, "the most beautiful girl in Saigon." It was in the midst of the actual battle that Nha threw in his lot with the Communists. At the urging of Ho Chi Minh, he became a secret agent whose cover was ordination as a Catholic priest.

Nha was evacuated from the north with one million other Catholic refugees who fled south in 1954. He picked grapes in France and worked as a parish priest in Saigon until he caught the attention of the Diem family and moved into Independence

Palace as President Diem's private confessor and confidant. After surviving the 1963 coup against Diem, Nha reemerged as a trusted adviser to President Nguyen Van Thieu, the general who led South Vietnam until the country ceased to exist in 1975. Nha successfully recruited a host of other spies into his network, including the top Vietnamese officials involved in planning strategic hamlets, pacification programs, troop deployments, and other tactical moves in the war.

In 1968, during the Têt Offensive—while Tu Cang and his commandos were attacking the Presidential Palace from the street—Vu Ngoc Nha was commanding the agents inside who were charged with capturing and killing Nguyen Van Thieu. Luckily for Thieu, he was off for the holidays visiting his wife's family when the palace was attacked. Hoping to distract the palace guard, Nha threw open the president's wine cellar. Unfortunately the timorous troops fought even better when they were drunk. On returning to Saigon and seeing that his cellar was the most heavily damaged part of the palace, Thieu commended his priestly adviser for using such a brilliant stratagem to rally morale.

When his cover was blown in 1969, Nha was arrested and tortured before being sent to the tiger cages on Poulo Condore. Pope Paul VI intervened on his behalf, recognizing Nha as a "filial son of God." Released in the prisoner exchange that followed the signing of the Paris Accords in 1973, Nha reemerged on the political scene as a "liberation bishop," supposedly supporting a third force to run Vietnam but actually working again as a Communist agent. When Duong Van Minh, South Vietnam's final president, surrendered on April 30, 1975, standing next to him as his trusted adviser was a smiling Vu Ngoc Nha.

The most brazen Communist agent in Vietnam was Albert Pham Ngoc Thao. Another member of the Catholic upper class, Thao, under the patronage of Dr. Tran Kim Tuyen, rose quickly through the ranks to become chief of Kien Hoa province in the Delta south of Saigon. He was so successful at building "strategic hamlets" that he was elevated to running the program throughout the country. His vigorous promotion of Diem's idea to build sixteen thousand forced labor camps was a master stroke of disinformation. A defoliated countryside filled with peasant gulags was ripe for Communist recruiting. While he was putting together the pieces for a peasant rebellion, Thao was damping down Communist activity in the areas under his control. Kien Hoa, long known as a Viet Minh stronghold, became the most peaceful of South Vietnam's provinces.

"Thao was a coup cooker," An says. He kept trying to knock over the government and spare Vietnam another decade of war, but his luck ran out in 1965, when he was captured at the end of a failed coup. An lowers his voice when he describes Thao's punishment. He reaches out his hand and gives his clenched fist a swift, clockwise jerk. "They crushed his testicles. Then they strangled him. This was done by General Loan." An holds a cocked finger to his head, reminding me that Loan was the Saigon police chief pictured in the famous Eddie Adams photo of a Vietcong prisoner assassinated at point blank range.

An never vaunted his own skills as a spy, attributing to luck what others would have claimed as cunning. An considered his work defensive rather than offensive in nature. He was not an aristocrat like Sir Anthony Blunt, who advised the Queen on her art collection while spying for the Soviet Union. He more closely resembled Richard Sorge, the German journalist who befriended all the top Nazis while spying for Stalin. Sorge was hung by the Japanese in 1944. The closest An got to playing on the world stage was his aborted posting to the United States. After 1975, as Vietnam blundered into wars against Cambodia and China and destroyed its own economy, three million people were forced to flee as refugees; An regretted not being able to lend his services to the government which obviously needed him. "No one listened to me," he complains of the apparatchik who came to power after 1975.

O ne night when I am visiting An, a typhoon blows in from the east, and the following morning, showers fall throughout the day. Now that the rains have come, An's room fills with the smell of damp dogs and bird droppings, and my ankles erupt with red dots and begin to swell from flea bites. By midmorning, the air thickens with the smell of spicy vegetables and then dissipates as An keeps talking through the lunch hour and into the afternoon. Fortunately, I have learned to eat a substantial breakfast before going to see him.

Great streaming sheets of water are puddling in the garden and filling the air with mist. I worry for An's yellowing books, which are getting foxed with mold and slowly dissolving into unreadable pulp. An pauses occasionally to get up and search for a quote or press a text into my hands to confirm his analysis. Many of An's books are signed, either by their authors or by the people who presented them to him. Of his two copies of Neil Sheehan's *A Bright Shining Lie,* one is inscribed by Sheehan, the other by CBS correspondent Morley Safer.

An's collection includes volumes in French and English, but very few in Vietnamese. "People here can't write freely," he explains. "This is one reason I won't write about my life. I'd get in trouble if I talked about my life or what I know."

I sometimes feel as if the books An presses in my hands are coded messages, ways of talking about experiences that are still too dangerous to confront directly. For each day's visit, An seems to have chosen a text or a passage around which to weave our conversation. One day it is Dickens writing, "It was the best of times, it was the worst of times." Another day, the lesson is drawn from the *Fables* of Jean de La Fontaine. An delights in these stories of beasts acting like men and men like beasts.

At one of our final meetings, An shows me a book by Gérard Tongas, a French educator who went to Hanoi to help the Communists establish a high school after their victory over the French in 1954. According to An, Tongas, like Edward

Lansdale, had an intelligent dog who one day saved him from being poisoned to death.

I see from the inscription on the flyleaf that Tongas's book was given to An by the head of the Asia Foundation, the CIA front organization that sponsored his travels in America. The title alone seems pregnant with meaning: *J'ai Vécu dans l'Enfer Communiste au Nord Viet Nam et J'ai Choisi la Liberté* (I Have Lived in the Communist Hell of North Vietnam, and I Have Chosen Liberty).

"It's a very important book, a true book," An says. "You must read it before you write anything."

In the afternoon, when the rains have blown off, An shuffles through the kitchen and out the back door into the driveway where his desk and files are stored under a plastic canopy. Opening his desk drawer to find some old photos, he dismissively flings aside some newer pictures that show him in his general's uniform standing next to the prime minister and other members of the Vietnamese Politburo. "They wanted to see what I looked like," he says. "They spent the war in the jungle and had never met me before."

I reach in the drawer to fish out a medal attached to a red ribbon. "What's this?" I ask.

"They just give me these things," he says. "I have no idea what they mean. I worked in obscurity. I die in obscurity," he says, shutting the drawer.

# A Brighter World

On Easter Sunday I wake at five in the morning to catch the flight from Saigon to Poulo Condore, also known as Con Dao, after the black Plutonic island at its center. This archipelago between Vietnam and Malaysia is the sunny purgatory that served as Vietnam's preeminent island prison. Pham Xuan An always presumed it would be his final resting place.

Our thirty-seater Antonov aircraft is piloted by two homesick Russians who miss their wives and children in Kamchatka. We land smoothly on the island's single runway and take a minivan to the Labor Union Rest House, the cheaper of the two places to stay on Con Dao. I am traveling with Kyle Hörst, a former U.N. official who works on refugee issues in Washington, and Dinh Nguyet Ha, a pleasant, forthright woman who is a former officer with the Vietnamese Ministry of Foreign Affairs. After checking in to the hotel, Kyle, who was trained as a geologist, pulls a topo map out of his backpack and starts quizzing the girls staffing the front desk. They describe the island's sites while giggling over the oddity of having a tall Vietnamese-speaking American in their midst.

From the balconies in front of our rooms we look through a leafy furze of tamarisk trees over a bay dotted with rock out-croppings and little volcanic islands. Anchored in the blue water are dozens of fishing boats. They fly red flags at their upturned bows and are outfitted with low, square cabins at their sterns. Surrounding the hotel's empty swimming pool and running along the beach is a profusion of bright pink, white, and red paper flowers which thrive here, I am told, because they are poisonous to moths. The temperature is already pushing into the nineties, and the air is so humid that my notebook has turned limp with moisture. Sweat drips off our faces as we begin the walk into town. Other than a handful of bars, an In-ternet café, and three restaurants, not counting the one serving dog meat, Con Dao's sole diversions are a museum devoted to the history of its prison camps and a dive shop. The dive shop owner's Finnish wife describes how the harbor fills with fishing boats whenever there is a storm. Sailors drunk on rice wine pass out in the streets "like beached porpoises." When the storm passes, they shake themselves out of their stupor and sail away.

We walk along the harbor front of great stone jetties and breakwalls built by prison labor before coming to the stone house, now tumbling into ruin, where Camille Saint-Saëns composed *Brunhilde*. A plaque on the wall informs us that Saint-Saëns's opera is "the sole beautiful mark left on this island by the French."

The Poulo Condore museum, housed in the governor's colonial house overlooking the harbor, is filled with engrav-ings, sketches, newspaper clippings, and black-and-white pho-tographs of the island's prisons. One photo shows a pile of naked bodies heaped on the floor of their cell. Another presents a hooded figure standing with his arms outstretched in the form of a cross. Many photos are of American advisers who visited the island frequently and supervised its operation after the French defeat at Dien Bien Phu. Also displayed are pictures of Paulo Condore's "graduates"—a wall of fame that includes virtually every top revolutionary leader in twentieth-century Vietnam.

On rented motorbikes we travel a kilometer down the island's main road to Poulo Condore's original French prison, called *bagne* or camp number one, which was built in 1862. Passing under a guard turret erected over high stone walls, we enter a courtyard decorated with a small white Catholic church and shaded walkways which give no hint of the horrors that are summoned as we enter cell block six. After our eyes have adjusted to the gloom in this cavernous chamber, we are surprised to find one hundred and fifty life-size mannequins of emaciated prisoners chained to the floor. Hundreds of prisoners lived in this one room, where many of them starved to death or died of diarrheal infections or other diseases. As a former prisoner wrote of Poulo Condore in 1934, "The air reeks from the stench of latrines and sweat from dozens of naked bodies." The food is "rotten, stinking, and full of maggots." The guards are "ferocious brutes" capable of beating prisoners to death with their bare hands. This prison can only be compared to "monkey cages in a zoo."

The courtyard is lined with six identical cells, some reserved for women and others for prisoners on death row. In a dark and airless cell used for solitary confinement we discover a small altar built on a concrete bench. For want of incense, pilgrims have left upright cigarettes to burn in memory of the souls who died here.

Modern Vietnam was born on this dark granitic island. Every colonial power that tried to rule Indochina began by laying claim to Poulo Condore. Marco Polo got swept onto these shores during his Asian explorations in the thirteenth century. The Portuguese landed here in 1560. The British landed here in 1702. In fact, it was the British East India Company that built the island's first prisons—a short-lived experiment that ended when the company's Sulawesi mercenaries revolted and murdered their British bosses. Most importantly, Poulo Condore was the toehold that allowed France to begin building its Asian empire.

Before becoming emperor of Vietnam, Gia Long, then known as Nguyen Anh, took refuge on Poulo Condore in 1783 during the Tay Son Rebellion. When the missionary soldier Pigneau de Béhaine sailed out to find him, this is where Nguyen Anh signed the deal that defined the shape of Vietnamese history for the next two hundred years. In exchange for ownership of Poulo Condore and other commercial concessions, Pierre Joseph Georges Pigneau, a tanner's son who called himself the bishop of Adran, would provide the emperor with guns, ships, and a mercenary army.

To secure the deal, Nguyen Anh loaned the bishop his seven-year-old son, and together they sailed off to the court of Louis XIV to arrange the necessary financing. After a year of exile on Poulo Condore, Nguyen Anh returned to the mainland and captured Saigon. Here he met up with the bishop and was reunited with his son. With the aid of Pigneau's mercenary force, Nguyen Anh marched north. He subdued Vietnam's disparate territories and founded his empire in the city of Hué, the historic center of Nguyen family rule. The French capitalized on Pigneau de Béhaine's toehold by attacking Hué and Danang in 1858 and Saigon the following year. By 1861 the Nguyen dynasty was ruling Vietnam in name only.

Nguyen Anh described his deal with the French as "setting the wolf to guard the sheep." Phi Yen, his concubine, opposed the strategy, and for her temerity she was banished to an even more remote island in Con Dao harbor, which is now another shrine visited by incense-bearing pilgrims.

Our second day on Con Dao, after breakfasting on soup with squid and shrimp and imbibing a strong dose of *café filtre*, we head to Hang Duong cemetery, which holds many of the island's twenty thousand graves. Among the white tombs is a sarcophagus covered by fresh flowers, barrettes, combs, mirrors, and other offerings. This is the tomb of Vo Thi Sau. At sixteen, she tried to kill some French colonists who were celebrating Bastille Day. At nineteen, she was shipped to Poulo Condore and executed. From the picture on her headstone, she was a beautiful young woman, and her grave has become another of the island's sites where people stop to light bundles of incense and pray for the souls of the dead.

Reading from her biography as we stand over her grave, Kyle tells us that Vo Thi Sau was one of fifty Vietnamese executed in reprisal for the death of General de Lattre de Tassigny's son, a lieutenant in the French army. In January 1952, she arrived at Poulo Condore with her hands tied and her feet chained to the deck. "The island's church bells rang on her arrival. But the face of god was blank at the moment of her execution," Kyle reads. The island's Eurasian and Senegalese guards placed her on death row in *bagne* one. In charge of executing her was a Frenchman of German ancestry named Petervol, who was married to a *congai*—a Vietnamienne who consorts with Europeans.

"The night before her execution, Vo Thi Sau bathed and carefully combed her long black hair. She donned an outfit of black silk pajamas, embroidered with purple flowers. She was allowed out of her cell for ten minutes, to see her beautiful land for the last time. She began to sing the old Viet Minh songs about freeing Vietnam from its colonial masters. She sang all night. All the prisoners on the island, with their voices raised from camp to camp, began singing with Vo Thi Sau."

In the morning, the camp chaplain came to visit. "Now I will baptize you and wash away your sins."

"I have no sins," she said. "Baptize the people who are about to kill me."

"Do you have any regrets?" he asked.

"I only regret that I have not yet exterminated the colonialists who stole Vietnam and the errand boys who sold it to them. I ask only for one thing. When you come to shoot me, don't cover my face. I am brave enough to look down the barrel of your guns. I want to see my beloved country up to the moment of my death."

Singing the song which is now the national anthem of the Socialist Republic of Vietnam, Vo Thi Sau was "taken to the cemetery, where she was surrounded by ten thousand bodies, lying underground in wave after wave of graves. She looked into the faces of the seven men—the assassins—in her firing squad. They were shaking. She yelled, 'Down with the French colonialists. Long live a free Vietnam. Long live Chairman Ho.'"

"Seven stray shots came from seven shaking gun barrels. Cries rose from the prisoners a hundred meters away on the southern beach. The firing squad ran away. The *congai* wives of the guards, who were watching nearby, fainted. As the smoke from the rifles dispersed, Vo Thi Sau was still standing. Two spots of blood showed where she had been injured on the shoulder and hand."

When his men refused to fire another round, the commander pulled out his pistol. "Thousands of prisoners, raising their voices from the *bagnes* around the cemetery, began shouting, 'Down with the colonialists. Long live Vo Thi Sau.' The director of the prison, a Frenchman named Passi, and the chief administrator, another Frenchman named Jarty, jumped into a Jeep and drove like crazy back to the governor's palace, fearing a general uprising." The squad leader walked up to Vo Thi Sau and put his pistol under her ear. He pulled the trigger and blew out her brains.

Traveling counterclockwise around the island, we reach *bagne trois bis* (Charity Prison), built in 1940. In the rear of the compound are what the French called "solaria," cells open to the sky where prisoners often died of dehydration. Behind the solaria is a large stone shed, pierced by black iron doors. Opening one of these doors, we peer into a small cell, fifteen feet deep, ten feet wide, in which five female mannequins are chained to a concrete bench. Bars form the roof and above these is another roof made of tile. Thirty cells flank each side of this ominous shed. These are the famous tiger cages, whose discovery in 1970 and exposure in a *Life* magazine photo essay marked another turning point in America's disillusionment with the Vietnam war.

Mounting a staircase at the end of the building, we walk onto the parapet that allowed guards to stare down through the bars at the prisoners chained below. Placed along the parapet are facsimiles of the wooden barrels that used to hold anhydrous lime powder made from coral. When thrown on the prisoners below, the lime would burn or blind them. The walls of the tiger cages are made of quarried stone eighteen inches thick. The metal doors, each weighing three hundred pounds, could have been recycled from the Bastille. *Bagne trois bis* was clearly meant to last through years of steady use. Graffiti carved on the walls record the names of prisoners and count down the days when they would be released for a breath of fresh air, once every six months.

Behind the tiger cages is another camp, *bagne* five, built in 1928. In a massive stone structure consisting of one large room with two windows pierced high in the looming walls, we find graffiti dating from as recently as the 1980s, when boat people trying to flee Vietnam were detained here. Kyle translates one of the inscriptions: "A sad night remembering my parents."

Built in the courtyard of camp five is a latter-day addition to Poulo Condore, an American cellblock with concrete walls and tin ceilings that throb in the tropical heat. Gray sheds like these were thrown up across South Vietnam by RMK-BRJ, the Texas-sunbelt consortium of America's four largest construction companies: Raymond International, Morrison-Knudsen, Brown & Root, and J. A. Jones. Melded into a huge juggernaut that thrived on no-bid contracts, RMK-BRJ built the airfields, harbors, highways, and prisons that went into creating the country called South Vietnam. The successor corporation to RMK-BRJ was Halliburton, whose CEO, before he was elected vice president of the United States, was Dick Cheney. Halliburton thrived on its own no-bid contracts to build prisons at Bagram air base in Afghanistan, Abu Ghraib in Iraq, Guantánamo Bay, Cuba, and other CIA "dark" sites around the world.

Farther out of town we come to *bagne* seven, Phu Binh camp, which holds the American tiger cages that were built in 1971, after the *Life* exposé closed down the island's original torture cells. We enter a narrow passageway that cuts down the middle of a long gray barracks and start opening the iron doors that lie on either side. We peer into cells with bars on the ceiling, like the French tiger cages, but here there is no overhead parapet for surveillance, just a narrow space for ventilation. The cells have no concrete shelves for sitting, so prisoners slept on the floor. With three hundred and eighty four cells, the building once held two thousand people. It is so hot inside these metal-roofed cages that within minutes we are forced outside, gasping for air.

Heading farther out on the island, we search for *bagnes* eight and nine, reported to be the latest American additions to Con Dao's penal regime. We pass through a small forest to discover the remains of *bagne* eight. Local islanders are squatting in a clearing and cultivating vegetables. All that remains of the old prison are the metal guard towers that once stood at its four corners and are now rusting into oblivion.

After entering another forest and passing the low stone wall that marks the northeast corner of Con Dao's extensive cemetery, we discover *bagne* nine, the half-finished prison that RMK-BRJ was building up to the last day of the war. Metal reinforcing bars and concrete pillars rise in the jungle like a mysterious temple, an American Angkor Wat, now overgrown with vines and flowers. Flying through the ruins are dozens of snowy egrets, large white birds that glide silently through the green trees. The islanders believe that these birds are the souls of dead people. The birds are nervous, as birds often are, and their agitation reminds me of this tropical island's inescapable history.

Back in Saigon, I visit An, who is retreating from the midday heat with air-conditioning and oxygen. Wearing his usual white short-sleeved shirt and gray slacks flapping around his bare ankles, he opens the gate and leads me through the garden into the downstairs room that holds his fish tanks and books and the hard seat located near the telephone, where he sits like a reporter at his post taking incoming calls.

"I have never been to Con Dao," he tells me. "But I used to get reports on conditions there. I knew it was bad. Just like today, we know how hard life is for prisoners at Abu Ghraib."

He tells me about one of his near misses from being sent to Poulo Condore. Using information from his colleagues in South Vietnamese intelligence, he had written an article in 1965 predicting the overthrow of Vietnam's then-prime minister, Phan Huy Quat. "He was head of the government, but I knew the real power lay in the hands of Nguyen Van Thieu and Nguyen Cao Ky. My sources were too good, which is why the police called me in. I soon learned that I couldn't practice journalism the way I had been taught in the United States. After that, I would type up my stories and then I would tear them up."

An reaches for his bronchial inhaler. He is gasping for breath in the late afternoon heat.

"My lung capacity is at thirty-five percent of normal," he says. "I had a collapsed lung the last time I went to the hospital in 2003. I'm supposed to go again later this week."

Returning to our conversation about Poulo Condore, An says, "I survived by luck and because of my protecting goddess. I believe in astrology. I was born under auspicious circumstances." He gets up and walks to his bookshelf, pulling down a copy of *Le Zodiaque* published by Editions du Seuil. He shows me how he was born under the sign of the Virgin, who has protected him all his life.

Pulling another book from the shelf, the maxims of Jean de La Bruyere, An tells me, "You have to read these when you are in a bad mood." He is about to quote from one of his favorites when a coughing fit forces him back into his chair.

"I haven't prepared for my death," he tells me. "I want to be cremated. I prefer to have my ashes dropped in the Dong Nai River, near where I was born. But it's up to them to decide." *Them* is the Communist Party. Through Asian indirection or a spy's aversion to naming names, An often leaves his old bosses unidentified. "I don't want anyone visiting my tomb," he says. "People should save their time and effort for more useful things. I'm like Ho Chi Minh; he didn't want a mausoleum either."

It was forbidden in his will, but Ho Chi Minh got a mausoleum anyway. An too will get a state funeral. I ask him what will become of his books and papers when he dies. "My son will choose what to do with them," he says.

As if on cue, Pham Xuan Hoang An, or Little An, as everyone calls him, arrives home from work and walks into the salon to greet me. He is an urbane young man, a rounder, fleshier, but at the same time more nervous and high-strung version of his father. A bachelor in his mid-forties, Hoang An lives at home in the converted garage behind the house. "He has been a student all his life, first in Russia, then America," An says to me one day about his son. (Little An spent six years in Russia and another six years in the United States, studying journalism at the University of North Carolina and law at Duke University.) "The only place he hasn't studied yet is China," An says. "It's a life I would like to have led."

An's two younger sons have not fared as well as Little An. Working sporadically as midlevel functionaries, they too live at home, where the youngest son is now in charge of training An's fighting cocks. An's daughter, a doctor who no longer practices, lives in California with her family. "I worked very hard too," An says. "In fact, I worked all the time, except for a five-day honeymoon when I married my wife. Since 1959, I had only five days of sick leave, because of the effects of tuberculosis."

An tells me that Little An, because he is not a member of the Communist Party, has reached a glass ceiling in his career. He earns a salary of two million Vietnamese *dong*, about a hundred and sixty dollars a month. When I ask An why his son is not a Party member, he pushes the question aside. "My son is too old to join the Party," he tells me. "It's very difficult to learn Marxism and Leninism. You have to start when you are young."

Is it more difficult to learn Marxism than to get a law degree from Duke University? I am wondering how to phrase this thought when An tells me that I am asking too many questions and writing too slowly.

"I too was a slow writer," he confesses, "but Bob Shaplen was very fast. He just took his notes and wrote them up, no problem."

When I mention other slow writers, An agrees that "writing slowly produced the best book on the Vietnam war. This is Graham Greene's *The Quiet American,* a book that revealed the American character."

And what is this character? "When Americans think something is right, they just barrel ahead and do it," he says. "They like having fun. They are helpful. They are nice and they play fair, but you have to fly under their radar if you want to survive their aggression. Of all the world's empires, the American empire is the best. It is better than the French, better than the British, but it is still an empire, nonetheless, and the Vietnamese have always preferred—in fact they have always fought to the death—to have their own empire."

I ask An if he would still throw himself into this fight as a revolutionary. "I was never a revolutionary," he says. "I was a romantic, in love with my country and willing to defend her to the death." An writes in my notebook the two words *lang man,* "romantic," and *cach mang,* "revolutionary." Someone later explains to me that he has written a play on words, a joke. While

An's biographers argue over his legacy, debating whether he was a romantic or a revolutionary, a lover of Americans or a Communist committed to killing them, the old man is cutting a caper and laughing at us, taking his secrets to the grave.

I ask An about another sensitive subject, the T4-TC2 affair, which is named after two competing factions in the Vietnamese government. The dispute pits pro-Chinese elements against old Vietnamese patriots like General Giap, who claim that China's threats and bribes have cowed Vietnam into a vassal state. As soon as I mention the affair, An walks over to the buffet under the window and opens the drawer to remove a seventeen-page letter from General Giap. "He is complaining about T4-TC2," An says of the letter. "I think he is correct, although I don't take sides. I was trained to be objective. What I should say is that he is correct in describing his side."

"I like politics. I don't like politicians," he adds. "If you want to kill the dog, say the dog has rabies. This is what they are trying to do with General Giap. What is the term they use in English? 'Character assassination.' It is hard to know if the Chinese have used bribes. This affair involves too many tricks. What we know is that the Vietnamese have buried the story about our war against China in 1979. We have wiped our memories clean."

An tells me that thirty generals have signed a petition in support of Giap. "It is dangerous to take sides," he muses, before turning to look at me. "The way you write, you could go to jail," he says. "The reason we have no history of Vietnam written by Vietnamese is that you can't tell the truth. That's why all the books on my shelf are written by foreigners."

I ask An about another sensitive subject. What would Vietnam look like if America had won the war? Bui Tin has put me up to asking this question. Tin is the North Vietnamese journalist who accepted the surrender of the South Vietnamese government and rose high in the Party ranks before defecting to France in 1990 as a pro-democracy advocate. Several times over the past few years I have ridden the train out to the working-class suburb north of Paris where Tin lives in a rooftop garret with his "sister," a young woman who spends her days sitting in the kitchen hemming silk scarves for Hermès. Tin has become the strange bedfellow of American revisionists who argue that if the United States had unleashed the full force of its military power in Vietnam—invading the north and pushing westward into Laos, bombing the dikes around Hanoi, and using nuclear weapons—it could have "won" the war. In this case, Tin thinks Vietnam would resemble Korea. "An impoverished North Vietnam would be looking across the border at a booming South Vietnam, which would be leading the pack as the most advanced of all the Asian Tigers."

An partially agrees with Tin. "Two times America came close to winning the war," he says. "Once, in the late 1950s, when I was studying in America. This is when they wiped out eighty percent of the north's security apparatus in the south. The second time was immediately after the Tết Offensive, which destroyed the Vietcong as a fighting force. Then the United States introduced the Phoenix Program, which was extremely effective in assassinating thousands of Vietnamese and neutralizing the opposition in the south."

"And what would Vietnam look like if America had won the war?"

"Vietnam would not look like Korea," An says. "North Vietnam would have been absorbed into China."

"And South Vietnam?"

"The South Vietnamese are not as ruthless as the Koreans. The south would have ended up as nothing more than a minor star in the Western orbit."

An sits near the telephone in his old office chair with metal rollers and a green plastic seat. He looks as if he is on duty, erect, pen at hand, ready to report on a major battle or an impending coup. The phone rings. Following a terse conversation in Vietnamese, he hops up from his chair and begins moving at a quick clip toward the garden. "My youngest son will be late from work, and it's time to feed the cocks," he explains, as I trot to keep up with him.

The night is sweet and balmy. A breeze has come up to chase away Saigon's diesel fumes and dust. The moon is nearly full, suffering only a small dent in its otherwise brilliant face, and the stars are out. Thu Nhan's flower beds are planted with Spathiphyllum. The white flowers and their spiky, cream-colored pistils shine in the evening light over a bed of dark green leaves. At the back of the garden two cocks stare at us with beady eyes. They are caged separately to keep them from killing each other. An begins talking to them in a low, reassuring voice. He fills a small bowl with corn and places it in the first cage. He repeats the process for the second bird. An's movements are swift and assured. I am reminded of the comparison he once made between birds and journalists. He used to feed the latter with the same care and precision, but the food he fed them was information.

Ten months after my trip to Poulo Condore, I pull the bell on An's green gate for what will be our last visit. I arrive at half past six in the evening, when An says it is easier for him to breathe. Thu Nhan opens the gate. Her round, normally placid face is drawn with worry. "It is nice to see you," I say. "How are you?"

"Not well," she says, on this humid night in January. She bustles through the garden and excuses herself after leading me into the salon. The room has been rearranged. In the place where An's desk used to be, under the window to the right of the door, stand a hospital bed and wheelchair. An is resting in bed on his side, with a fan blowing on him. His skin is so translucent I can see the blood coursing through his veins. His ears protrude from his skull. His Adam's apple bobs up and down as he gulps for breath. His white pajamas billow around him as he sits up and reaches for a cup of ginseng tea. An tells me that he is taking rhinoceros horn to cure his emphysema. He is no longer joking about his death. His brown eyes are liquid and large. Trying to catch his breath, he grimaces with pain. Summoning the reserves of willpower and energy for which he is famous, he starts talking, and he is still talking two hours later, when I insist on leaving.

An tells me this is the last time we will meet. He gives various reasons, none of them convincing, and I sense that the decision to break off our conversations has been made elsewhere. We talk about my *New Yorker* article published in May 2005. An complains that the photographer nearly killed him in a photo shoot that lasted half a day. Following this ordeal, his favorite lark lost all his feathers and didn't sing for a week. Then the magazine's fact checker pestered him with phone calls but she still misidentified his great-grandfather's birthplace in North Vietnam.

"I know what happened to you," a Vietnamese friend later tells me. "You published information that should not have gotten out. It violated the protection of state secrets. After you let the cat out of the bag, someone made the decision to close you down." I am saddened to think that an old man taking rhinoceros horn and gasping for breath can still be considered dangerous to state security. I am also unnerved by realizing that An is still taking orders from his superiors. Like An's other American friends, I believed he was his own man, the one free soul in Vietnam who could speak his mind while flying the flag of liberty.

An returns to complaining about my *New Yorker* article. "Lots of people are no longer talking to me, and many others are spreading lies and rumors." He mentions attacks on his family but refuses to give any details.

"You were only doing your duty. You were a patriot," I say, trying to calm him down.

"All Vietnamese are patriots, even if they disagree with the party in power," he says. "Many others were braver and did more than I did. They sacrificed their families. They sacrificed their lives. People only know about me because of my American friends, and because I speak English."

I give him the stack of books and handful of magazines I have brought as presents. An picks up the latest copy of *Foreign Affairs,* intrigued to see a cover story on "Vietnam and Iraq" by former defense secretary Melvin Laird. "He was very smart," An says. "He was the architect of Vietnamization."

"But Vietnamization was a failure," I say.

"Not because it was a bad policy," An says. "It failed because of mistakes made by the Vietnamese."

Looking like a heap of bones covered with the cement paper on which he used to write his secret messages, An gathers every ounce of breath left in him to spend the night talking and joking about his beloved Vietnam. He is the perfect confessional subject. Out tumbles a torrent of talk, brilliantly mixing everything from military strategy to bawdy jokes. How could An be hiding anything when he talked so freely about everything? He seemed the most guileless and forthcoming guy in Vietnam. So convincingly did he don the persona of a pro-American, westernized, English-speaking journalist, no one ever suspected his allegiances lay elsewhere. An spent a lifetime hiding with words the place where his true self was operating, and by now the method has become a habit so ingrained in his character that he can't keep himself from filling the night with talk and more talk.

Some photos lying on the coffee table near An's bed show him in his white pajamas surrounded by three of the surviving members of his network, Chin Chi and her sister Tam Thao and a smiling Mai Chi Tho, the former head of Communist intelligence in the south, Vietnamese minister of the interior, and mayor of Saigon. An tells me that their gathering was a command performance, filmed for the twelve-part TV series the Party is making about him. The old spy, having come in from the cold, must now fend off the warm embrace of the state.

Before I say good-bye, An returns to discussing his death, telling me that he wants to be cremated and have his ashes scattered in the Dong Nai River near Bien Hoa, where he was born. The army, on the other hand, is insisting on giving him a state funeral.

The house fills with the smell of rice cooking in the kitchen. I look to the far end of the salon to see that the dining room table is out of commission. It is groaning under enormous piles of books and magazines that have metastasized as if An's friends, afraid of losing him, have built a paper fortress against the lord of the underworld. Dinnertime comes and goes, and An is still "yakking, yakking," until he collapses onto his bed, breathless. I say good-bye and rise to walk through the garden on my own, passing the porcelain statue of An's beloved German shepherd and the cages that hold his fighting cocks. I leave with a heavy heart, knowing that this is the last time I will speak with An.

An was not always a reliable narrator; he refused to talk about some parts of his life. He had a story he told about himself—about being a strategic rather than a tactical spy—which I have come to doubt. But encapsulated in his life are fundamental truths about the war in Vietnam and its after-math. I persist in thinking that the particular story of this one Vietnamese spy, who also happened to be a journalist, is our key to understanding the contemporary world of embedded re-porters. After all, what reporter is not embedded, either in a military unit or in a clan or culture, and who better than An to help us understand the moral perils and sheer terror of trying to report on a world at war?

The Saigon streets are bustling with people buying presents and getting ready for the new year's festivities at Tết. It is also the season of weddings, when it is not unusual to get invited to two weddings a day. These sumptuous affairs in Saigon's hotels involve hundreds of guests, live bands, fountains of champagne, and emcees who jolly everyone into drinking enormous quan-tities of beer and cognac. After being filmed raising their glasses to toast the happy couple, the guests stand up and wobble onto their motorbikes before heading into the crush of Saigon traffic.

As Vietnam whirls from Communism to consumerism, the Virgin Mary in front of Saigon's red-brick cathedral offers a sign of discontent. She graces a small oval park planted with flowers, which is a favorite spot for the city's brides to have their pictures taken. Lately, this scenic park has been drawing a different sort of crowd. Hundreds of visitors have started coming to see the strange events of the day. The Virgin Mary is crying. People have seen tears streaming down her cheeks. If you doubt it, the city's paparazzi will press in your hands photos which show quite clearly the tears welled up in her eyes and their glistening tracks down her face. Surrounded by brides in white tulle and curious crowds, the photographers are doing a brisk business.

At the urging of the Communist Party's Central Committee, the bishop has declared that the Virgin's tears are a natural phenomenon resulting from excessive rainwater and last season's strenuous monsoons. No one believes him. The Virgin is crying because she is sad. She feels the people's pain. She sees the growing disparity in Vietnam between rich and poor, the mounting corruption and venality. She sympathizes with the farmers who were forced to kill their chickens after an outbreak of bird flu. She supports the laborers in the Nike shoe factories who have gone on strike, demanding that their Korean bosses stop beating them and pay fair wages. She supports the country's garment workers, who are paid even less than the Nike shoe workers—forty dollars a month in the cities and a mere thirty dollars a month in the country—and who have also gone on strike. She knows the sorrow of 9/11 and regrets that the world is terrorizing itself with feuds that kill mainly women and children. The Virgin's tender embrace, her charity and forgiveness, are no longer sufficient to heal this world out of whack.

The Madonna in the park has become a pilgrimage site for Vietnamese from as far away as Hanoi. The bishop tries to shoo them off, but everyone assumes his statements are scripted for him by the government. "The Vietnamese have a 'deep' explanation for everything," a friend explains. If nothing else, they are great confabulators. They fill the city's cafés and street-side beer parlors with animated knots of people talking nonstop. In an avid torrent of jokes, aphorisms, and gossip, they dissect politics, analyze world affairs, share recipes, sing songs, recite poems. The only time I hear this chatter stilled is when I stand among the crowd peering into the face of the Virgin.

One night, strolling back to the Continental Hotel after dinner, some friends and I find the usual crowd standing in front of the Virgin. "I'm sure what they saw on her face was pigeon droppings," Thang says. Vietnam suffered prolonged rains in the fall, lasting through Christmas Day. It has also been unusually cold, leaving the country damp and somber. The *mai* apricot blossoms, which normally appear around the Vietnamese New Year and symbolize the country's prosperity and happiness, will not be blooming this year. "Maybe there is something to it," he admits. "First we had an earthquake in Saigon. Then came the bird flu. Now we have workers on strike and government officials being executed for corruption. These are not easy times."

In the summer of 2006, An was admitted twice to Military Hospital 175. A friend who went to visit him reported that An was joking about wanting to find a place in hell next to a good storyteller so that he would have someone to talk to. On his second visit, An's friend found him with a tracheotomy tube stuck in his windpipe. *You wouldn't stop talking, An,* he said. *So they finally had to shut you up.* An smiled with his eyebrows. On the third visit, An's friend found him in a coma. On Wednesday, September 20, at 11:20 in the morning, on the twenty-eighth day of the seventh month of the Year of the Dog, Pham Xuan An, age seventy-nine, died. He was put in a coffin and carried back to his house for three days of viewing. Visitors to the

family brought flowers, fruit, and incense. They placed their offerings on the family altar. Then they prayed with their palms
touching and bowed three times.

On display beside the open coffin, framed behind glass and
pinned on a field of black cloth, were An's sixteen medals. Previously it had been reported that he had won four military
medals, but the actual number was now revealed to be fourteen,
not including the medal naming him a Hero of the People's
Armed Forces and the award for fifty years of service to the
Communist Party. The medals were awarded for specific battles and campaigns which had been won thanks to An's tactical
engagement. The world had known about An's role in the battle of Ap Bac and at Tết, but not about two more First Class
medals. One was awarded in 1970 for giving advance warning
to the Communist command, which allowed them to avoid
being bombed or captured during Richard Nixon's invasion of
Cambodia. Another confirmed that An was a key player in Lam
Son 719, when the South Vietnamese army was decimated
after its failed attempt to invade Laos and cut off the Ho Chi
Minh Trail in 1971.

"As soon as we saw all of An's medals, we knew he was responsible for a big string of American defeats," Kyle Hörst tells
me. "There's a one-to-one correspondence between specific
battles and each one of these medals. An used to say to me, 'If
I tell my story, people will lose heart.' For a long time I wondered, 'Who are these people who will lose heart?' Then I realized, it was his American friends who had trusted him for so
many years while he fought against them. This is not the work
of someone who was exclusively a strategic analyst. It is the
work of a master tactician."

An was buried with full military honors on September 23,
2006. The ceremony included a color guard carrying the framed
display of his medals. Traditionally in Vietnam, a funeral entails
a procession through the streets, with blowing horns and preg-

nant women rushing up to touch the casket for good luck. An would have loved the horns and pregnant women, but he was loaded onto a military truck and driven to the Ministry of Defense funeral facility in Go Vap near the Thu Duc cemetery reserved for military heroes. An's picture in military uniform was placed in front of his ornately decorated red coffin. His family wore white tunics and head bands. Sticks of incense, gathered into big bundles and stuck into trays of sand, filled the air with smoke. Attending the memorial service were Vo Van Kiet, Vietnam's former prime minister, and a host of generals, including Nguyen Chi Vinh, the head of TC2 (Defense Intelligence), who delivered the *bai dieu van,* An's life history. Calling him "the assault spearhead and main attack force" of his intelligence cell—here identified by its code name, H.63—Vinh enumerated An's "extraordinary military achievements," accomplished while he lived "in the bowels of the enemy."

One observer described the scene as "a gathering of spooks. An was being admitted into the Pantheon of military intelligence." The process had already begun months earlier, when a twenty-seven-inch Sony TV was delivered to his house with a sign on it saying, "From your friends at Tong Cuc *hai*" (TC2).

Following the memorial service at Go Vap, rain was falling heavily as Tu Cang and An's wife and children followed his coffin out of the building. They walked through a parade of soldiers with bayonets mounted on their guns, and watched as the coffin was loaded back into the glass compartment on the military truck. The cortege drove to the cemetery along the highway to Bien Hoa, where An was to be buried next to Ba Quoc and other colleagues in military intelligence. This burial ground, with about five hundred graves, is maintained like a park. Across the highway lies a cemetery reserved for South Vietnamese soldiers who fought on the losing side of the war. The Republican graveyard is overrun with weeds, and the tombstones are cracked and tumbling onto the ground.

Dozens of obituaries marked An's death. He had not been forgotten by his friends in the press. His was the lead obituary in the *New York Times* and *Le Monde*, and even *Time* broke its years of embarrassed silence to give An his due as a great correspondent. An was "a first-class journalist . . . part Confucian scholar, part medieval monk," wrote Stanley Cloud, a former Saigon bureau chief. Cloud knocked down the charge that An planted disinformation, saying that he "saved us from reporting things that weren't true." Cloud went on to say that An was a nationalist, a patriot, someone who loved his country and culture. This did not exclude his loving America or France. He loved French literature. He admired American culture. But there was not a servile bone in his body, and the only relationship he wished to have with outsiders was one of mutual respect. Vietnam had been repulsing invaders for thousands of years, and to expect anything else of a Vietnamese patriot was to imagine a leopard with no spots. People looked at An and imagined he was spotless. They thought he was on their side, and he never told them otherwise, but he was most assuredly a spotted Vietnamese, who placed the love of his country above his own self-interest. As Cloud wrote at the end of his obituary, "During the war, a colleague of ours said to me, 'I think Pham Xuan An is the perfect example of the very best in Vietnamese society.' I felt that way, too. I still do."

In another obituary, An's first boss at *Time*, Frank McCulloch wrote, "Not once in the years he worked for me in the *Time* bureau did An ever slant or shade his reporting to favor the Communists. Paradoxically, he truly loved the U.S. and its democracy, and he also vastly respected and treasured good journalism in the American context of that phrase." McCulloch ended his obituary on a personal note, writing, "I still salute you, An, as a friend, a journalist, a complex and contradictory lover of democracy, a husband and father, and perhaps, above all, as a Vietnamese patriot who may, or may not, have placed his biggest bet on the wrong horse."

On the third day after An's burial, his family traveled back to the cemetery for the symbolic "opening of the grave." Bringing flowers and food, they prayed for the release of his soul. They also brought an umbrella that they raised to protect him from the sun. The last thing they carried was a model ladder, which they propped against the grave to help his soul ascend to heaven. I imagine An made good use of this ladder, clambering out of hell as fast as possible to look for a brighter world with good conversation.

# *Acknowledgments*

Since this is a book about spies and spy craft, not everyone who helped me can be thanked in public. You might try rubbing the pages with a solution of water, iodine, and alcohol to see if any names appear between the lines. Named or unnamed, my debt to these people is very large.

The Cheshire Cat grinning down on this project is Pham Xuan An. Since our first meeting in 1992 he was a generous host, and even after his disappearance he had lessons to teach. I also wish to thank An's family, particularly his wife, Hoang Thi Thu Nhan, and his eldest son, Pham Xuan Hoang An, for the hours I spent as a guest in their house and for their help with this project.

For her aid in Ho Chi Minh City—and for inviting me to so many Vietnamese weddings—I thank Duong Hanh Dung. Other assistance came from Dinh Nguyet Ha, who accompanied me to the island of Poulo Condore and who was still smiling when I left her behind because there was no room on the flight home.

I wish to thank the members of Pham Xuan An's H.63 intelligence network, who shared with me their memories of working together during the war: Mai Chi Tho, Nguyen Van Tau (Tu Cang), Nguyen Xuan Manh (Muoi Nho), Nguyen Thi My Nhung (Tam Thao), Nguyen Thi My Linh (Chin Chi), Nguyen Van Thuong, and Nguyen Thi Se.

I am grateful for having been invited to Vietnam twice as an official guest. My thanks to Le Thanh Ha, chairman of the Ho Chi Minh City People's Committee, and Nguyen Thien Nhan, vice-chairman, for inviting me to attend the press events surrounding the thirtieth anniversary of the end of the Second Indochina War, and to Bach Ngoc Chien and his colleagues at Vietnam Television for organizing my visit to Hanoi in 2008. I also appreciate the assistance I have received over the years from the press section and the consular staff at Vietnam's Washington embassy.

I am indebted to the Vietnamese authors and journalists who have written about Pham Xuan An, some of whom generously shared with me their notes and other material. These include Hoang Hai Van and Tan Tu; Nguyen Thi Ngoc Hai; and Truong Giang, Viet Ha, and The Vinh. Another colleague whose help I gratefully acknowledge is filmmaker Le Phong Lan.

To the friends who accompanied me over the years, I was always pleased to spend time with Phuong Thao and Ngoc Le, Tran Van Hong (Viet), Le Ly Hayslip, Henry Nguyen Bao Hoang, Thuyen Nguyen, and Du Thi Thanh Nga (Tiana). I thank with invisible ink another friend who wishes to remain anonymous. "Chu tai lien voi chu tai mot van."

I owe a great debt to my able translator Thuy Duong Nach, who is also a very good cook, and to her husband Jim Nach, who shared with me his knowledge of Vietnam. I am grateful for the aid of other scholars and experts, including James Fisher, Christopher Goscha, Francois Guillemot, Tom Heenan, Gerald Hickey, Joyce Hoffman, Hy Van Luong, Maurice Isserman, Loch Johnson, Wayne Karlin, Stanley Kutler, Jack Langguth, Jonathan Nashel, Ngo Vinh Long, John Prados, Andrew Rotter,

Nicolas Roussellier, Keith Taylor, Tim Weiner, Hugh Wilford, and Peter Zinoman.

The journalists and writers who shared with me their memories of working in Vietnam during the war include Peter Arnett, Robert Sam Anson, Kevin Buckley, Stanley Cloud, Robert Olen Butler, Nayan Chanda, Gloria Emerson, George Esper, Frances FitzGerald, Zalin Grant, David Greenway, David Halberstam, Barry Hillenbrand, Richard Hornik, Henry Kamm, Stanley Karnow, Jonathan Larsen, John Laurence, Don Luce, Frank McCulloch, Richard Pyle, Jon Randal, Peter Ross Range, Roy Rowan, Morley Safer, Peter Shaplen, Neil Sheehan, Frank Snepp, Germaine Loc Swanson, Dick Swanson, and Nick Turner.

Other colleagues who aided me in this project include Daniel Ellsberg, Philippe Franchini, Earl Gustkey, Chris Hedges, Ellida Maki, Nguyen Ngoc Bich, Rick Perlstein, Rufus Phillips, Doug Ramsey, Peter Scheid, Tranh Tu Thanh, Bui Tin, Seymour Topping, Tom Vallely, and Sesto Vecchi. Three filmmakers generously shared with me the transcripts of taped interviews and other material: David Felsen at NBC, Thomas Herman, producer of *Shoot the Messenger,* and Alain Taieb in Paris.

I am grateful for the help of many archivists and librarians, including Bill Hooper at Time Inc., Evan Hocker at the Center for American History at the University of Texas at Austin, Alan Messmer at the *Christian Science Monitor;* Harry Miller and Heather Richmond at the Wisconsin Historical Society, Carl Morgan at Orange Coast College, Stephen Plotkin at the John F. Kennedy Presidential Library; Dan Reasor at the *International Herald Tribune,* and Margie D'Aprix, Glynis Asu, Rebecca Hewitt, Reid Larson, Lynn Mayo, Joan Wolek, Sharon Britton, and Kristin Strohmeyer at Hamilton College's Burke Library.

I thank Jeffrey Ward for drawing my maps; Jim Nachtwey and the Richard Avedon Foundation for permission to use their photos; Henri Bovet, editorial director at Editions Tallandier in

Paris; and my capable editors at Public Affairs in New York, Clive Priddle and Morgen Van Vorst. The journey from manuscript to published book was beautifully orchestrated by Peter Garceau, Lindsay Goodman, Lisa Kaufman, Whitney Peeling, Melissa Raymond, Chrisona Schmidt, Meredith Smith, and Susan Weinberg.

I owe a special note of thanks to readers who read and commented on early drafts of the manuscript: Frank Anechiarico, Tom Cohen, Alex Kodat, Mary Mackay, and Jim and Thuy Nach. My inspiring editors at *The New Yorker*, John Bennet and David Remnick, published an early version of this story in May 2005.

I am lucky to have two literary agents who are literary: Michael Carlisle in New York and Michelle Lapautre in Paris. I am grateful for financial support from the Fund for Investigative Journalism, the Research Foundation of the State University of New York, and the Dean of the College of Arts and Sciences at the University at Albany.

My loving family was infinitely patient and supportive. I am nurtured by their good cheer and good ideas. Along with thanking my wife Bonnie and daughter Maude, I dedicate this book to my sons Tristan and Julian, who are coming of age in a world far from but perhaps not unlike the one described in this book.

# *Notes*

## A CAUTIONARY NOTE ON AGENT Z.21

2    **four hundred and ninety-eight reports:** The number of re-
     ports authored by Pham Xuan An was revealed in a multipart
     series of articles written by Truong Giang, Viet Ha, and The
     Vinh, which began appearing on VietNamNet on August
     17, 2007.

5    **'official' biography:** See Larry Berman, *Perfect Spy: The
     Incredible Double Life of Pham Xuan An,* Time *Magazine
     Reporter and Vietnamese Communist Agent* (New York:
     Smithsonian Books, 2007).

6    **crushing military defeat for Republican forces:** As noted by
     Kyle Hörst in remarks delivered at the Vietnam Center,
     there is an inverse relationship between the significance of
     An's deeds and the amount of time he spent talking about
     them. "What An failed to mention in the hundreds of hours
     of detailed discussions with the various Western biogra-
     phers are the two First Class Battle Exploit medals that he
     earned, the highest-level Battle Exploit medal awarded, given
     only for unusual accomplishments of national significance.

Neither of these was for analysis or strategic intelligence, and they establish that An's greatest contributions to the cause were not for analysis or reporting but for work as a tactical intelligence operative who secured specific information on impending military operations and, in the words of the official citation making him a Hero of the People's Armed Forces in January 1976, 'provided in a timely fashion' much information 'of great value.'" Kyle Hörst, "Imagining Viet Nam: Misunderstanding Pham Xuan An" (talk delivered at the Vietnam Center, 6th Triennial Vietnam Symposium, Lubbock, Texas, March 13, 2008).

## BAPTISM BY FIRE

23    death rates higher than twenty percent: See Ngo Vinh Long, *Before the Revolution: The Vietnamese Peasants Under the French* (New York: Columbia University Press, 1991), 113.

36    "What we know today as Saigon": See William L. Cassidy, *Southern Viet-Nam's Criminal Traditions* (Washington, D.C.: International Association of Asian Crime Investigators, 1991), 8.

## THE WORK OF HUNTING DOGS

49    Diaries written by Jack and Bobby Kennedy: My thanks to the Kennedy Library in Boston, Massachusetts, for access to the diaries and other personal papers of John F. Kennedy and Robert F. Kennedy.

72    "Indochina became a vast chessboard": See Alfred W. McCoy, *The Politics of Heroin: CIA Complicity in the Global Drug Trade* (Chicago: Chicago Review Press, 1991), 132.

72    **The proceeds from this operation:** Financing its colonial ad-
      ministration through the sale of opium was standard practice
      in Indochina. In the early 1900s, twenty-five percent of the
      colony's gross general budget came from the sale of opium.
      At its peak in 1918, the figure rose to forty-two percent.
      Chantal Descours-Gatin, *Quand l'opium finançait la colo-
      nization en Indochine* (Paris: l'Harmattan, 1992), 222–225;
      Philippe Le Failler, "Le movement international anti-opium
      et l'Indochine (1906–1940)," Ph.D. diss., Institut d'Histoire
      des Pays d'Outre-Mer, Université de Provence-Aix Mar-
      seille 1, 1993; and Jean Michaud, "The Montagnards and the
      State in Northern Vietnam from 1802 to 1975: A Historical
      Overview. *Ethnohistory* 47, no. 2 (2000): 345.


## BRAIN GRAFT

76    **Lansdale writes in his autobiography:** Written accounts of
      Edward Lansdale's intelligence work are highly unreliable,
      with the least reliable being his autobiography. See Edward
      Lansdale, *In the Midst of Wars: An American Mission to
      Southeast Asia* (1972; New York: Fordham University Press,
      1991); and Cecil B. Currey, *Edward Lansdale: The Unquiet
      American* (Boston: Houghton Mifflin, 1988). See also
      Richard Drinnon, *Facing West: The Metaphysics of Indian-
      Hating and Empire Building* (Minneapolis: University of
      Minnesota Press, 1980); and Jonathan Nashel, *Edward Lans-
      dale's Cold War* (Amherst: University of Massachusetts
      Press, 2005).

79    **Daniel Ellsberg released the Pentagon Papers:** *The History
      of United States Decisionmaking on Vietnam,* a forty-seven
      volume, seven thousand word study of U.S. involvement in
      the Vietnam war from 1945 to 1968, has never been pub-
      lished in its entirety. The *New York Times* rushed a volume
      of selected material into print in 1971. This was followed by

the five-volume Senator Gravel edition and the twelve-volume U.S. Government Printing Office edition, which was heavily expurgated.

The last four volumes of the Pentagon Papers, the so-called diplomatic volumes, describing U.S. negotiations to end the war, were released partially in 1983 and then fully in 2002 as a result of Freedom of Information Act (FOIA) requests. While the secret diplomatic volumes of the Pentagon Papers are now available to the public, the original forty-three volumes leaked by Ellsberg—which exist only in partial or expurgated versions—have never been released by the U.S. government.

See Neil Sheehan, Hedrick Smith, E. W. Kenworthy, and Fox Butterfield, eds., *The Pentagon Papers* (New York: Quadrangle, 1971); *The Pentagon Papers: The Defense Department History of United States Decisionmaking on Vietnam,* Senator Gravel ed., 5 vols. (Boston: Beacon, 1971); and *United States-Vietnam Relations, 1945–1967,* Study Prepared by the Department of Defense, 12 vols. (Washington, D.C.: U.S. Government Printing Office, 1971). For a discussion of Ellsberg's decision to release the Pentagon Papers and their publishing history, see Daniel Ellsberg, *Secrets: A Memoir of Vietnam and the Pentagon Papers* (New York: Viking, 2002); and John Prados and Margaret Pratt Porter, eds., *Inside the Pentagon Papers* (Lawrence: University Press of Kansas, 2004).

80    "They must have had someone on the inside": See Sedgewick Tourison, *Project Alpha: Washington's Secret Military Operations in North Vietnam* (New York: St. Martin's, 1997), 12.

82    "located Vietnam on the new world map": See James Fisher, *Dr. America: The Lives of Thomas A. Dooley, 1927–1961* (Amherst: University of Massachusetts Press, 1997), 35.

84      Lansdale scripting battles: See L. Fletcher Prouty, *The Secret Team: The CIA and Its Allies in Control of the United
States and the World* (Costa Mesa, CA: Institute for Historical Review, 1973), 12; and *JFK: The CIA, Vietnam, and
the Plot to Assassinate John F. Kennedy* (New York: Citadel,
1996), 65.

89      "three Lansdales": See Zalin Grant, *Facing the Phoenix*
(New York: Norton, 1991), 98.

91      "band of superterrorists": See Prouty, *JFK*, 60. See also A.
J. Langguth, *Our Vietnam: The War, 1954–1975* (New York:
Simon & Schuster, 2000), 93.

91      denied Mankiewicz permission to film in Vietnam: See
Fisher, *Dr. America*, 157–158.

92      "let it be finally revealed that the Communists did it":
Letter from Edward Lansdale to Joseph Mankiewicz, March
17, 1956, reproduced in Graham Greene, *The Quiet American*, Viking Critical Edition, ed. John Clark Pratt (New
York: Penguin, 1996), 301.

93      "I would never have chosen Colonel Lansdale": See
Greene, *Quiet American*, 319.

96      "The South Vietnamese government existed in name
only": See Christian Appy, *Patriots: The Vietnam War Remembered from All Sides* (New York: Viking, 2002), 51.

## CONFIDENCE GAME

139     assassinated in Dallas, Texas: Conspiracy theorists who are
struck by the propinquity of Ngo Dinh Diem's and John F.
Kennedy's assassinations should consult the writings of Lansdale's former assistant, L. Fletcher Prouty, particularly his
book *JFK: The CIA, Vietnam, and the Plot to Assassinate
John F. Kennedy*. Other intriguing connections between the
two events are presented in *The Tears of Autumn*, a novel by
former CIA agent turned novelist, Charles McCarry.

## RELIABLE SOURCES

149    "I felt extremely angry with this traitor": See Hoang Van Hai and Tan Tu, *Pham Xuan An: A General of the Secret Service* (Hanoi: The Gioi, 2003), 97.

156    Harriman asked Shaplen to contact North Vietnam: See Tom Heenan, *From Traveler to Traitor: The Life of Wilfred Burchett* (Melbourne: Melbourne University Press, 2006), 204.

157    "most highly respected Vietnamese journalist": See Robert Shaplen, "We Have Always Survived," *The New Yorker,* April 15, 1972. Reprinted in *Reporting Vietnam,* pt. 2 (New York: Library of America, 1998), 281–334.

158    An explained to a reporter for *Le Monde*: See Jean-Claude Pomonti, *Un Vietnamien bien tranquille : L'extraordinaire histoire de l'espion qui défia l'Amérique* (Paris: Editions des Equateurs, 2006), 72.

160    "surely one of the best-informed men in town": See Robert Shaplen, *Bitter Victory* (New York: Harper & Row, 1986), 11.

## THE PERFECT CRIME

190    "the first known case of a Communist agent": See Zalin Grant, *Facing the Phoenix: The CIA and the Political Defeat of the United States in Vietnam* (New York: Norton, 1991), 256.

191    the relationship between *Time* and the Agency was so close: See Hugh Wilford, *The Mighty Wurlitzer: How the CIA Played America* (Cambridge: Harvard University Press, 2008), 232.

192    "more than four hundred American journalists": See Carl Bernstein, "The CIA and the Media," *Rolling Stone,* October 20, 1977, 55–67.

193     "Oh sure, all the time": Cited by Daniel Brandt in "Journalism and the CIA: The Mighty Wurlitzer," NameBase NewsLine, April-June 1997.

## NEW YEAR

198     **Westmoreland cabled Wheeler:** Cited by Larry Berman in "The Tet Offensive," in Andrew J. Rotter, ed., *Light at the End of the Tunnel: A Vietnam War Anthology,* rev. ed. (Wilmington, DE: Scholarly Resources, 1999), 111.

202     **sent to Hanoi for display in the museum of military intelligence:** The only report by Pham Xuan An to see the light of day is a memo he wrote to headquarters in 1995 describing his Renault 4CV, before it was put on a flatbed truck and shipped to Hanoi for display in the military intelligence museum. Using his code name, Hai Trung, An describes how he bought the car because it looked like the taxis then being driven in Saigon. It was a good car for avoiding undue attention from "enemy security forces," he wrote.

## A COUNTRY CREATED BY SALVADOR DALI

224     **An was put in the political deep freeze for a decade:** In 2008, I traveled to Vietnam and France, trying to learn what Pham Xuan An had done as an active duty military officer and intelligence agent from the end of the war in 1975 until his death in 2006. Opinion divided between an orthodox view, presented in Hanoi, and a more skeptical view offered by An's friends in Saigon and outside Vietnam.

    Officials in Hanoi informed me that Western writers misunderstand An's position. He assumed new duties after 1975 and was kept from public view like the rest of the

country's high officials. The surveillance he faced was standard operating procedure for an intelligence officer with
security clearances. Apart from his military service in 1945,
An had never worn a uniform or saluted commanding officers. He may have been irked about restarting this business in 1978, but his being sent to Hanoi's Nguyen Ai Quoc
Political Institute was an honor comparable to enrolling for
a year at the U.S. Army War College or Saint-Cyr. It signaled
that An was beginning to move up the ranks into the general
staff.

The Vietnamese who make this argument imply that
An, after his cover was blown in 1975, adopted a *second*
cover—the face he presented to Western visitors as an accidental Communist who remained steadfast in his love for
the West. An neglected to mention to these visitors that he
was still a working intelligence agent and Communist Party
member, and none of his friends seems to have inquired
too deeply about what exactly he was doing for the last thirty
years of his career as a spy.

The contrary view is argued most forcefully by An's
friend and fellow journalist Bui Tin, who was himself a
colonel and high-ranking Party official until he defected to
France in 1990. During the year that An was enrolled at
the Nguyen Ai Quoc Political Institute, he spent his Sundays
at Tin's house in Hanoi lunching, napping, and complaining
about the curriculum, which Tin describes as "a steady diet
of political cant and Communist propaganda."

According to Tin, An's military promotions came late
and begrudgingly. (Even the dates of these promotions are
a matter of dispute.) From 1945 to 1947, An was a battalion
commander fighting the French in the south, Tin says. By
1955 he held a rank in the Communist forces equivalent to
that of major. He remained at this rank for the next twenty
years, while working as Vietnam's preeminent spy. According to Tin, An was promoted to Trung Ta, Lieutenant

Colonel, in 1976, the same year he was named a Hero of the People's Armed Forces. "This was a big insult," Tin says. "Lots of people at the end of the war were jumped up the ranks, straight to the top. They should have made An a full colonel right away."

"The Communists were suspicious of him," Tin says. "He bred dogs—a bourgeois pastime—and he had too many Western friends. They prevented him from leaving the country and seeing visitors, and they put him under heavy surveillance." Even after these restraints were loosened in the 1990s, An could not receive guests without permission, and he had to write reports on his conversations. In 1980, following his year of political indoctrination, An was promoted to Thuong Ta, Senior Lieutenant Colonel. Only in 1982 was he made a Dai Ta, a full Colonel. Then in 1990, at the age of sixty-three, he was promoted to General.

226    "I'd like to kill him": See Grant, *Facing the Phoenix*, 257.

231    sufficiently accessible to commission a biography: See Nguyen Thi Ngoc Hai, *Pham Xuan An: Ten Nguoi Nhu Cuoc Doi* (Hanoi: Nha Xuat Ban Cong An Nhan Dan, 2002).

233    "a short course in the history of Vietnam": See Truong Nhu Tang, *A Vietcong Memoir,* trans. David Chanoff and Doan Van Toai (New York: Harcourt Brace Jovanovich, 1985), 15.

## A BRIGHTER WORLD

260    An's sixteen medals: Not until they were displayed next to his open casket was it revealed that An had won sixteen military medals, not four, as previously reported by his biographers. *Quan Cong* are Military Exploit medals, and *Chien Cong* are Battle Exploit medals. Each medal is awarded in one of three classes. A First Class medal recognizes a major contribution to the nation. A Second Class

medal recognizes a contribution to a particular ministry or department. In An's case, this would have been either military intelligence (Tong Cuc II, TC2) or the People's Army of Vietnam (PAVN). A Third Class medal recognizes achievement at the regional level, popular acclaim, or a contribution to one's military group. For An, this would have been the Central Office for South Vietnam (COSVN), military intelligence unit H.63, or some other military entity.

As we learned from the official eulogy delivered at his funeral, An won two Battle Exploit medals, First Class. These were awarded for warning COSVN in advance of Richard Nixon's invasion of Cambodia in 1970, thereby allowing the Communist military commanders to escape being bombed or captured, and for obtaining the battle plans for Lam Son 719. This attempt by the South Vietnamese army to invade Laos and cut the Ho Chi Minh Trail resulted in a crushing military defeat for the south in 1971. An's First Class medals represent major feats of tactical intelligence. They undermine his story—his ultimate cover—that he did only strategic intelligence, after-action reports, and long-range planning.

An won his first military medal in the 1950s for opposing France after the signing of the Geneva Accords. The cease-fire agreement of 1954, which marked the end of the First Indochina War, would be followed by preparations for what would become the Second Indochina War. An, at the time, was working in the psychological warfare department of the newly formed South Vietnamese general staff. This medal is a *Chien Thang*, a Battle Victory medal, Third Class.

An's second medal was awarded for his work during the battle of Ap Bac in 1963. The Communists' ability to set a trap and inflict serious damage on South Vietnam's better equipped forces resulted in An receiving a *Chien Cong*, a Battle Exploit medal, Second Class.

An was awarded another Battle Exploit medal, Second Class, for similar work in 1966. This was for obtaining the battle plans and other tactical intelligence supplied for the battle of Ia Drang. This engagement in November 1965 marked the first major battle in the American phase of the war. Three hundred and five soldiers, primarily from the U.S. 7th Cavalry—the same unit that had been massacred at the Battle of Little Big Horn—were killed after four days of fighting in the Central Highlands near the Cambodian border.

An received three Battle Exploit medals, Third Class, for advance warning on America's plans to increase its military presence in 1965; for his work during the Tết Offensive in 1968; and for providing secret documents detailing the Christmas 1972 B-52 attacks against Hanoi. One source describes these three accomplishments as the reason, collectively, for An's being named a Hero of the People's Armed Forces in 1976. This medal, Vietnam's highest military honor, is awarded for "exceptionally outstanding merits in combat or in combat support." It is equivalent to the French Legion of Honor or the U.S. Medal of Honor.

For intelligence provided during the Ho Chi Minh campaign, the final battle in the war, and for his "after-action" reports and other undisclosed work—which may have continued up to his death in 2006—An received six more medals sometime after 1975. These include an Independence medal (*Doc Lap*), Second Class; a Resolved-to-Win Military Flag medal (*Quan Ky Quyet Thang*); a Resistance medal (*Khang Chien*), First Class; and three Liberation Soldier medals (*Chien Sy Giai Phong*), which were awarded in the First, Second, and Third Class. The final medal on display at An's funeral commemorated his fifty years of service as a member of the Communist Party.

262     **"Dozens of obituaries marked An's death.":** An's death also invited the rebroadcasting of errors about the man and

his country. The process had already begun before his death. Most of the statements on the Web in which An is quoted criticizing Vietnam's Communist government are fake. Tracking down the original sources, for example, Morley Safer's interview with An, published in the *New York Times Magazine* and then in his book *Flashbacks*, one discovers that remarks made by Safer are misattributed to An.

# Index

# A Note on the Type

The text of this book is set in New Caledonia, a modern typeface released by Linotype-Hell in 1979. New Caledonia originates from William Anderson Dwiggens's 1938 design for linotype production—a method of setting hot metal type in lines of words or slugs. Called Caledonia, the Roman name for Scotland, Dwiggens's typeface added a touch of calligraphic style and fluidity to earlier Scotch typefaces that were designed to be set by hand, one letter at a time. W. A. Dwiggens (1880–1956) was one of America's foremost graphic designers. He championed the revival of fine bookmaking, which began in England with the work of the nineteenth-century social reformer and printer William Morris. An accomplished puppeteer and illustrator and the designer of twelve widely used typefaces, Dwiggens is also known for his articles attacking the leading publishers of his day, whom he mocked for the poor design of modern books.

**THOMAS A. BASS** is the author of *The Eudae-monic Pie*, *Vietnamerica*, *The Predictors*, and other books. An award-winning correspondent cited by the Overseas Press Club for his foreign report-ing, he is a frequent contributor to *The New Yorker*, *Wired*, *Smithsonian*, the *New York Times*, and other publications. He is a professor of Eng-lish and Journalism at the State University of New York in Albany.

PublicAffairs is a publishing house founded in 1997. It is a tribute to the standards, values, and flair of three persons who have served as mentors to countless reporters, writers, editors, and book people of all kinds, including me.

I. F. STONE, proprietor of *I. F. Stone's Weekly*, combined a commitment to the First Amendment with entrepreneurial zeal and reporting skill and became one of the great independent journalists in American history. At the age of eighty, Izzy published *The Trial of Socrates*, which was a national bestseller. He wrote the book after he taught himself ancient Greek.

BENJAMIN C. BRADLEE was for nearly thirty years the charismatic editorial leader of *The Washington Post*. It was Ben who gave the *Post* the range and courage to pursue such historic issues as Watergate. He supported his reporters with a tenacity that made them fearless and it is no accident that so many became authors of influential, best-selling books.

ROBERT L. BERNSTEIN, the chief executive of Random House for more than a quarter century, guided one of the nation's premier publishing houses. Bob was personally responsible for many books of political dissent and argument that challenged tyranny around the globe. He is also the founder and longtime chair of Human Rights Watch, one of the most respected human rights organizations in the world.

·     ·     ·

For fifty years, the banner of Public Affairs Press was carried by its owner Morris B. Schnapper, who published Gandhi, Nasser, Toynbee, Truman, and about 1,500 other authors. In 1983, Schnapper was described by *The Washington Post* as "a redoubtable gadfly." His legacy will endure in the books to come.

Peter Osnos, *Founder and Editor-at-Large*